THE NANNY AND DOMESTIC HELP LEGAL KIT

J. Alexander Tanford
Professor of Law

Brian A.P. Mooij
C.P.A.

Sphinx® Publishing
A Division of Sourcebooks, Inc.
Naperville, IL • Clearwater, FL

First edition, 1999

Published by: **Sphinx® Publishing, A Division of Sourcebooks, Inc.®**

Naperville Office	Clearwater Office
P.O. Box 372	P.O. Box 25
Naperville, Illinois 60566	Clearwater, Florida 33757
630-961-3900	727-587-0999
Fax: 630-961-2168	Fax: 727-586-5088

Cover Design: Andrew Sardina/Dominique Raccah, Sourcebooks, Inc.®
Interior Design and Production: Edward A. Haman and Amy S. Hall, Sourcebooks, Inc.®

This publication is designed to provide accurate and authoritative information in regard to the subject matter covered. It is sold with the understanding that the publisher is not engaged in rendering legal, accounting, or other professional service. If legal advice or other expert assistance is required, the services of a competent professional person should be sought.

From a Declaration of Principles Jointly Adopted by a Committee of the
American Bar Association and a Committee of Publishers and Associations

Library of Congress Cataloging-in-Publication Data
Tanford, J. Alexander.
     The nanny and domestic help legal kit / J. Alexander Tanford,
Brian A.P. Mooij.
          p.   cm.
     Includes index.
     ISBN 1-57248-098-X (pbk.)
     1. Domestics--Legal status, laws, etc.--United States Popular
works.   2. Domestics--Taxation--Law and legislation--United States
Popular works.   I. Mooij, Brian A.P.   II. Title.
KF3580,D64T36   1999
344.7301'764046--dc21   99-41756
                                                                        CIP

Printed and bound in the United States of America.

Paperback — 10 9 8 7 6 5 4 3 2 1

CONTENTS

ACKNOWLEDGMENTS

The authors wish to express their appreciation to attorneys Lynne Ellis and Sandra Hamilton, whose legal research assistance on chapters 1, 2, 3, and 7 essentially amounted to co-authorship; Beatrice Guarneschelle-Holt, Esq., for additional legal research; and Jeanine Hullinger Wiese for tirelessly tracking down brochures, forms, and information on taxes and unemployment insurance from all fifty states.

DEDICATION

To Philippa and Jamie,
without whom we never would have started this project

Using Self-Help
Law Books

Whenever you shop for a product or service, you are faced with various levels of quality and price. In deciding what product or service to buy, you make a cost/value analysis on the basis of your willingness to pay and the quality you desire.

When buying a car, you decide whether you want transportation, comfort, status, or sex appeal. Accordingly, you decide among such choices as a Neon, a Lincoln, a Rolls Royce, or a Porsche. Before making a decision, you usually weigh the merits of each option against the cost.

When you get a headache, you can take a pain reliever (such as aspirin) or visit a medical specialist for a neurological examination. Given this choice, most people, of course, take a pain reliever, since it costs only pennies; whereas a medical examination costs hundreds of dollars and takes a lot of time. This is often the most logical choice: it's rare to need anything more than a pain reliever for a headache. But in some cases, a headache may indicate a brain tumor, and failing to see a specialist right away can result in complications. Should everyone with a headache go to a specialist? Of course not, but people treating their own illnesses must realize that they are betting on the basis of their cost/value analysis of the situation; they are taking the most logical option.

The same cost/value analysis must be made in deciding to do one's own legal work. Many legal situations are very straight forward, requiring a simple form and no complicated analysis. Anyone with a little intelligence and a book of instructions can handle the matter without outside help.

But there is always the chance that complications are involved that only an attorney would notice. To simplify the law into a book like this, several legal cases often must be condensed into a single sentence or paragraph. Otherwise, the book would be several hundred pages long and too complicated for most people. However, this simplification necessarily leaves out many details and nuances that would apply to special or unusual situations. Also, there are many ways to interpret most legal questions. Your case may come before a judge who disagrees with the analysis of our authors.

Therefore, in deciding to use a self-help law book and to do your own legal work, you must realize that you are making a cost/value analysis. You have decided that the money you will save in doing it yourself outweighs the chance your case will not turn out to your satisfaction. Most people handling their own simple legal matters never have a problem, but occasionally people find that it ended up costing them more to have an attorney straighten out the situation than it would have if they had hired an attorney in the beginning. Furthermore, you may not be able to undo some mistakes. Keep this in mind while handling your case. Also, be sure to consult an attorney if you feel you might need further guidance.

INTRODUCTION

The idea for this book arose when the Tanfords had a baby and decided to hire a full-time nanny. They turned to their tax accountants, Mooij and Associates, for help. Their request was simple: "We want to hire a nanny, pay her a fair salary, and comply with laws concerning withholding income and social security taxes. Will you tell us which tax forms to complete?"

The answer, as it turned out, was far more complicated. Despite the fact that the authors are lawyers and accountants, the task proved daunting. The standard tax guides were no help. The local IRS office had no current forms, and gave us incorrect information—telling us at one point that we needed to open an account with the Federal Reserve Bank!

Along the way, we discovered that we were covered by more than just tax laws—we also needed to be concerned with immigration laws, state and federal labor laws, and state tax codes. Hiring a nanny proved to be a legal and accounting thicket that took dozens of hours to traverse. Because we, the authors, have legal and tax training, we were able to do the research ourselves, but a non-lawyer might have had to pay several thousand dollars in legal bills. It is no wonder that fewer than one in four families who employ nannies and other domestics bother to comply with the employment and tax laws.

We survived the process. Once we finally figured out what we had to do, when we had to do it, and which forms to fill out; the ongoing process of record keeping and compliance proved not to be difficult. We decided to write this book to try to save other families the trouble we went through at the beginning.

For years, parents who needed household help simply identified someone, either by word of mouth or through a simple advertisement in the local paper, and started paying them to take care of the children, clean, cook, or tend the garden. Payments were in cash, no records were kept, and no one paid much attention. In major urban areas, these nannies, maids, and gardeners were often recent immigrants, willing to work long hours for relatively low pay. No one cared about their immigration status. No one worried about their social security. Many families were simply unaware that they were in violation of tax, immigration, and employment laws.

This picture changed dramatically in 1993, when President Clinton nominated Zoe Baird to be the first woman Attorney General of the United States. She was on her way toward easy confirmation, when it was discovered that she had employed a nanny without complying with federal tax laws. She was forced to withdraw. The next potential nominees were Judge Kimba Wood, one of the most respected federal judges in the country, and prominent Washington attorney Charles Ruff. They, too, had problems with illegal domestic help. In rapid succession, Secretary of Commerce Ron Brown confessed to not paying taxes on a maid, Surgeon General Joycelyn Elders revealed that her husband did not pay taxes on an aide for his ailing mother, and Stephen Breyer lost his first opportunity for a Supreme Court appointment because of unpaid taxes on a domestic employee. The headlines were full of references to "Nannygate."

Suddenly, the most popular topics at cocktail parties and parent-teacher organization meetings were green cards and whether to start paying social security taxes on household help. In the Washington, DC, and San Francisco areas, consulting firms emerged offering to handle the legalities of domestic employment (for a price!). There was a small surge in tax compliance in Washington, and Congress briefly turned its attention to trying to simplify the laws—by creating additional tax forms, of course. After a year or so, however, interest died down and Nannygate was off the front pages. Then in 1997, national attention was drawn to nannies again by the trial of a British *au pair*, Louise Woodward, who was accused of killing one of the children in her care.

This book will lead you through the thicket of federal and state tax and employment laws affecting the hiring, employing, and firing of household help. It will explain the important legal consequences to you if your employee causes harm or injury. While every attempt has been made to provide a clear and accurate explanation of the laws relating to household help, this book cannot explain all of the law's nuances. Also, laws change, and there is always a possibility that they have changed since this book was printed. Therefore, this book is no substitute for up-to-the-minute legal research, or advice from your tax accountant or an attorney who specializes in employment law. But this book will point you in the right direction, help get you started, and flag particular topics on which you may need to consult an attorney.

In this book, we take you through the basic laws and forms you have to cope with when hiring a nanny or other household employee. These include:

- ☞ Federal immigration rules and filling out an "I-9" form proving that your employee is not an illegal alien
- ☞ Federal and labor laws which require you to pay unemployment taxes
- ☞ Federal income tax laws and regulations concerning:
  - Your employee filling out a W-4 form
  - Calculating, deducting and withholding the correct amount of income taxes
  - Paying withheld taxes to the I.R.S. four times a year as estimated taxes, filing a 1040-ES form

- Providing your employee with a W-2 form and filing copies with the Social Security Administration
- Reporting annual household employment taxes on Schedule H
- Obtaining a Federal Employer's Identification Number

☞ Federal social security laws concerning:

- Calculating, deducting and withholding FICA taxes (social security and medicare)
- Paying the withheld taxes to the I.R.S. four times a year as estimated taxes, filing a 1040-ES form
- Properly reporting the information on a W-2 and W-3 form
- Making your own matching contribution to your employee's social security fund over and above what you withheld

☞ Federal minimum wage laws requiring you to pay $5.15 per hour plus overtime

☞ State tax laws and whether you are required to calculate, withhold and pay state and local income taxes

☞ State employment law concerning:

- Registering with the state department of employment security as an employer
- Paying state unemployment taxes quarterly
- Obtaining worker's compensation insurance
- Reporting new hires

Cheer up! This is not as difficult as it seems. If you keep good records of your employee's wages and follow the instructions in this book, compliance takes less than fifteen minutes per paycheck and adds no more than an hour or two to the time you already spend figuring out your tax return.

HIRING HOUSEHOLD HELP 1

You probably wouldn't be reading this book unless you had already made the decision to hire a nanny, maid, gardener, or some other type of household help. This chapter starts at the beginning and guides you through the hiring process.

DO YOU NEED TO WORRY ABOUT HOUSEHOLD EMPLOYMENT LAWS?

WHY SHOULD YOU COMPLY WITH EMPLOYMENT AND TAX LAWS?

Complying with all the applicable laws concerning household help can be a big pain! If you never intend to run for public office, why not just skip all the hassle and pay your nanny in cash? If you do not report the payment and she does not report the income, who's to know? Isn't it simpler and cheaper to forget the whole thing?

There is a very good reason to comply: Noncompliance is illegal, dangerous, and potentially costly. Government officials are not amused by people who break the law and will not necessarily be lenient on you because you are a nice person. There are several ways to get caught:

☛ To claim the child care tax credit on your federal tax return, you must give the nanny's name and social security number. If she failed to report the income, or is working illegally, the IRS may discover it.

☞ If you claim the child care credit on your federal tax form but do not report any withheld taxes or social security on Schedule H, the discrepancy will be obvious to IRS auditors.

☞ If immigration authorities apprehend your gardener for working illegally, they will ask him for whom he was working.

☞ Your neighbor might turn you in to the authorities. The IRS has a reward system that gives the neighbor a ten percent bounty of all money collected from a tax evader he or she reports.

☞ A former household employee may file for unemployment benefits. If the state finds no record that you ever paid state unemployment taxes, they may assign an investigator to look into it.

☞ Your former maid may find out she was entitled to minimum wage and overtime and sue you for back wages or complain to the Department of Labor.

If they catch you, the penalties can be high:

☞ The civil penalty for hiring or continuing to employ an illegal alien is $250 to $10,000. In addition, the Immigration and Naturalization Service can press criminal charges against you, in which case you face another potential fine up to $3,000 and six months in jail.

☞ The penalty for failing to collect federal withholding taxes on a household employee's salary ranges from two percent to fifteen percent of the amount owed.

☞ Failing to make quarterly payments of the taxes collected (plus your contribution to your employee's social security fund) could make you liable for penalties from five to twenty-five percent of the unpaid taxes, plus 0.5% more for each whole or part month the tax remains unpaid.

☞ Failing to pay annual Federal Unemployment taxes is the same as failing to pay any federal tax and carries a maximum penalty of $100,000!

● Failure to withhold and pay state taxes have similar penalties.

● Violations of minimum wage laws and overtime provisions are subject to civil penalties of $1,000 per violation, and criminal penalties of a fine up to $10,000 and six months in jail.

You might think you can avoid personal liability by setting up a family corporation to employ household help. Then, a disgruntled employee or government agency could only sue the corporation. Unfortunately, this scheme won't work. The IRS can collect the taxes and penalties from any "responsible person," which means you would still be personally liable for them. The IRS has even been known to seize homes and cars to enforce their judgments.

IF YOU HAVE NOT BEEN COMPLYING, SHOULD YOU START NOW?

What if you are one of the more than two million families who have not been complying with all the laws concerning household help? Is it better to continue to evade the laws, or "come clean" and start complying?

The better course of action is generally to "turn yourself in" and begin complying. The current policy of the Internal Revenue Service is to bring non-payers into the system, not to scare them away by being punitive. The IRS has recognized in the last few years that many people have not been paying household employee taxes and has taken a lenient attitude toward those who wish to begin complying. In general, you can approach any regional IRS office and explain the situation. You will be liable for your portion of back FICA (Social Security) taxes, but not for back income taxes or your employee's social security contribution. There may be interest or civil penalties due, but these are negotiable and will tend to be small if you cooperate. The longer you wait, the more likely it is that the government will treat you like a tax evader and take a hard line toward you.

ARE YOU AN EMPLOYER?

Only *employers* need to comply with the employment laws. Just because you hire someone to do work around the house does not necessarily make you an employer. If all you do is pay kids in the neighborhood to mow your lawn or babysit on Saturdays, you probably are not considered an employer and do not need this book. But the determination of your legal status is not necessarily simple. It does not depend on the age of the person you hire nor the number of hours they work.

Employees vs. Independent Contractors

Every person you hire falls into one of two categories: they are either an *employee* or an *independent contractor*. If your nanny is legally an employee, you are her employer and must comply with these laws. If your nanny is an independent contractor, you are not her employer— she works for herself.

What is the difference between an employee and an independent contractor? An employee is a person who works for you (the number of hours is not usually important), takes her instructions from you, uses tools and equipment supplied by you, and is expected to defer to your judgment and guidance. An independent contractor works for himself and may have many customers, makes his own decisions how to accomplish a job, uses his own tools and equipment, and is expected to use his own experience and judgment to guide him. There is no simple litmus test for distinguishing between these statuses. It is a question of fact that will be determined by looking at all the circumstances surrounding that person's duties, not by what you call the relationship.

In some cases, the status of a person who works for you may be unclear. For example, a housekeeper may have some characteristics of an employee and some characteristics of an independent contractor. Like an employee, she may follow your general instructions, use cleaning equipment you provide, and work during hours you determine. Like a contractor, she may work for several different families, determine which cleaning products you are to buy, and use her own discretion and experience in deciding how to clean something.

When in doubt, treat the person as an employee and comply with tax withholding, employment, and social security laws. You only run the risk of legal penalties if you mistakenly treat her as an independent contractor. The IRS will be happy to make this determination for you if you fill out and send them Form SS-8 (see form 10 in appendix B, which includes instructions as part of the form).

The following two illustrations may help:

Example 1: Hiring a Nanny for Your Children

Evidence that she is an employee	Evidence that she is an independent contractor
When she is on duty, she only takes care of your children	She takes care of your children and the children of another family at the same time
She comes to your home	You take the children to her home
You supply food for the kids' lunch, books, toys, and playground equipment	She supplies lunch, buys the books and toys, and has her own playground equipment
You determine the lunch menu, nap schedule, and maximum number of hours the children may watch TV	She decides what to serve for lunch, when the children should nap, and when they may watch TV
She must personally take care of your children	She may hire assistants who take care of your children some of the time.
You set the hours she works	She sets the hours she works

Example 2: Hiring a Housekeeper

Evidence that she is an employee	Evidence that she is an independent contractor
She works for you a substantial part of each week and has only one other cleaning job	She works for you one afternoon a week and also cleans ten other houses
She uses your vacuum cleaner and cleaning supplies	She brings her own vacuum cleaner and supplies
She does both routine cleaning and special jobs at your request	She doesn't do windows
She comes to work in her family car	She comes to work in a car with a sign saying "The Merry Maid" on it
You can instruct her to use only organic non-toxic cleaning products even though they make her job harder	She leaves you instructions on which specific cleaning products to buy or brings her own

PART-TIME
EMPLOYEES

Do household employment laws apply to a part-time person? Maybe. Whether you must comply with employment laws depends primarily on whether the person you hire is your employee or an independent contractor. It does not depend on whether they are full or part-time. Although people employed full time are usually considered employees, it is not necessarily so. Similarly, people who work for you only occasionally (like babysitters) or only part-time (ten hours per week) are usually independent contractors but not necessarily so. You must look at all the facts and circumstances of their working conditions.

Under federal and most state laws, you must comply with tax and employment laws even for part-time help under any of the following conditions:

☛ The person you hire is an employee, not an independent contractor

☛ The person works for you eight hours or more per week

☛ You have a payroll of $1,000 or more (for all employees) in any quarter of the year, or pay more than $1,100 to any one employee in a year

SUMMER OR
SEASONAL
EMPLOYEES

Do household employment laws apply to summer help? Yes. Many employers who run farms, summer camps, ski resorts, and other seasonal businesses depend on temporary employees. They still must comply with employment laws during the times when they are operating and have employees. You are an employer subject to these laws if the person who works for you is an employee and not an independent contractor, works more than eight hours a week during the season they work for you, and if you have a payroll of $1,000 or more in any quarter of the year, even if you have no payroll during other time periods. The seasonal nature of their work is irrelevant.

AU PAIRS

Do household employment laws apply to an "au pair"? A special set of rules covers *au pairs*. The term *au pair* is a French idiom, meaning *on equal basis*. In an official *au pair* arrangement, you arrange through a government-approved agency to host a young person from a foreign country who agrees to exchange her domestic services for an introduction to American culture—a kind of barter arrangement. You provide air fare, private room, board, $139 per week spending money, English language instruction, and an introduction to American culture. She provides up to forty-five hours a week of child care. The services you provide to her are equal to the child care services she provides to you, and no money changes hands for salary. The $139 per week spending money you supply is not considered *income*, so you do not generally need to report or withhold taxes and social security on it. Official *au pair* contracts may only be arranged through one of eight exchange programs approved by the United States Information Agency. The *au pair* will arrive with the proper J-1 visa. Further information on the *au pair* program can be found under the topic "General Counsel" at: www.usia.gov

Unofficial *au pair* arrangements are also theoretically possible, where you make your own arrangements with someone from a foreign country; but laws against employing non-citizens make it an unattractive option. See the section on "Immigration Laws" in chapter 3 before you decide to make your own *au pair* arrangement. Also, unofficial *au pairs* are considered employees, which will obligate you to comply with laws on minimum wage, income reporting, tax withholding, etc.

HIRING
RELATIVES

Do household employment laws apply if you hire a relative? In general, employment laws do apply if you hire and pay a member of your family to do a job. However, a relative who provides services to family members, including extensive child care, is presumed to do so out of love and affection for the family—not for money. For example, if your sister picks the kids up from school every day and watches them until 5:30 P.M. for free, she is not an employee. If you pay her, however, she is then an employee and you must comply with most employment laws, such as minimum wage and workers compensation requirements. Hiring family members does not fall under anti-discrimination laws.

If you hire your own spouse, or your child (under age twenty-one), to perform household work, that family member will have to pay income taxes but is exempt from social security, medicare, and unemployment taxes.

DISCRIMINATION IN HIRING

If a major corporation refused to hire African-Americans, it could be sued for race discrimination. If a national hotel chain refused to rent rooms to Jews, it could be sued for religious discrimination. If an airline hired only young, attractive women as flight attendants; it would be violating federal civil rights laws which prohibit gender and age discrimination. Do such restrictions apply to you, or may you discriminate in your selection of household employees? The answer depends on the type of discrimination.

Three separate federal laws prohibit discrimination in employment:

1. Section 1981 of the Civil Rights Act, which prohibits racial discrimination.

2. Title VII of the Civil Rights Act, which prohibits discrimination based on gender, religion, age, and ethnicity.

3. The Americans with Disabilities Act (ADA), which prohibits discrimination against people with a variety of physical, medical, and mental disabilities.

Only the first of these laws applies to you. No employer may make a hiring decision based upon the applicant's race. The other discrimination laws apply only to people who have fifteen or more employees. If you are wealthy enough to have fifteen or more household employees, you already have at least one lawyer on retainer and should refer this question to your lawyer.

The courts have established a five part test for determining if racial discrimination in hiring exists. All five of these factors must be met:

1. A member of a racial minority group applied for a job

2. The applicant had the necessary qualifications for the job

3. The applicant was not hired

4. The employer (you) hired a white person with lesser qualifications, or continued the job search and eventually hired a white person whose qualifications were the same as the rejected applicant's

5. You are unable to provide a legitimate nonracial explanation for your decision

Bear in mind that the race discrimination laws do not require you to hire a non-white applicant or give him or her a preference. Regardless of your race and the race of the applicants, you may hire the person who is best qualified for the job. What you may not do is intentionally refuse to hire an applicant because of his or her race. In other words, you must act in good faith and consider all applicants equally.

Also, hiring a nanny is different from hiring other household help. Because child care involves all sorts of intimate and emotional factors, you have the right to hire a nanny based on personal traits such as how well you and she get along, the similarity of your values, and whether your personalities fit well together. If you feel instinctively that a particular white applicant will bond with your children better than a particular black applicant, you may base your hiring decision on that feeling. What you cannot do is decide in advance, before you have even interviewed anyone, that a white nanny would be better for your child than a black nanny.

Employment discrimination lawsuits are difficult to prove and expensive to bring, so they are rarely brought against individuals with limited resources. Your chances of being sued are small. However, you can take a few simple steps to protect yourself against even the small possibility of a lawsuit:

1. Advertise the job in the newspaper; don't rely just on word of mouth.

2. Before you begin any interviewing, have written guidelines describing what you are looking for—how many years' experience, educational level, scheduling flexibility, own transportation,

willingness to work occasional weekends, etc. Conduct the interview according to those guidelines and try to avoid talking about irrelevant personal topics (except for hiring nannies, where personality is a relevant job criteria).

3. Keep track of the information you learn, so that you will be able to explain how well different applicants fit your "ideal employee" profile.

4. Don't discuss race during the interview or mention it in advertising. If asked, make it clear that race is not part of your criteria.

5. Hire the best qualified person regardless of race.

AGE LIMITS

MINIMUM AGE

Federal law sets a minimum age. You may not "employ" children under the age of sixteen in any occupation. However, using teenagers for occasional babysitting and lawn mowing less than eight hours per week is permitted because they do not qualify as *employees*. Many states also have their own child labor laws.

MAXIMUM AGE

There is no maximum age for an employee. No law says anyone has to retire at age sixty-five or seventy. Many senior citizens now work part time to supplement their social security. A grandmother may be just what you are looking for as a part-time nanny! You may hire them, however old they are.

SCREENING AND INTERVIEWING JOB APPLICANTS

When we hired our nanny, we did not advertise, invite applications, interview candidates, or conduct background checks. We were hiring a woman we had known for years.

You may not be so fortunate. Hiring a total stranger and entrusting them with your children is a scary thing to do. What if she has a hidden history of violence, drug abuse, or child molestation? The employing of a stranger as a cook or maid poses risks because she will have substantial access to your home, your valuables, and your desk drawers. How do you know she was not fired from her previous job for forging checks she stole from her boss's desk? What steps can you take to screen applicants and investigate their backgrounds? The sections that follow discuss the laws that balance your right to discover relevant information and the applicant's right to privacy.

EMPLOYMENT
APPLICATIONS

If someone were applying for a job at the grocery store, they would have to fill out a job application form. There is a reason employers use these forms: they facilitate the gathering of relevant background information. Why not use one yourself?

Employment application forms commonly ask a job applicant for the following basic information:

- ☞ Full name
- ☞ Whether they have ever been known by a different name
- ☞ Complete address
- ☞ Previous address if they have recently moved
- ☞ Date and place of birth
- ☞ Social security number

You have the right to request an applicant's social security number in connection with a job application (social security numbers are not private or confidential, as many people believe). You can explain to an applicant who feels uneasy about this that you will need their social security number eventually in order to issue them a paycheck. The form should not ask about race and probably should not ask for sex or ethnic background, since it may be illegal to discriminate on those bases. Check appendix A to see if any other kinds of discrimination are illegal in your state and make sure your application form does not ask for that information either.

Many forms also ask for some or all of the following information:

- ☞ Any criminal convictions
- ☞ Education information—name of school, dates attended, degrees
- ☞ Apprenticeships, training programs, or technical education
- ☞ Work experience—name, address, dates, job descriptions, reason for leaving
- ☞ Driver's license number (if applicant will be driving for you)
- ☞ Personal references—names, addresses
- ☞ Starting date availability
- ☞ Ability to work nights and weekends if needed

Application forms generally end with two standard provisions: a statement by you promising to keep the information confidential, and an affirmation by the applicant that they are being truthful. For example:

All information will be kept strictly confidential.

I certify that the statements I have made are true and correct to the best of my knowledge.

Signed: _____

An employment application form is included in appendix B (form 1). Standardized forms are also readily available at most office supply stores.

CONDUCTING AN INTERVIEW

Chances are you are not an experienced interviewer. People who screen applicants in a corporate human resources department may conduct hundreds of job interviews a year. This may be the first one you have ever conducted.

Professional job interviewers stick to a standard series of questions and do not improvise. They only ask about matters related to the qualifications needed for the job they are filling. They do not ask personal and family questions which are irrelevant to the job description because they know that asking personal questions is the easiest way to get sued for discrimination if you do not hire the person.

For example, consider a young woman applying for a job selling cars. The interviewer (to be friendly) asks her if she is married and what her husband does. Then he asks, "Are you planning a family?" She says yes. The applicant is not hired and she sues for gender and pregnancy discrimination. The interviewer, of course, denies that the decision not to hire her had anything to do with gender. But why, then, did he ask about marital status and pregnancy? These issues are not germane to selling cars. The obvious implication is that either intentionally or subconsciously, the employer did not hire her because he was concerned that she might quit when she became pregnant.

You should follow the lead of these professional interviewers. Have a pre-determined list of topics to discuss and do not use the interview for small talk or trying to make friends. It is okay to ask about anything connected to an applicant's ability to perform the job; however, you should not talk about any topics that are closely related to grounds for illegal discrimination. For example:

- ☛ Don't ask a woman what her husband does for a living. Because if this question is usually asked only of women, it may be evidence of gender discrimination.

- ☛ Don't ask a woman about her children and the arrangements she has made for child care. It is gender discrimination to assume that a woman will have to shoulder the burden of child care in her family and to not hire her because she might not be able to come to work when her children are sick.

- ☛ Don't ask a woman about pregnancy or whether she plans to have a family in the future.

☞ Don't ask a person's ethnic background, especially if they look "exotic." The question may seem innocuous to you ("You have unusual skin coloring. Are you Indian?"), but may later be used as evidence of discrimination if you do not hire that person.

☞ Similarly, don't ask where an applicant is from originally, as this may lead to ethnic information.

☞ Don't discuss age, except if necessary to ascertain that the applicant is over eighteen. If a person appears elderly and you worry whether they can do the tasks, ask about ability ("One of my children weighs forty pounds. Will you be able to lift her up?") rather than age ("One of my children weighs forty pounds. Do you think your age will interfere with your picking her up?").

☞ Don't ask about religion unless it is directly relevant to the job. For example, you could ask a prospective nanny, "We will want you to say the same grace before lunch that we say at dinner. Will you have any problem doing this?" However, do not, however, ask, "So what church do you attend?" merely as a topic of social conversation. Even though you may prefer to employ a member of the same religious faith as you, in many states, this is illegal discrimination.

☞ Don't ask about disabilities, even if they are obvious, unless they are related to the job. If you are hiring a nanny, you can safely ask, "I see that you walk with a cane. How do you think this would affect your ability to take the children for walks or play games with them?" If you are hiring a cook, don't ask, "I see you walk with a cane. What happened to you?"

☞ Don't ask about whether the applicant smokes tobacco or drinks alcohol. Even if you would prefer to have an employee who never smokes or drinks, what they do in their own home is irrelevant, and a growing number of states make discrimination based on off-the-job conduct illegal. You may worry that a nanny who smokes at home will smoke occasionally on the job (say, at a park), and you do not want your child exposed to a smoker as a role model, but that does not justify your asking about the applicant's conduct at home. You may ask only about on-the-job hours ("I do not want anyone smoking near my child. Does this pose any problems for you? Are you able to go a full eight-hour day without smoking?"). If you are hiring a live-in employee, you may ask if they can refrain from smoking anywhere in your house.

☛ We suggest you do not ask about sexual orientation. In some states, discrimination based on sexual orientation is illegal. In other states, there are gay rights cases pending in the courts that could change the law. These laws are based on the principle that sexual orientation is irrelevant to most household jobs, such as cooks, gardeners, and elder care providers, and is therefore irrelevant to an employment decision. The issue is more complicated when you are hiring a nanny, but again, sexual orientation is largely irrelevant. Scientific evidence shows clearly that the sexual orientation of children is not affected by the sexual orientation of their caregivers. If you nevertheless have strong feelings about the sexual orientation of your nanny, you may wish to consult a local attorney who specializes in employment law and discuss the issue with him or her before you start interviewing.

☛ Don't ask about current membership in the National Guard or military reserves. It is illegal in most states not to hire a member of these forces because they might be called to duty and miss work.

If you need a topic for "small talk" purposes, safe ones include books they have read, television shows or movies they have enjoyed, favorite restaurants, what they think of your local sports team's latest scandal, or something recent in the news. Better yet, ask about their general attitudes toward the job for which they are applying. You could ask a prospective nanny, "Tell me your own views on how children ought to be raised. What kinds of values should we instill in them?" You could ask an applicant for a gardener job to talk about his favorite types of plants or his favorite city park, and what it is about them he likes.

Remember—you're hiring an employee, not making a new friend; so keep it businesslike!

BACKGROUND INVESTIGATION

After the application and interview, you may want to verify the background of good prospects. Such an investigation may include verifying their basic credentials, checking their character and criminal records, and following up on references. Once an applicant has completed the job application form, you have the necessary personal information on the applicant to conduct such checks.

The easiest and most reliable way to do this is to hire a private detective. Running background checks is a common activity for a detective agency. They will have the necessary forms and know how to get information from law enforcement and other agencies. They may even have sources of information not available to you. Of course, this costs money. If you prefer to undertake this task yourself, some guidelines follow.

CRIMINAL BACKGROUND CHECKS

Checking criminal records seems like a basic step in any investigation. Especially for hiring a nanny, this is a good way to help reduce the chance that you or your children will be victimized by the person you hire. A criminal record may be some indication of a tendency toward dishonesty or violent behavior. You certainly want to screen out anyone with a history of past crimes against children.

In general, criminal records are public and may be accessed by anyone with a legitimate need to know the information. Hiring a new employee is considered a legitimate reason to do a criminal record check. You should call or visit your local police department, sheriff's office, or state police office; explain your purpose; and ask for a form to request a criminal record check. Fill it out with all the information you have, return it to the police station, and they will run a computerized criminal record check for you. There is usually a small charge ($7 to $10) for this service, which takes about twenty-four hours.

There are limits to what you can find out from criminal records. Juvenile records, or even serious offenses, are confidential and will not appear. Convictions from other states might not appear. The record also will not list crimes for which the person was accused, but the charges were dropped or the person was found not guilty.

In addition to conducting a criminal background check, you may want to check the sex offender registry for your state, especially when hiring a nanny. In 1996, a federal law, commonly called "Megan's Law," was enacted; this law requires local law enforcement agencies in all fifty states to develop registries of convicted child molesters and to notify parents about their presence. Many states have made it easy to check on a potential nanny or other household employee to see if they have any sex offenses in their backgrounds. You will need to know the person's name, date of birth, and social security number—all of which should be on their employment application form. It is likely that your local law enforcement office can conduct this check at the same time as they conduct the general criminal records check. Be sure to ask specifically.

You also can easily check this information yourself in most places. Many states have put their sex offender registries on the Internet. Others have installed "hotline" telephone numbers that enable you to quickly access the information. If there is a do-it-yourself way of checking for sexual offenders in your state, information is included in appendix A.

DRIVING RECORD CHECKS

If you are hiring a chauffeur or a nanny who will drive your children places, you may want to check their driving record. Incidents of reckless or drunk driving will probably not be reflected on their general criminal record, so you will need to see their driving record. You should generally be able to get this from the police department at the same time as you run the general criminal record check, or you can obtain it directly from your state department of motor vehicles. A driver's license check will also help you verify that the applicant gave you his or her true identity. You will need to know the applicant's full name, address, date of birth and driver's license number—all information asked for on the employment application form. There is usually a charge for obtaining these records ($3–$10), so you will want to call the department before you send them a request.

CREDIT CHECKS

There is a lot of controversy concerning so-called *credit checks*. We're all familiar with them. They range from the extensive reports obtained by mortgage lenders to brief phone call checks made by department stores issuing credit cards. Can you run a credit check on an applicant? Yes, although the process is cumbersome and the area is extensively regulated by federal law. Also, we've seen our credit reports, and frankly they are boring. You are unlikely to get much information relevant to your hiring decision, so you may sensibly skip this process if you prefer.

Credit reports generally contain the following information: bankruptcies, tax liens, court judgments, child support obligations, loans (including past defaults), credit cards (including amounts in arrears), department store charge account information, and the names of other employers or lenders who have requested the file. The reports will probably not contain information on backgrounds, bank accounts, character, criminal history, or medical history. You may have seen a copy of your own credit report when you applied for a mortgage or car loan.

There are two ways you can obtain these types of reports. The first option is simpler—ask your applicant to obtain a copy of her own credit report and bring it to you when it arrives. A person can order their own report for about $8 from any of the three leading credit agencies by calling their toll-free numbers:

- ☞ Equifax Information Service Center: 1-800-685-1111
- ☞ Experian Consumer Assistance (formerly TRW): 1-800-682-7654
- ☞ Trans Union Corporation: 1-800-916-8800

There are two drawbacks to this approach. First, there is always the danger that the applicant will remove a damaging piece of information and deliver only a partial report to you. Second, if you are hiring someone to be a maid, cook or gardener, the applicant may not have the sophistication or language skills necessary to get their own credit report.

The second option is to do it yourself. As a prospective employer, you are authorized by federal law to obtain someone else's credit history.

However, before a credit reporting agency can send this information to you, you may have to open an account with them and obtain their forms. The major companies will not serve you directly—they charge large fees and have minimum monthly inquiry requirements that you will not satisfy. However, they also use *resellers*—local credit agencies that handle small accounts and single inquiries. You can find these small credit agencies in your Yellow Pages under *Credit Reporting Agencies*. Their fees vary considerably and may prove more expensive than you think the information is worth. All you can do is call and ask. Be sure to tell them you want this information for employment purposes.

If you decide to use a credit reporting agency, federal law requires that you adhere to these guidelines:

☞ You must give the applicant a clear and conspicuous written disclosure advising her "that a consumer report may be obtained for employment purposes." This disclosure must be written on a document that contains nothing but the disclosure.

☞ The applicant must give you written authorization to procure the report.

☞ You may not use this information against the applicant without first providing her with a copy of the report and a statement of her rights afforded by Federal law.

☞ You may not use the information in the report "in violation of any applicable Federal or State equal employment opportunity law or regulation."

What does this mean for you? If you intend to obtain a consumer report on your prospective employee, you should follow these six steps:

1. Ask the applicant to fill out your standard Employment Application (form 1 in appendix B).

2. Give the applicant a separate page containing a statement in large, bold print that you intend to obtain a copy of his or her consumer credit report. The credit agency you contact may have copies of

such forms for you, or you may use the Disclosure of Intent to Request Consumer Report (form 2).

3. Obtain the applicant's written consent to disclosure of his or her credit report. This should be on a separate piece of paper from the notice itself. If no appropriate form is included in the materials supplied to you by the credit agency, use the Consent to Disclosure of Consumer Credit Report (form 3).

4. Prepare a document called a "certification," in which you swear that you are a bona fide employer seeking the information only for employment purposes. If no form is included in the materials supplied by the credit reporting agency, you may use the Certification to Credit Reporting Agency (form 5).

5. Prepare a cover letter (form 6) or fill out the agency's request form.

6. Attach copies of the disclosure and consent forms to the cover letter or agency request form, and mail these documents to the credit reporting agency of your choice.

If you decide to obtain a credit report on your potential nanny or cook, make sure you use the report only for employment purposes. You cannot show the report to someone else or use it for any other purpose. The potential penalties can be severe:

☛ Willful noncompliance—this means that you know the requirements and deliberately decide not to comply with them.

• If this is the case, you can be held liable to the consumer for actual damages the consumer incurs of "not less than $100 and not more than $1,000."

• If you obtain "a consumer report under false pretenses or knowingly without a permissible purpose," you may have to pay the consumer the actual damages she sustained "or $1,000, whichever is greater," punitive damages, and all court costs and attorney fees associated with the lawsuit. You could potentially be imprisoned for two years.

- You may also be held liable to the consumer reporting agency for the greater amount of either $1,000 or the actual damages incurred by the agency.

☛ Negligent noncompliance—this means that you failed to comply with the regulations when you knew or should have known that the regulations applied to your actions. If this is the case, you may be held liable to the consumer for actual damages she has incurred and reasonable attorney fees.

If you decide not to hire someone based on their credit report, federal law requires that you give the applicant a copy of the credit report, along with a written explanation that the person has the right to obtain a free copy of their own report (include the phone numbers listed previously for the various credit agencies), and has the right to request the correction of erroneous information.

FRAUD CHECKS

Just because your applicant comes through a background check with flying colors, you should not end your inquiry. You need to verify one final thing: is your applicant who she says she is? How do you protect yourself against the possibility that the applicant is a thief casing your home, or a child molester who has changed his name?

Credit agencies offer a wonderful service called a Fraud Alert Notification. This service checks to see whether an applicant's Social Security number matches her name, whether the person to whom the number was issued has been reported dead, whether the person's telephone numbers and zip codes match at her current and former addresses, and so forth. It is not foolproof, but it is a simple and inexpensive way of verifying the applicant's identity.

Drug Testing

The issue of drug testing is controversial. It has been and will continue to be the subject of extensive regulation and is the kind of hot political issue that causes state legislatures to pass laws changing the rules in almost every session. We suggest that you do not attempt to require a job applicant to submit to a drug test without first checking with an attorney who specializes in employment and labor law.

We are talking here only about a pre-employment drug test. Asking for periodic drug tests after you hire someone is covered in chapter 2. In general, you can assume that you probably can require pre-employment drug screening under the following conditions:

☛ Drug use by the employee would pose a legitimate safety concern. For example, if the person is applying for a job such as nanny or chauffeur, or would ever be carrying a gun or providing personal security for the family, you can probably require a drug test, but not if she is applying to be a gardener or maid.

☛ You test only the person you have decided to hire. If you do intend to ask your applicant to undergo a drug screening test, you should wait until you have decided on a particular applicant, and offer her the job conditioned on passing a drug screening exam.

Most "doc-in-the-box" prompt-care facilities offer a walk-in drug screening test. Other medical and nursing facilities that provide these services will be listed in the Yellow Pages under *Drug Abuse Testing*, or some similar title. The cost may range from $35 to more than $100.

AIDS/HIV Testing

Some parents who are very concerned about AIDS have considered having nanny applicants screened for the virus. Like drug screening, pre-employment blood tests for AIDS or HIV are currently permitted by federal law but may be regulated or prohibited by state law. In some states, there is an absolute right to privacy concerning AIDS, and you probably cannot force a person to take such a test. It may even be improper for you to ask a job applicant to waive their right of privacy and voluntarily take such a test. This is a rapidly changing area of law, so if you plan to ask applicants to take an AIDS test, you should check with a local attorney who specializes in employment law before you do. The same labs and medical facilities that can provide a drug screening test can usually also do a blood test for AIDS/HIV.

If this issue is a concern for you, and you would like to get the latest information about the disease, check the Centers for Disease Control (CDC) web site at http://www.cdc.gov/nchstp/hiv_aids or call the CDC National AIDS Clearinghouse at 1-800-458-5231.

OBTAINING REFERENCES

By far the most common kind of background check is the letter (or phone call) of reference. You ask your applicant to provide the names of personal references and the names of people she used to work for, and you contact them. You want to know whether she is a person of good character and can be trusted, and whether she performed well at her last job.

But there's a problem. People may be reluctant to talk to you. They may say only general things about your applicant, carefully avoiding saying anything negative about their former employee. They may have heard stories about someone getting sued for giving a bad reference and be scared to give you the information you need. How do you get them to talk?

In some states, a former employer is required to provide a "service letter" stating the dates of service, nature of the job, and the reasons the person left or was fired. To see if there is such a law in your state, check the listing for your state in appendix A. In other states, there is no such law, so it is entirely up to the former employer to decide whether to provide a reference. In either case, you can facilitate the process with a little advance planning. At the application stage, ask that the applicant sign a consent form permitting you to contact their references. You may then contact each reference, tell them you have been given consent to talk to them, and offer to send or fax the form. You may use the Consent to Release of Information from References (form 4).

When you contact a former employer or other reference, what can you ask about? We suggest that you follow the guidelines for interviewing the candidates themselves, discussed previously in this chapter. Ask only about job-related matters and avoid the personal topics listed in that section.

The Employment Contract 2

Entering into a Contract

Once you have decided to offer a job to a particular candidate, you and your new employee will have to agree on an employment contract. In legal terms, a *contract* is an agreement between two parties concerning the rights and duties of each. You will spell out what you expect your new employee to do and how you will compensate her for her job. Contracts may be either oral or written—there is no rule that requires a contract to be in writing. However, we recommend, both as professionals and as parents who have employed a nanny, that you put this contract into written form to avoid any later misunderstanding. A general Employment Agreement (form 8), and a specialized Employment Agreement (form 9) for a nanny, are included in appendix B.

There are two kinds of contracts. Both are legally binding.

1. A "take-it-or-leave-it" contract, where one side spells out the rules and the other side either accepts them or turns down the job. This type of contract is used in everything from opening a bank account to buying insurance—a big company has one standard product available, and you either accept their terms or go elsewhere.

2. A mutually negotiated contract, where two people sit down and discuss the terms and conditions of a contract that would be

important to them, they resolve any differences, and only then does one person put the agreement in writing.

You may prefer the first type (the take-it-or-leave-it contract) because you have clear ideas about exactly what you want a household employee to do.

We successfully used the second type (the mutual agreement) when hiring our nanny. She wanted to begin work after 8:15 A.M. because she had to get her own children ready for school, and she wanted certain holiday periods off and flexibility to take other days off as needed. We wanted her to occasionally help on the weekend or stay late if we could not get home from work and to give us thirty days notice if she decided to quit. We negotiated over her salary, number of vacation days, and a procedure for what would happen if she got sick. We then wrote down our understanding of the agreement.

You should understand, however, that there are limits to what a contract can do. It can help avoid misunderstandings and act as a job description, but it cannot "force" an employee to abide by its terms. It gives you a good basis for evaluating job performance and some protection against a wrongful termination suit (see the section on "Firing an Employee" in chapter 6) if you fire an employee for failing to do the work to which they agreed. Your only practical recourse against an employee who does not do the job they promised is to fire them.

At the same time, a contract binds you. You must live up to your promises or you may be sued for damages. If you promise to pay your cook $7.50 an hour, you cannot later decide that she eats so much of the food she prepares that you will reduce it to $6.50 an hour. If you promise your nanny that she may take the week off between Christmas and New Year's, you cannot change your mind and force her to work because your boss unexpectedly sends you to Europe that week. Household employees are not slaves who work at your whim and must do whatever you want. They are employees whose jobs are defined by your agreement (contract) with them, whether it is a written or oral agreement.

One final note: In many states, a take-it-or-leave-it contract that is unfair or takes advantage of the person in the weaker position (often called a *contract of adhesion*) may be either unenforceable or interpreted against you in court. You have all the bargaining power. If you attempt to force an unfair contract on a household employee, especially a person who has limited education, the courts may not enforce it. They will not permit you to take advantage of someone's need for a job and limited sophistication to write into a contract a whole bunch of clauses that turn her into your vassal.

Do You Need a Written Contract?

You don't need a written contract. In most states, you may hire, set job requirements, and fire employees *at will*. Nevertheless, you may want a written contract. We recommend them. There are numerous issues other than an employee's basic duties and the circumstances under which she can be fired that need to be addressed. A written contract protects you from misunderstandings that might lead to lawsuits over the terms and conditions of employment. The contract can itemize exactly what duties you expect from your employee, what days and times you expect these duties to be performed, what the rate of pay will be, how overtime pay will be computed, what you consider to be holidays and whether they are paid or unpaid, whether your nanny can use corporal punishment, and so forth. The list of items that can be placed in an employment contract is endless.

There is a potential downside to an employment contract. In many states, having a contract can hinder your ability to terminate an employee whenever you want, or to suddenly change her duties. Depending on how the contract is worded, you may only be allowed to terminate employment for breach of the written agreement. For example, suppose your contract states that your ex-husband is allowed to visit the children only on Fridays while they are in your nanny's care. One week, you and your ex-husband agree to change his visitation to Thursday. You explain this to your nanny. Despite this, your nanny refuses to let your ex-husband see the children on Thursday, and he hauls you back into court complaining that you are interfering with his visitation. You are mad at the nanny for getting you into trouble, and you want to fire her. Can you? Probably not. The contract clearly stated that the ex-husband could only visit on Fridays, and the nanny was just performing her contractual duties.

The lesson here is that a written contract is useful in spelling out the basic duties of the job but should not be too specific. It should also include a provision giving you the power to supplement the contract with additional oral or written instructions. Without this final clause, the language of the contract cannot be modified by oral or written instructions from you. We have included a modification clause as section F in the Employment Agreement (form 8) and section H in the nanny Employment Agreement (form 9).

A written contract is also useful to specify what type of notice you require if your employee quits. Without a contract, she may walk off the job any time without notice, leaving you stranded the week of your big business trip to London. This might not matter if the person who quits is your gardener. The azaleas will survive. But it can be a major inconvenience if the person quitting is your nanny. Alternative child care cannot be arranged overnight. For this reason alone, a written contract with a nanny is important. Typically, employers require two weeks notice, but you can decide on any time-frame upon which you and the nanny can agree. New nannies are hard to find; therefore, you may want thirty days' notice from a nanny. The beauty of a written contract is that you and your employee can agree to almost anything as long as it is legal.

Don't forget that both you and your employee should sign and date the contract. It is not necessary to get it notarized.

In the sections that follow, we discuss the major issues that you will need to discuss with your new employee and on which you will need to reach agreement. Your agreement can then be expressed in an employment contract—salary, benefits, and the terms and conditions of the job itself.

There is nothing magical about writing an employment contract. By using form 8 or form 9 in appendix B, and filling in your agreement in your own words, you will have a valid contract.

COMPENSATION

The federal Fair Labor Standards Act regulates minimum wage, overtime pay, and record-keeping and requires equal pay for equal work regardless of gender. Anyone who employs another person must comply with this Act. Its terms apply to nannies and other household employees, but not to occasional babysitters or lawn mowers who work for you less than eight hours a week.

MINIMUM WAGE

Nannies, gardeners, maids, chauffeurs, nurses, and other household help are called *domestic service employees* under the Fair Labor Standards Acts. All must be paid at least the federal minimum wage. At the time this book was printed, the federal minimum wage was $5.15 per hour for anyone who works more than eight hours a week. However, Congress was considering a bill to raise the minimum wage, and we cannot predict exactly what the minimum wage will be when you decide to hire your employee. You can verify the current minimum wage by calling the reference desk at your public library or checking the Department of Labor's web site at:

www.dol.gov/dol/esa/public/minwage/main.htm

In addition, some states may have a minimum wage more than $5.15 an hour. Most states have their own minimum wage laws. They either tie their rate to the federal level or set a state minimum wage lower than

$5.15, in which case the federal wage is the one that applies. You cannot pay your employees less than federal minimum wage. However, at the time we went to press, eight states had set their minimum wage higher than the federal rate, in which case you will have to pay the higher state wage. See the listing for your state in appendix A, but remember that minimum wage is the kind of hot topic that leads to frequent changes in state law, so the wage information might be out of date by the time you refer to this. There is a useful Internet site that summarizes current state minimum wage laws at:

www.toolkit.cch.com/text/p05_4046.asp

One category of household employee is exempt from federal minimum wage laws: an employee who provides companionship services to the aged or infirm who cannot care for themselves. Note that this does not include employees who care for children. Nannies are fully subject to minimum wage laws. Eldercare employees are exempt as long as at least eighty percent of their working time is devoted solely to providing companionship. Services like bed making, dressing, bathing, and cooking are not considered companionship and may constitute no more than twenty percent of the employee's work day.

OVERTIME   Chances are you will be faced with overtime situations on a regular basis. The Federal overtime laws are different for three classes of domestic employees:

1. So-called "come-and-go" employees who do not live with you and are paid an hourly wage

2. Live-in household employees

3. Salaried employees

The most common type of employee is the come-and-go employee who works for an hourly wage. For these employees, you must pay one and one-half times their regular hourly rate for each hour of overtime they work. Anything over forty hours in a week requires overtime pay, and overtime must be calculated on a weekly basis. If your nanny works forty-five hours one week and thirty-five hours the next week, you still must pay her overtime for the five extra hours the first week. However, overtime is not required on a daily basis (except in California). If she works ten hours one day and six hours the next, no overtime is required for the ten-hour day.

Overtime rates are based on your employee's basic hourly wage as set forth in your contract, not on minimum wage. If you pay your employee $5.15 minimum wage, her overtime rate is $7.73 per hour (1.5 x $5.15). If you pay your Nanny $10.00 per hour, however, her overtime rate is $15.00 (1.5 x $10.00). You can't change this by contract.

If the nanny lives with you, calculating overtime is more complicated. As long as she is only "on duty" forty hours a week, she is not entitled to overtime for the extra hours she is on-call on the premises. On-call time must generally be compensated, but is exempt from the overtime requirement. The problem is calculating how many hours a day she is really working. The issue needs to be clarified in your contract.

Salaried workers are not entitled to overtime at all. However, their total compensation for the year must satisfy minimum wage laws. A salaried employee is entitled at least to what they would make if they were hourly workers receiving minimum wage plus time-and-a-half for over-time. Sound confusing? It's not that bad. If a nanny works for you all year, her yearly salary must be at least minimum wage ($5.15 per hour) times forty hours per week, for fifty-two weeks, or $10,712 per year. If you expect her to work more than that—for example, from 8:00 A.M. to 5:00 P.M., or nine hours a day—then her salary must be at least what she would make on an hourly basis including overtime. In this example, her salary minimum at an hourly basis would be calculated as follows:

$5.15/hour (minimum wage) x 40 hours = $206.00

plus

$7.73/hour (minimum overtime wage) x 5 hours = $38.65

which equals

$244.65/week minimum ($206.00 + $38.65)

times 52 weeks equals

$12,721.80/year minimum salary

In other words, you cannot put someone on a yearly salary as a trick to evade minimum wage laws and pay your employees less than they would make as hourly employees. Take the extreme example of the quintessential nanny: Mary Poppins. She was a live-in nanny for the Banks family. This meant that Mary was required to sleep in a room adjacent to the nursery; take care of the children from 6:30 A.M when they got up, until 8:00 P.M. when they went to bed (a thirteen-hour day, or eight regular hours and five overtime hours); and to handle illnesses, drinks of water, and other night-time events (one extra overtime hour per day). She worked six days a week (one extra thirteen hour day, all overtime). Her minimum weekly salary would have to be:

40 hours at minimum wage = $206.00

plus

46 hours of overtime = $355.58

equals

$561.58 per week

times 52 weeks per year equals

$29,202.16 minimum yearly salary.

If you were paying Mary Poppins $20,000 a year salary and requiring her to be on duty those hours, you would be in violation of federal law.

COMP TIME

Your employees are entitled to overtime pay if they work more than forty hours a week; not if they work more than eight hours a day. If you have regular business meetings on Mondays that always run late, so you ask your nanny to work from 8:00 A.M. to 8:00 P.M. on Mondays, you are allowed to give her four hours of *compensatory time*, or *comp time*, instead of four hours of overtime. Comp time is time off from work given to compensate for extra hours worked so the employee's work week remains under forty hours. However, there is a big condition put on comp time: you must give it, and the nanny must take it, in the same week in which she put in overtime hours.

For example: Suppose your nanny's normal work week is eight hours per day, Monday through Friday. You leave town at 8:00 A.M. Monday morning on a business trip and don't get home until Wednesday at 3:00 P.M., leaving the nanny in charge of the children for fifty-four hours. Thus, by Wednesday evening, the nanny has already put in fifty-four hours in three days and is on the verge of a nervous breakdown. That's thirty extra hours (yes, you have to pay her for sleeping on the job) beyond the twenty-four hours she would normally have worked those three days. If you pay your nanny $10 an hour, thirty hours of overtime would cost you $450! You have two choices: If you make your nanny work the rest of the week, you must pay the overtime rate on the full thirty hours. If you give the nanny Thursday and Friday off (sixteen hours of comp time), you pay the regular hourly rate for those sixteen hours ($160). However, even if you give her the rest of the week off, she still has an additional fourteen hours of overtime due to her. You cannot eliminate it by giving her an additional two days off next week. Comp time must be taken in the same week as the overtime.

If your employee has fixed regular hours, you must pay overtime when she works extra time whether she is technically hourly or salaried. For example, if your nanny regularly works a forty-hour week, and you pay her $10 an hour, you will have to pay her five hours of overtime at $15 per hour if she works forty-five hours one week. You cannot avoid paying this overtime by giving nanny a "salary" of $400 per week for a forty-hour week, and then paying her the same $400 in a week in which she works forty-five hours. You are still required to pay her overtime for the extra five hours. The rate is calculated by converting her weekly rate into an hourly rate—taking $400 per week and dividing it by forty hours, which equals a basic rate of $10 per hour. You owe her five hours of overtime at $15 an hour.

In your contract, you should spell out whether you will pay overtime or give comp time and whether you or your employee has any choice in the matter.

Overtime is not required if your employee is on a genuine yearly or monthly salary. In a genuine salary arrangement, the hours required week by week vary, and your contract specifies that the employee is required to work as many hours as reasonably necessary to get the job done. It is common to hire a gardener this way. His job is to "keep the grounds looking nice." In winter, he may work only a few hours per week. In the spring, he may put in twelve hour days. Following a storm, he may have to work around the clock to get debris cleared away.

Hours of Employment

Is there a maximum number of hours an employee can work? No. You can ask your employees to work as many hours a week as they are willing to work and you are willing to pay them. As we just saw, however, every hour over forty per week must be paid time and a half, so working your employees long hours is expensive.

Also, be careful about designating a specific number of hours in the contract. If you describe the job as customarily a forty-hour week, it could be interpreted as setting a maximum number of hours by contract. So make it clear that the employee will work overtime at your request.

Employee Benefits

GENERALLY   Generally, an employer is not required to provide employee fringe benefits, such as health insurance, vacations, or holidays. If you want to keep your employees happy, you may decide that they deserve some benefits. You should specify what you are willing to provide in your written employment contract.

MATERNITY
AND FAMILY
EMERGENCY
LEAVE   In most states, you are not required to provide time off to an employee for maternity leave or family medical emergencies. The federal Family and Medical Leave Act of 1993 entitles employees to take reasonable unpaid leave for medical reasons, the birth or adoption of a child, or to care for a seriously ill family member. However, it applies only if you

have fifty or more employees (full or part-time), so will not affect most household employers.

A number of states have their own family and medical leave acts, but most of them also do not apply to an employer with only a few employees. However, if you live in the District of Columbia, Iowa, Maine, or Montana, you may be required to provide reasonable pregnancy, maternity or adoption leave. Such leave does not have to be paid, and you generally will not have to guarantee to hold the position open if the demands of the job preclude it. For example, if you employ a nanny five days a week to care for your children, and she wishes to take eight weeks of maternity leave, you do not have to go without child care for eight weeks waiting for her to return. The nature of the job requires that the children have constant care and supervision, and temporary care is virtually unavailable. On the other hand, if your housekeeper wants three weeks of family leave, you may be required to grant it and hold her job open for her. Nothing bad will happen to the house while she's gone and commercial cleaning services are readily available to fill in for her. If you live in one of the four states with family leave acts that apply to small employers, and you think you cannot hold a job open for an employee who wants parental leave, you should check with a local attorney who specializes in employment law to determine your options.

VOTING, JURY SERVICE, AND NATIONAL GUARD DUTY

The only "fringe benefit" you are required to provide is time off for important civil obligations: voting, serving on jury duty, and training or active service in the National Guard or military reserves.

OTHER SUBJECTS FOR EMPLOYMENT CONTRACTS

REIMBURSEMENT FOR EXPENSES

Who pays the bill when your nanny takes your children to the movies or the swimming pool? If your cook picks up some fresh thyme from the farmer's market on her way to work, how will you reimburse her?

There is no legal restriction—you may work this arrangement any way you want. You can leave a supply of "petty cash" at home and your nanny or cook can use it as needed and remind you when it is running low. This works well if you trust the employee and remember to replenish the cash drawer. You may also include a notebook in the cash drawer and ask your employee to record her expenses or leave the receipts.

Alternatively, you can expect your household help to spend their own money and be reimbursed. Many businesses use this system, reimbursing their employees as needed. You can reimburse at the end of a day in which expenses are incurred, or for convenience, you can reimburse on a weekly basis at the same time you calculate the paycheck. If you are going to reimburse, you should decide whether you will take the nanny's word for it or require receipts. Whatever you decide should be included in the contract to avoid later misunderstanding.

PERIODIC DRUG TESTS

You may require your household employees to undergo periodic drug screening as far as federal law is concerned. You have too few employees to be covered by the Americans with Disabilities Act. You are probably okay under most state laws if you require a nanny or a chauffeur to have periodic tests, because both those jobs qualify under the "safety" exception. There is a significant risk to your children if the nanny becomes incapacitated by drug use, and a significant risk to the public if your chauffeur does. However, state laws vary considerably and change often, so if you decide you want to require drug testing, you should contact a local attorney who specializes in employment law.

One common provision in an employment contract you may want to include is a paragraph that gives you the right to ask for a drug-screening test at some time in the future if you have a reasonable suspicion that the employee is affected by drug use. You would still want to contact an employment lawyer before actually invoking this clause to force your chauffeur to get a drug test, but you would at least head off any argument that you cannot ask for one because there was no provision in the contract concerning it.

Your Obligations As a New Employer 3

Immigration Laws

Whatever other decisions you make about following or ignoring the advice in this book, do not skip this stage. The federal Immigration Reform and Control Act requires all employers to verify the identity and work eligibility of all persons hired. In recent years, under political pressure to minimize the number of jobs held by illegal aliens, the Immigration and Naturalization Service (INS) has been serious about this rule. Indeed, household employment as maids, cooks, gardeners, and nannies (often at low wages) has traditionally been one of the main sources of jobs for illegal aliens. Household employers rarely bother to check citizenship and are often willing to look the other way even if they know the applicant is an illegal alien if she is willing to work for less than the going rate.

The fine for employing an undocumented worker is $3,000 per worker and up to six months in jail. Of course, it is unlikely that the Federal Government would impose a heavy fine or jail time on a first-offender household employer, but why take the chance? Just because it is current INS policy not to actively pursue families hiring illegal domestic workers, the policy could change at any time. It is almost always a bad idea to break the law based on the government's assurances they will not prosecute you. Besides, someone (including your employee) may report you, bringing you to the attention of the INS without their doing anything.

FORM I-9
Basically, the law requires that you be able to prove that your employees are legally entitled to work—either because they are U.S. citizens or are *documented* aliens who have been given permission to work by the government. To prove this, you are required to make your employees produce identification and fill out a federal "Employment Eligibility Verification" form, also called an "I-9." A sample filled-in I-9, along with its instructions, can be found on pages 58 through 60. Form 11 in appendix B is a blank I-9 form. For more information, including obtaining I-9 forms and a copy of the booklet titled *Handbook for Employers and Instructions for Completing Form I-9*, check one or more of the following:

☞ INS web sites: http://www.ins.usdoj.gov

http://www.us-immigration.com

To download blank I-9 forms:

http://www.ins.usdoj.gov/forms/download/i-9.htm

☞ INS phone numbers: 1-800-870-3675 or 1-202-514-2000

☞ INS address: U.S. Department of Justice
Immigration and Naturalization Service
425 I Street, NW
Washington, DC 20536

As soon as you have hired a new employee, you must provide him or her with a copy of the I-9 form to fill out and ask the employee to provide proper documentation proving identity and citizenship. A complete list of the various types of acceptable documentation can be found in the instructions to the I-9 form on page 60. The employee has three days to provide either one piece of primary identification (from "List A") or two pieces of secondary identification (one from "List B" and one from "List C").

The most common form of primary identification is a United States passport. The other types of identification mentioned in List A are forms issued by the government to foreigners, authorizing them to work in the United States. However, be aware that List A of acceptable forms described in the instructions to form I-9 is not entirely accurate due to recent changes in the immigration laws.

Warning

You will note that List A includes ten items. Several of these items are no longer acceptable, however, the government has not yet changed the I-9 form. The Illegal Immigration Reform and Immigrant Responsibility Act of 1996 resulted in the following changes:

☛ Documents 2, 3, 8, and 9 in List A are no longer acceptable.

☛ Document 4 is only acceptable for an alien who is authorized to work for a specific employer.

However, as of the printing of this book, the government was not making any new forms or instructions available; and employers were not yet being prosecuted for violating the new rules.

Many U.S. citizens do not possess any of the primary documents described in List A. Therefore, a new employee may instead provide you two secondary documents. The first type of secondary document must establish the employee's identity. The documents that are acceptable to prove identity are found in List B. The second type of secondary document must establish the employee's eligibility for employment. The documents that are acceptable to prove employment eligibility are found in List C.

The instructions to Form I-9 spell out exactly what kinds of identification are acceptable. Follow these guidelines to the letter—accept no substitutes! You will need to make a photocopy of the documents the employee provides you, and keep them on file.

There are two things you do not have to do. First, you don't have to verify the authenticity of a document used to prove identity. As long as the document looks reasonably genuine (examples are shown in the *Handbook for Employers and Instructions for Completing Form I-9*), you have satisfied the law. Second, you don't send Form I-9 anywhere. Instead, you must keep it on file for as long as the employee works for you and at least one year thereafter. This may tempt you to ignore this step because the INS is not likely to ever check up on a family employing a nanny. The problem is that the nanny may be picked up for deportation and asked where she was working—and then the INS may come knocking on your door.

The penalty for failing to fill out the I-9 and keep it for the required time period is a fine of at least $100 but not more than $1,000 for each employee for whom you do not have a completed I-9.

NOT ALL
FOREIGNERS
ARE ILLEGAL
ALIENS

Just because an applicant is from a foreign country and has not become a U.S. citizen, does not mean he or she is an illegal alien who cannot be hired. Many non-Americans are in this country legally and have been given permission to work by the government. This is the world of green cards (which are not actually green), work permits, and visas.

It is much easier for you to hire a nanny or gardener who is already a citizen of the United States. But the best applicant for a job might be a non-citizen, or you may want a foreign nanny who can teach your children French or Spanish. You may only legally hire a foreigner if the person has the right immigration status.

Is your employee a citizen of the United States despite being "foreign"? A person is a citizen if any one of the following apply:

☞ The person was born in the United States. It does not matter whether his or her parents were citizens, or whether he or she has been living in a foreign country

☞ The person was born abroad, both parents were United States citizens, and at least one of the parents lived in the United States at some point in their life

☞ The person was born abroad, one parent was a United States citizen who lived at least five years in the United States before his or her birth, and two of the five years in the United States were after this parent's fourteenth birthday

☞ The person is from Puerto Rico

If your employee falls into one of these categories, he or she is entitled to U.S. citizenship, and you may hire the person.

NON-IMMIGRANT VISAS

Non-immigrant visas give someone temporary residence in the United States for any one of a number of purposes, including employment. However, these visas are given for very specific purposes (work, study, travel) and are not transferable. A non-citizen on a student visa cannot work; a person on an employment visa cannot quit work and go to school.

There are two temporary visas that permit a person to work while they are here:

1. The "H-2B" visa for unskilled workers

2. The "J-1" visa for exchange visitors

H-2B Visas. H-2B visas are limited to 66,000 per year for all unskilled workers coming into the United States. Most are taken up by U.S. companies with international facilities who need to bring their foreign workers to the United States for temporary periods to learn how the U.S. operations work. Only about 6,000 visas are available for domestic employees.

To get an H-2B visa, a non-citizen must already have a temporary job offer in the U.S. Thus, if you particularly wanted to hire a nanny from France who could teach your children to speak French while taking care of them, you would first have to hire one through an advertisement or agency in France and then have her apply for the visa. Once you have hired her, you are considered an employer and she is eligible for the visa. However, before she can request it, you must obtain a certification of need from the U.S. Department of Labor. You must demonstrate that the position you are filling satisfies prevailing wage and conditions standards, but that American workers are unavailable. To prove this, you must jump through several hoops, including verification that you have advertised the position, considered all American applicants, and have a justifiable reason for rejecting all U.S. citizens who have applied for the job (for example, no U.S. applicant willing to work as a nanny is fluent in French). Once you have jumped through these hoops, you send the documentation to the French nanny you have found, and she must apply for the visa at the U.S. Embassy in her country.

The process is complicated and time consuming and your nanny might not get one of the few visas given in any year. In the unlikely event that your nanny is granted a visa, it is good for only one year. Thereafter, she must apply to the INS for an extension of the visa on an annual basis. Employees are limited to two extensions, which means your nanny could stay in the U.S. for a maximum of three years. Obviously, this slow and cumbersome process is not very practical for hiring non-citizens for most household jobs. Nevertheless, this is a plausible approach if you especially want a foreign nanny who can teach your children a different language, and you can wait for the endless federal bureaucracy to process the application. You probably should obtain the assistance of a lawyer who specializes in Immigration law to facilitate the process.

J-1 Visa. The J-1 visa allows American families to host a foreign youth as an *au pair*. An official *au pair* relationship is not technically employment—it is an exchange, in which you provide air fare, lodging, food, parental supervision, $139 per week spending money, and an introduction to American culture to the *au pair*; and she provides child care. This sounds good to many parents, who think it will enable them to obtain the services of a nanny cheaply. There are two potential drawbacks:

☞ The J-1 visa is granted strictly to young people between eighteen and twenty-seven years old, so you may be getting a nanny with no child-raising experience. Louise Woodward was such an *au pair*, and her inexperience led to tragic results for the family who hired her.

☛ There are some strict federal guidelines that must be followed:

1. *Au pairs* can spend no more than forty-five hours per week on child care activities.

2. You are required to provide room, board, and $139 per week "pocket money."

3. You must take the *au pair* to cultural events to promote cross-cultural awareness. This may sound like fun, but if you had the time to do this, you wouldn't have required an *au pair*.

4. You are not allowed to choose your *au pair*; instead, she is chosen for you by the organizing agency which oversees the program. This means you have no way of investigating her background or checking her references.

5. The maximum time an *au pair* is allowed to stay in the country is one year, and it cannot be extended. This time restriction puts you in the "nanny hunting mode" more often than the H-2B Visa.

6. Your actual chances of getting an *au pair* are slim because only 2,840 American families are allowed an *au pair* each year.

IMMIGRANT
VISAS

An immigrant is a "legal alien"—a person who has been granted permission to immigrate to the U.S. for the purpose of eventually becoming a citizen. They are called *Permanent Resident Aliens*, and may work at any job they want. They possess an *Immigrant Visa*, commonly called a *green card*, although it is no longer actually green. A bona fide green card looks like a credit card with a holographic image on the front and an optical memory stripe on the back.

Immigration is strictly controlled by a series of quotas. An applicant for a household job might hold an immigrant visa because they have relatives or a spouse already living in the United States, or because they have been on a waiting list for several years in their home country for one of the few immigrant visas allotted to it.

In theory, a foreign worker could also obtain an immigrant visa through her prospective employer. As an employer, you may request such a visa for a worker you wish to bring to the U.S. by promising that there is a job waiting for them. We say "in theory" because this is not at present a very practical alternative. Current law limits immigrant visas to 10,000 per year for household employees, and the current waiting period is approximately five years.

REFUGEES

There is one final non-citizen status that permits employment—a refugee who has been granted asylum. A *refugee* is a person who has been driven out of their own country and cannot return because he or she will be persecuted. A refugee can seek asylum if the persecution is based on race, religion, nationality, membership in a particular social group, or political opinion. For example, in 1999, ethnic Albanians coming to the U.S. from Kosovo qualified for temporary asylum because of the extermination campaign (so-called *ethnic cleansing*) waged against them by the majority Serbs in their native land.

Some non-citizens who are here on student, travel, or work visas do not want to go home. They may justifiably fear persecution or may simply not want to return to a more impoverished life. If you decide to help such a person try to claim refugee status, be aware that the process of applying for asylum is complicated and requires an attorney who specializes in Immigration law.

REGISTERING AS A NEW EMPLOYER

If this is your first household employee, you will need to fill out some registration forms for both the federal and state government. The process is discussed in the following sections.

FEDERAL
EMPLOYER
IDENTIFICATION
NUMBER

The Ford Motor Company does not have a social security number, so what does it put down on its tax form? It uses something called a *Federal Employer Identification Number*. These have the same number of digits as a social security number, but are written in the form 12-3456789 instead of 123-45-6789. As an employer, you must get an employer identification number just like Ford! It will be needed for a number of state and federal reports and forms that you will fill out later.

Luckily, employer identification numbers are easy to obtain. Just visit your local IRS office and ask for an SS-4 form or use the blank form we have included as form 12 in appendix B. A sample filled-in SS-4 form, along with its instructions, can be found on pages 61 through 64.

STATE LAW
INFORMATION
FOR NEW
EMPLOYERS

Many states have information packets for new employers that contain instructions on what kinds of reporting are required. If such a packet is available in your state, the listing for your state in appendix A will explain how to obtain it. The packets generally include W-4 forms which your employee must complete, forms needed to report new hires, forms to obtain an account number for paying withheld income taxes, and a form for registering with the employment security commission and paying unemployment taxes.

If your state does not have a comprehensive information packet, you will have to obtain the necessary forms for tax withholding and paying unemployment insurance taxes directly from the relevant state agencies, which are listed in appendix A.

STATE
REGISTRATION

In all states, you are supposed to register with your state employment agency as a new employer. In many states, you must also register with the state tax department so they can set up a withholding account for you. You will have to obtain the necessary forms from both agencies unless you are lucky enough to live in one of the fifteen states that use a combined registration form. The listing for your state in appendix A explains with which agencies you must register, and where you can obtain the necessary forms.

The primary reason you must register is to establish an account with your state employment security commission for purposes of tracking employment, reporting new hires, and paying the unemployment tax (FUTA). To establish a tax rate for unemployment insurance taxes, you will have to fill out something called a "Status Report" or a "Report to Determine Liability." Based on the information you provide, the state agency will determine how much you must pay into the state unemployment insurance fund. Your rate depends on the history of your business—how many former employees have filed for unemployment? If this is your first employee, you will start at a general rate (commonly 2.7% of your total payroll), which will rise or fall over the years depending on whether any of your employees file for unemployment. These forms are generally due promptly at the end of the first quarter in which you have paid out $1,000 or more to your household employees.

When filling out these registration forms, you may be asked to identify what type of business entity you are. Obviously, you are not a "business" in the usual sense. If there is an option to indicate "individual" or "household employer," select that. If not, select "sole proprietorship," and if there is space to describe your business, put "private household employer."

Some forms will ask you whether you are required to file a federal Employer's Annual Federal Unemployment Tax Return (Form 940). You should answer "no." Instead of using Form 940, you will report on and pay Federal Unemployment Tax (FUTA) on Schedule H for Household Employers. This is discussed later in chapter 5.

You will eventually be issued an account number. Don't lose it and don't be tempted to skip this stage. Like your new federal taxpayer identification number, you will be asked for your state number on forms the government wants you to fill out, including Schedule H on your federal income tax return.

DISCUSSING TAX WITHHOLDING WITH YOUR EMPLOYEE

You are not required to withhold federal income taxes from the paycheck of a household employee. In one of those rare situations in which Congress actually simplified the tax laws, they exempted household employers from the general rule requiring businesses to withhold their employees' income taxes. Many states also do not require income tax withholding. However, you have the option to voluntarily withhold state and federal income taxes from your employee's paycheck.

You may ask: If I don't have to do it, why on earth would I want to? Withholding income taxes will present little difficulty for you and require little extra paperwork because you are required to withhold social security taxes anyway. If you do not withhold income taxes, your employee must make quarterly estimated tax payments. Especially if your household employees have limited education, they may have trouble complying with the estimated tax system. When you hire an employee, you should sit down with them and discuss whether they prefer to make the estimated payments themselves or prefer that you withhold the taxes. Make sure they understand that the taxes must be paid and that you will be required at the end of the year to tell the IRS how much they have earned. If you have not withheld taxes and they have not made estimated tax payments, they may have to pay interest and civil fines or criminal penalties. Why run the risk of losing a good employee or getting them into trouble with the IRS? For that reason, we encourage you to withhold taxes from your employee's paycheck.

W-4 FORM

If you will be withholding taxes (federal or state) from your employee's paycheck, he or she must fill out a W-4 form. You filled one out yourself when you started your own job. A W-4 is the form that asks an employee how many "allowances" he or she will be claiming, so that the correct amount of federal and state income tax can be withheld from the paycheck. These forms also must be filled out in most states even if you will not be withholding taxes, because they are used to report new hires.

A copy of the "alternate" federal W-4 form, and its instructions, can be found on pages 65 and 66. This alternate form includes space for noting the additional information needed to report a new hire. If you are unsure whether to use the regular or alternate version of the W-4, use the alternate version. You also may get a state version of the W-4 in your packet of information for new employers, or be able to easily download one from the Internet. See the listing for your state in appendix A for Internet addresses for state tax forms. You may use any W-4 form as far as federal taxes are concerned. For state tax and new hire reporting, it will generally be preferable to use the state version if one is available, or the alternate version.

You should give the W-4 form to your new employee and ask him or her to complete it. Do not fill it out yourself, even if the employee is of limited education. If your new employee is unable to fill out the form, you may assist him or her, but the employee should be the one to actually fill out the form.

When your new employee returns the form, check to make sure it is completely filled out and contains his or her full name, social security number, address, and signature. Also look at line 5. The total number of allowances the employee is claiming should be approximately equal to the number of people in his or her immediate family (spouse and children). If the number is either zero or very high, you may want to make sure the employee understood how to fill out the form, or it may result in over-withholding or under-withholding. If the number is ten or more, you must send the W-4 to the IRS; otherwise it is for your own benefit as an employer. The W-4 form will be used in conjunction with the withholding tables to tell you exactly how much federal and state income tax must be withheld from your employee's paycheck.

REPORTING YOUR "NEW HIRE"

State and federal governments are keeping increasingly close track of the workforce for a variety of economic and political purposes. State agencies need to know who is eligible for welfare and unemployment compensation. Law enforcement and welfare agencies are trying to prevent parents from evading child support payments by switching jobs. For these and other reasons, the state government will want you to report that you have hired someone. This is called a *new hire*.

In most states, you will have to send a copy of the W-4 form your employee filled out to a designated state agency. Some states also require you to report the employee's date of birth and the date of hire. Boxes for including this information are listed as "optional" information on the W-4. Make sure your employee fills in this information when you first hire him or her if you will be sending it to your state new hire agency. Information about the requirements for your state, including where to get and send the forms, is included in appendix A. Some states permit registration over the Internet, and those web sites are also listed.

In general, you will have to report your new hire within twenty days of the date you hire someone, but a few states require the report sooner. Hawaii, for example, requires the report within five days. Deadlines for each state are specified in appendix A. Because each state varies in exactly what information it wants, it is impossible to give specific instructions here. Wherever possible, we have included in appendix A a phone number for each state where you can call for assistance.

NOTIFY YOUR INSURANCE COMPANY

Bringing an employee into your home raises liability and insurance issues. If the nanny falls down your poorly lit basement stairs, will her injuries be covered on your homeowner's policy? If you fire the nanny and she sues you for breach of contract, will any damages or the cost of defending yourself be covered by your umbrella policy? If she has an accident while driving your car, will your automobile insurance cover it? If your maid orders ten thousand dollars worth of merchandise using your credit card number, will your insurance cover you?

To answer these questions, you must talk to your insurance agent. Some homeowner and automobile policies exclude "employees" from some kinds of general coverage. Others require that you notify your company or your entire policy is void. If you hire a nanny or chauffeur to drive your car, you will need to report the addition of a new "regular driver," and your rates may rise.

Notifying your insurance company is very important. Otherwise, you may find out only after an accident, damage, or lawsuit that you have no coverage, and then it is too late. This issue is covered in more detail in chapter 7.

WORKERS' COMPENSATION INSURANCE

In most states, household employers are exempt from the requirement that all employers must provide workers' compensation insurance. In other states, household employers must obtain insurance only if there are three or more employees. However, be sure to check the listing for your state in appendix A because in a few states you are required to obtain this insurance. There is usually a state insurance pool for small employers with only one or two employees. You can find out by contacting a general business insurance agency or by calling the state department of labor whose number is listed in appendix A.

In some states, your homeowner's insurance policy will cover household employees and be an acceptable substitute for the required workers' compensation insurance. You will need to review this with your insurance agent.

Deferred Compensation Plans Through Your Employer

Many large corporations offer deferred compensation plans that permit their employees to put up to $5,000 a year into a special account used to pay for child care. Check to see if your company has such a plan. If you select it, the $5,000 is deducted from your gross income before taxes are computed, which reduces your adjusted gross income. It is therefore advantageous from a tax standpoint to use this system for paying nanny, rather than just paying her from your after-tax income and taking the child-care tax credit.

If your employer does not offer this tax saver benefit program, you are not hurt too badly. You can still take a tax credit for child care. This is discussed later in chapter 5 concerning tax returns.

Deferred compensation plans are available only for child care employees, not for other kinds of household help. You are limited to $5,000 per year per family. If you and your spouse both work, and both have deferred compensation plans available, it makes no difference which plan you use. It is probably administratively easier to defer the full $5,000 through one employer rather than deferring $2,500 through each, but it makes no tax difference.

U.S. Department of Justice
Immigration and Naturalization Service

OMB No. 1115-0136
Employment Eligibility Verification

Please read instructions carefully before completing this form. The instructions must be available during completion of this form. **ANTI-DISCRIMINATION NOTICE. It is illegal to discriminate against work eligible individuals. Employers CANNOT specify which document(s) they will accept from an employee. The refusal to hire an individual because of a future expiration date may also constitute illegal discrimination.**

Section 1. Employee Information and Verification. To be completed and signed by employee at the time employment begins

Print Name:	Last	First	Middle Initial	Maiden Name
	Poppins	Merry	I.	Poppins

Address *(Street Name and Number)*	Apt. #	Date of Birth *(month/day/year)*
4569 George Lane	345	6/7/67

City	State	Zip Code	Social Security #
Ocala	FL	00000	789-10-2345

I am aware that federal law provides for imprisonment and/or fines for false statements or *use of false documents* in connection with the completion of this form.

I attest, under penalty of perjury, that I am (check one of the following):
☒ A citizen or national of the United States
☐ A Lawful Permanent Resident (Alien # A _____)
☐ An alien authorized to work until ____/____/____
(Alien # or Admission # _____)

Employee's Signature	Date *(month/day/year)*
Merry I. Poppins	10/9/00

Preparer and/or Translator Certification. *(To be completed and signed if Section 1 is prepared by a person other than the employee.) I attest, under penalty of perjury, that I have assisted in the completion of this form and that to the best of my knowledge the information is true and correct.*

Preparer's/Translator's Signature	Print Name

Address *(Street Name and Number, City, State, Zip Code)*	Date *(month/day/year)*

Section 2. Employer Review and Verification. To be completed and signed by employer. **Examine one document from List A OR examine one document from List B and one from List C** as listed on the reverse of this form and record the title, number and expiration date, if any, of the document(s)

	List A	OR	List B	AND	List C
Document title:	Passport		_____		_____
Issuing authority:	_____		_____		_____
Document #:	123456789		_____		_____
Expiration Date *(if any)*:	10/6/06		___/___/___		___/___/___
Document #:	_____				
Expiration Date *(if any)*:	___/___/___				

CERTIFICATION - I attest, under penalty of perjury, that I have examined the document(s) presented by the above-named employee, that the above-listed document(s) appear to be genuine and to relate to the employee named, that the employee began employment on *(month/day/year)* **10/9/00** **and that to the best of my knowledge the employee is eligible to work in the United States.** (State employment agencies may omit the date the employee began employment).

Signature of Employer or Authorized Representative	Print Name	Title
Renee Fjord	Renee Fjord	owner

Business or Organization Name	Address *(Street Name and Number, City, State, Zip Code)*	Date *(month/day/year)*
	1238 Minnie Drive, Ocala, FL 00000	10/9/00

Section 3. Updating and Reverification. To be completed and signed by employer

A. New Name *(if applicable)*	B. Date of rehire *(month/day/year) (if applicable)*

C. If employee's previous grant of work authorization has expired, provide the information below for the document that establishes current employment eligibility.

Document Title:_____ Document #:_____ Expiration Date (if any): ___/___/___

I attest, under penalty of perjury, that to the best of my knowledge, this employee is eligible to work in the United States, and if the employee presented document(s), the document(s) I have examined appear to be genuine and to relate to the individual.

Signature of Employer or Authorized Representative	Date *(month/day/year)*

Form I-9 (Rev. 11-21-91) N

U.S. Department of Justice
Immigration and Naturalization Service

OMB No. 1115-0136
Employment Eligibility Verification

INSTRUCTIONS
PLEASE READ ALL INSTRUCTIONS CAREFULLY BEFORE COMPLETING THIS FORM.

Anti-Discrimination Notice. It is illegal to discriminate against any individual (other than an alien not authorized to work in the U.S.) in hiring, discharging, or recruiting or referring for a fee because of that individual's national origin or citizenship status. It is illegal to discriminate against work eligible individuals. Employers **CANNOT** specify which document(s) they will accept from an employee. The refusal to hire an individual because of a future expiration date may also constitute illegal discrimination.

Section 1 - Employee. All employees, citizens and noncitizens, hired after November 6, 1986, must complete Section 1 of this form at the time of hire, which is the actual beginning of employment. **The employer is responsible for ensuring that Section 1 is timely and properly completed.**

Preparer/Translator Certification. The Preparer/Translator Certification must be completed if Section 1 is prepared by a person other than the employee. A preparer/translator may be used only when the employee is unable to complete Section 1 on his/her own. However, the employee must still sign Section 1 personally.

Section 2 - Employer. For the purpose of completing this form, the term "employer" includes those recruiters and referrers for a fee who are agricultural associations, agricultural employers, or farm labor contractors.

Employers must complete Section 2 by examining evidence of identity and employment eligibility within three (3) business days of the date employment begins. If employees are authorized to work, but are unable to present the required document(s) within three business days, they must present a receipt for the application of the document(s) within three business days and the actual document(s) within ninety (90) days. However, if employers hire individuals for a duration of less than three business days, Section 2 must be completed at the time employment begins. **Employers must record: 1)** document title; **2)** issuing authority; **3)** document number, **4)** expiration date, if any; and **5)** the date employment begins. Employers must sign and date the certification. Employees must present original documents. Employers may, but are not required to, photocopy the document(s) presented. These photocopies may only be used for the verification process and must be retained with the I-9. **However, employers are still responsible for completing the I-9.**

Section 3 - Updating and Reverification. Employers must complete Section 3 when updating and/or reverifying the I-9. Employers must reverify employment eligibility of their employees on or before the expiration date recorded in Section 1. Employers **CANNOT** specify which document(s) they will accept from an employee.

- If an employee's name has changed at the time this form is being updated/ reverified, complete Block A.

- If an employee is rehired within three (3) years of the date this form was originally completed and the employee is still eligible to be employed on the same basis as previously indicated on this form (updating), complete Block B and the signature block.

- If an employee is rehired within three (3) years of the date this form was originally completed and the employee's work authorization has expired or if a current employee's work authorization is about to expire (reverification), complete Block B and:
  - examine any document that reflects that the employee is authorized to work in the U.S. (see List **A** or C),
  - record the document title, document number and expiration date (if any) in Block C, and
  - complete the signature block.

Photocopying and Retaining Form I-9. A blank I-9 may be reproduced provided both sides are copied. The Instructions must be available to all employees completing this form. Employers must retain completed I-9s for three (3) years after the date of hire **or** one (1) year after the date employment ends, whichever is later.

For more detailed information, you may refer to the INS Handbook for Employers, (Form M-274). You may obtain the handbook at your local INS office.

Privacy Act Notice. The authority for collecting this information is the Immigration Reform and Control Act of 1986, Pub. L. 99-603 (8 U.S.C. 1324a).

This information is for employers to verify the eligibility of individuals for employment to preclude the unlawful hiring, or recruiting or referring for a fee, of aliens who are not authorized to work in the United States.

This information will be used by employers as a record of their basis for determining eligibility of an employee to work in the United States. The form will be kept by the employer and made available for inspection by officials of the U.S. Immigration and Naturalization Service, the Department of Labor, and the Office of Special Counsel for Immigration Related Unfair Employment Practices.

Submission of the information required in this form is voluntary. However, an individual may not begin employment unless this form is completed since employers are subject to civil or criminal penalties if they do not comply with the Immigration Reform and Control Act of 1986.

Reporting Burden. We try to create forms and instructions that are accurate, can be easily understood, and which impose the least possible burden on you to provide us with information. Often this is difficult because some immigration laws are very complex. Accordingly, the reporting burden for this collection of information is computed as follows: **1)** learning about this form, 5 minutes; **2)** completing the form, 5 minutes; and 3) assembling and filing (recordkeeping) the form, 5 minutes, for an average of 15 minutes per response. If you have comments regarding the accuracy of this burden estimate, or suggestions for making this form simpler, you can write to both the Immigration and Naturalization Service, 425 I Street, N.W., Room 5304, Washington, D. C. 20536; and the Office of Management and Budget, Paperwork Reduction Project, OMB No. 1115-0136, Washington, D.C. 20503.

Form I-9 (Rev. 11-21-91) N

EMPLOYERS MUST RETAIN COMPLETED I-9
PLEASE DO NOT MAIL COMPLETED I-9 TO INS

LISTS OF ACCEPTABLE DOCUMENTS

LIST A		LIST B		LIST C
Documents that Establish Both Identity and Employment Eligibility	**OR**	**Documents that Establish Identity**	**AND**	**Documents that Establish Employment Eligibility**

LIST A

1. U.S. Passport (unexpired or expired)

2. Certificate of U.S. Citizenship (INS Form N-560 or N-561)

3. Certificate of Naturalization (INS Form N-550 or N-570)

4. Unexpired foreign passport, with I-551 stamp or attached INS Form I-94 indicating unexpired employment authorization

5. Alien Registration Receipt Card with photograph (INS Form I-151 or I-551)

6. Unexpired Temporary Resident Card (INS Form I-688)

7. Unexpired Employment Authorization Card (INS Form I-688A)

8. Unexpired Reentry Permit (INS Form I-327)

9. Unexpired Refugee Travel Document (INS Form I-571)

10. Unexpired Employment Authorization Document issued by the INS which contains a photograph (INS Form I-688B)

LIST B

1. Driver's license or ID card issued by a state or outlying possession of the United States provided it contains a photograph or information such as name, date of birth, sex, height, eye color, and address

2. ID card issued by federal, state, or local government agencies or entities provided it contains a photograph or information such as name, date of birth, sex, height, eye color, and address

3. School ID card with a photograph

4. Voter's registration card

5. U.S. Military card or draft record

6. Military dependent's ID card

7. U.S. Coast Guard Merchant Mariner Card

8. Native American tribal document

9. Driver's license issued by a Canadian government authority

For persons under age 18 who are unable to present a document listed above:

10. School record or report card

11. Clinic, doctor, or hospital record

12. Day-care or nursery school record

LIST C

1. U.S. social security card issued by the Social Security Administration (other than a card stating it is not valid for employment)

2. Certification of Birth Abroad issued by the Department of State (Form FS-545 or Form DS-1350)

3. Original or certified copy of a birth certificate issued by a state, county, municipal authority or outlying possession of the United States bearing an official seal

4. Native American tribal document

5. U.S. Citizen ID Card (INS Form I-197)

6. ID Card for use of Resident Citizen in the United States (INS Form I-179)

7. Unexpired employment authorization document issued by the INS (other than those listed under List A)

Illustrations of many of these documents appear in Part 8 of the Handbook for Employers (M-274)

Form I-9 (Rev. 11-21-91) N
FPI-RBK

Form **SS-4** (Rev. February 1998) Department of the Treasury Internal Revenue Service	**Application for Employer Identification Number** (For use by employers, corporations, partnerships, trusts, estates, churches, government agencies, certain individuals, and others. See instructions.) ▶ **Keep a copy for your records.**	EIN OMB No. 1545-0003

Please type or print clearly.

1 Name of applicant (legal name) (see instructions)
Renee Fjord

2 Trade name of business (if different from name on line 1)	**3** Executor, trustee, "care of" name

4a Mailing address (street address) (room, apt., or suite no.) 1238 Minnie Drive	**5a** Business address (if different from address on lines 4a and 4b)
4b City, state, and ZIP code Ocala, FL 00000	**5b** City, state, and ZIP code

6 County and state where principal business is located
Bradford, Florida

7 Name of principal officer, general partner, grantor, owner, or trustor—SSN or ITIN may be required (see instructions) ▶ 345-67-8910
Renee Fjord

8a Type of entity (Check only one box.) (see instructions)

Caution: *If applicant is a limited liability company, see the instructions for line 8a.*

☒ Sole proprietor (SSN) 345 : 67 : 8910
☐ Partnership   ☐ Personal service corp.
☐ REMIC   ☐ National Guard
☐ State/local government   ☐ Farmers' cooperative
☐ Church or church-controlled organization
☐ Other nonprofit organization (specify) ▶ _____
☐ Other (specify) ▶ _____

☐ Estate (SSN of decedent) _____
☐ Plan administrator (SSN) _____
☐ Other corporation (specify) ▶ _____
☐ Trust
☐ Federal government/military
(enter GEN if applicable) _____

8b If a corporation, name the state or foreign country (if applicable) where incorporated

State	Foreign country

9 Reason for applying (Check only one box.) (see instructions)
☐ Started new business (specify type) ▶ _____
☒ Hired employees (Check the box and see line 12.)
☐ Created a pension plan (specify type) ▶

☐ Banking purpose (specify purpose) ▶ _____
☐ Changed type of organization (specify new type) ▶ _____
☐ Purchased going business
☐ Created a trust (specify type) ▶ _____
☐ Other (specify) ▶ _____

10 Date business started or acquired (month, day, year) (see instructions)

11 Closing month of accounting year (see instructions)
12/31/00

12 First date wages or annuities were paid or will be paid (month, day, year). **Note:** *If applicant is a withholding agent, enter date income will first be paid to nonresident alien. (month, day, year)* . . . . ▶ 10/20/00

13 Highest number of employees expected in the next 12 months. **Note:** *If the applicant does not expect to have any employees during the period, enter -0-. (see instructions)* . . . . ▶

Nonagricultural	Agricultural	Household

14 Principal activity (see instructions) ▶

15 Is the principal business activity manufacturing? . . . . ☐ Yes ☒ No
If "Yes," principal product and raw material used ▶

16 To whom are most of the products or services sold? Please check one box.   ☐ Business (wholesale)
☐ Public (retail)   ☐ Other (specify) ▶   ☐ N/A

17a Has the applicant ever applied for an employer identification number for this or any other business? . . . . ☐ Yes ☐ No
Note: *If "Yes," please complete lines 17b and 17c.*

17b If you checked "Yes" on line 17a, give applicant's legal name and trade name shown on prior application, if different from line 1 or 2 above.
Legal name ▶   Trade name ▶

17c Approximate date when and city and state where the application was filed. Enter previous employer identification number if known.

Approximate date when filed (mo., day, year)	City and state where filed	Previous EIN

Under penalties of perjury, I declare that I have examined this application, and to the best of my knowledge and belief, it is true, correct, and complete.

	Business telephone number (include area code) 404-567-8900
	Fax telephone number (include area code) 404-567-8900

Name and title (Please type or print clearly.) ▶ Renee Fjord

Signature ▶ *Renee Fjord*   Date ▶ 10/06/00

Note: *Do not write below this line. For official use only.*

Please leave blank ▶	Geo.	Ind.	Class	Size	Reason for applying

For Paperwork Reduction Act Notice, see page 4.   Cat. No. 16055N   Form **SS-4** (Rev. 2-98)

Form SS-4 (Rev. 2-98)

General Instructions

Section references are to the Internal Revenue Code unless otherwise noted.

Purpose of Form

Use Form SS-4 to apply for an employer identification number (EIN). An EIN is a nine-digit number (for example, 12-3456789) assigned to sole proprietors, corporations, partnerships, estates, trusts, and other entities for tax filing and reporting purposes. The information you provide on this form will establish your business tax account.

Caution: *An EIN is for use in connection with your business activities only. Do NOT use your EIN in place of your social security number (SSN).*

Who Must File

You must file this form if you have not been assigned an EIN before and:

• You pay wages to one or more employees including household employees.

• You are required to have an EIN to use on any return, statement, or other document, even if you are not an employer.

• You are a withholding agent required to withhold taxes on income, other than wages, paid to a nonresident alien (individual, corporation, partnership, etc.). A withholding agent may be an agent, broker, fiduciary, manager, tenant, or spouse, and is required to file **Form 1042**, Annual Withholding Tax Return for U.S. Source Income of Foreign Persons.

• You file **Schedule C**, Profit or Loss From Business, **Schedule C-EZ**, Net Profit From Business, or **Schedule F**, Profit or Loss From Farming, of **Form 1040**, U.S. Individual Income Tax Return, **and** have a Keogh plan or are required to file excise, employment, or alcohol, tobacco, or firearms returns.

The following must use EINs even if they do not have any employees:

• State and local agencies who serve as tax reporting agents for public assistance recipients, under Rev. Proc. 80-4, 1980-1 C.B. 581, should obtain a separate EIN for this reporting. See **Household employer** on page 3.

• Trusts, except the following:

   1. Certain grantor-owned trusts. (See the **Instructions for Form 1041**.)

   2. Individual Retirement Arrangement (IRA) trusts, unless the trust has to file **Form 990-T**, Exempt Organization Business Income Tax Return. (See the **Instructions for Form 990-T**.)

• Estates

• Partnerships

• REMICs (real estate mortgage investment conduits) (See the **Instructions for Form 1066**, U.S. Real Estate Mortgage Investment Conduit Income Tax Return.)

• Corporations

• Nonprofit organizations (churches, clubs, etc.)

• Farmers' cooperatives

• Plan administrators (A plan administrator is the person or group of persons specified as the administrator by the instrument under which the plan is operated.)

When To Apply for a New EIN

New Business. If you become the new owner of an existing business, **do not** use the EIN of the former owner. IF YOU ALREADY HAVE AN EIN, USE THAT NUMBER. If you do not have an EIN, apply for one on this form. If you become the "owner" of a corporation by acquiring its stock, use the corporation's EIN.

Changes in Organization or Ownership. If you already have an EIN, you may need to get a new one if either the organization or ownership of your business changes. If you incorporate a sole proprietorship or form a partnership, you must get a new EIN. However, **do not** apply for a new EIN if:

• You change only the name of your business,

• You elected on **Form 8832**, Entity Classification Election, to change the way the entity is taxed, or

• A partnership terminates because at least 50% of the total interests in partnership capital and profits were sold or exchanged within a 12-month period. (See Regulations section 301.6109-1(d)(2)(iii).) The EIN for the terminated partnership should continue to be used. This rule applies to terminations occurring after May 8, 1997. If the termination took place after May 8, 1996, and before May 9, 1997, a new EIN must be obtained for the new partnership unless the partnership and its partners are consistent in using the old EIN.

Note: *If you are electing to be an "S corporation," be sure you file* **Form 2553**, *Election by a Small Business Corporation.*

File Only One Form SS-4. File only one Form SS-4, regardless of the number of businesses operated or trade names under which a business operates. However, each corporation in an affiliated group must file a separate application.

EIN Applied for, But Not Received. If you do not have an EIN by the time a return is due, write "Applied for" and the date you applied in the space shown for the number. **Do not** show your social security number (SSN) as an EIN on returns.

If you do not have an EIN by the time a tax deposit is due, send your payment to the Internal Revenue Service Center for your filing area. (See **Where To Apply** below.) Make your check or money order payable to Internal Revenue Service and show your name (as shown on Form SS-4), address, type of tax, period covered, and date you applied for an EIN. Send an explanation with the deposit.

For more information about EINs, see **Pub. 583**, Starting a Business and Keeping Records, and **Pub. 1635**, Understanding your EIN.

How To Apply

You can apply for an EIN either by mail or by telephone. You can get an EIN immediately by calling the Tele-TIN number for the service center for your state, or you can send the completed Form SS-4 directly to the service center to receive your EIN by mail.

Application by Tele-TIN. Under the Tele-TIN program, you can receive your EIN by telephone and use it immediately to file a return or make a payment. To receive an EIN by telephone, complete Form SS-4, then call the Tele-TIN number listed for your state under **Where To Apply**. The person making the call must be authorized to sign the form. (See **Signature** on page 4.)

An IRS representative will use the information from the Form SS-4 to establish your account and assign you an EIN. Write the number you are given on the upper right corner of the form and sign and date it.

Mail or fax (facsimile) the signed SS-4 within 24 hours to the Tele-TIN Unit at the service center address for your state. The IRS representative will give you the fax number. The fax numbers are also listed in Pub. 1635.

Taxpayer representatives can receive their client's EIN by telephone if they first send a fax of a completed **Form 2848**, Power of Attorney and Declaration of Representative, or **Form 8821**, Tax Information Authorization, to the Tele-TIN unit. The Form 2848 or Form 8821 will be used solely to release the EIN to the representative authorized on the form.

Application by Mail. Complete Form SS-4 at least 4 to 5 weeks before you will need an EIN. Sign and date the application and mail it to the service center address for your state. You will receive your EIN in the mail in approximately 4 weeks.

Where To Apply

The Tele-TIN numbers listed below will involve a long-distance charge to callers outside of the local calling area and can be used only to apply for an EIN. THE NUMBERS MAY CHANGE WITHOUT NOTICE. Call 1-800-829-1040 to verify a number or to ask about the status of an application by mail.

If your principal business, office or agency, or legal residence in the case of an individual, is located in:	Call the Tele-TIN number shown or file with the Internal Revenue Service Center at:
Florida, Georgia, South Carolina	Attn: Entity Control Atlanta, GA 39901 770-455-2360
New Jersey, New York City and counties of Nassau, Rockland, Suffolk, and Westchester	Attn: Entity Control Holtsville, NY 00501 516-447-4955
New York (all other counties), Connecticut, Maine, Massachusetts, New Hampshire, Rhode Island, Vermont	Attn: Entity Control Andover, MA 05501 978-474-9717
Illinois, Iowa, Minnesota, Missouri, Wisconsin	Attn: Entity Control Stop 6800 2306 E. Bannister Rd. Kansas City, MO 64999 816-926-5999
Delaware, District of Columbia, Maryland, Pennsylvania, Virginia	Attn: Entity Control Philadelphia, PA 19255 215-516-6999
Indiana, Kentucky, Michigan, Ohio, West Virginia	Attn: Entity Control Cincinnati, OH 45999 606-292-5467

Kansas, New Mexico, Oklahoma, Texas	Attn: Entity Control Austin, TX 73301 512-460-7843
Alaska, Arizona, California (counties of Alpine, Amador, Butte, Calaveras, Colusa, Contra Costa, Del Norte, El Dorado, Glenn, Humboldt, Lake, Lassen, Marin, Mendocino, Modoc, Napa, Nevada, Placer, Plumas, Sacramento, San Joaquin, Shasta, Sierra, Siskiyou, Solano, Sonoma, Sutter, Tehama, Trinity, Yolo, and Yuba), Colorado, Idaho, Montana, Nebraska, Nevada, North Dakota, Oregon, South Dakota, Utah, Washington, Wyoming	Attn: Entity Control Mail Stop 6271 P.O. Box 9941 Ogden, UT 84201 801-620-7645
California (all other counties), Hawaii	Attn: Entity Control Fresno, CA 93888 209-452-4010
Alabama, Arkansas, Louisiana, Mississippi, North Carolina, Tennessee	Attn: Entity Control Memphis, TN 37501 901-546-3920
If you have no legal residence, principal place of business, or principal office or agency in any state	Attn: Entity Control Philadelphia, PA 19255 215-516-6999

Specific Instructions

The instructions that follow are for those items that are not self-explanatory. Enter N/A (nonapplicable) on the lines that do not apply.

Line 1. Enter the legal name of the entity applying for the EIN exactly as it appears on the social security card, charter, or other applicable legal document.

Individuals. Enter your first name, middle initial, and last name. If you are a sole proprietor, enter your individual name, not your business name. Enter your business name on line 2. Do not use abbreviations or nicknames on line 1.

Trusts. Enter the name of the trust.

Estate of a decedent. Enter the name of the estate.

Partnerships. Enter the legal name of the partnership as it appears in the partnership agreement. **Do not** list the names of the partners on line 1. See the specific instructions for line 7.

Corporations. Enter the corporate name as it appears in the corporation charter or other legal document creating it.

Plan administrators. Enter the name of the plan administrator. A plan administrator who already has an EIN should use that number.

Line 2. Enter the trade name of the business if different from the legal name. The trade name is the "doing business as" name.

Note: *Use the full legal name on line 1 on all tax returns filed for the entity. However, if you enter a trade name on line 2 and choose to use the trade name instead of the legal name, enter the trade name on all returns you file. To prevent processing delays and errors, **always** use either the legal name only or the trade name only on all tax returns.*

Line 3. Trusts enter the name of the trustee. Estates enter the name of the executor, administrator, or other fiduciary. If the entity applying has a designated person to receive tax information, enter that person's name as the "care of" person. Print or type the first name, middle initial, and last name.

Line 7. Enter the first name, middle initial, last name, and SSN of a principal officer if the business is a corporation; of a general partner if a partnership; of the owner of a single member entity that is disregarded as an entity separate from its owner; or of a grantor, owner, or trustor if a trust. If the person in question is an alien individual with a previously assigned individual taxpayer identification number (ITIN), enter the ITIN in the space provided, instead of an SSN. You are not required to enter an SSN or ITIN if the reason you are applying for an EIN is to make an entity classification election (see Regulations section 301.7701-1 through 301.7701-3), and you are a nonresident alien with no effectively connected income from sources within the United States.

Line 8a. Check the box that best describes the type of entity applying for the EIN. If you are an alien individual with an ITIN previously assigned to you, enter the ITIN in place of a requested SSN.

Caution: *This is not an election for a tax classification of an entity. See "Limited liability company" below.*

If not specifically mentioned, check the "Other" box, enter the type of entity and the type of return that will be filed (for example, common trust fund, Form 1065). Do not enter N/A. If you are an alien individual applying for an EIN, see the **Line 7** instructions above.

Sole proprietor. Check this box if you file Schedule C, C-EZ, or F (Form 1040) and have a Keogh plan, or are required to file excise, employment, or alcohol, tobacco, or firearms returns, or are a payer of gambling

winnings. Enter your SSN (or ITIN) in the space provided. If you are a nonresident alien with no effectively connected income from sources within the United States, you do not need to enter an SSN or ITIN.

REMIC. Check this box if the entity has elected to be treated as a real estate mortgage investment conduit (REMIC). See the **Instructions for Form 1066** for more information.

Other nonprofit organization. Check this box if the nonprofit organization is other than a church or church-controlled organization and specify the type of nonprofit organization (for example, an educational organization).

If the organization also seeks tax-exempt status, you must file either **Package 1023,** Application for Recognition of Exemption, or **Package 1024,** Application for Recognition of Exemption Under Section 501(a). Get **Pub. 557,** Tax Exempt Status for Your Organization, for more information.

Group exemption number (GEN). If the organization is covered by a group exemption letter, enter the four-digit GEN. (Do not confuse the GEN with the nine-digit EIN.) If you do not know the GEN, contact the parent organization. Get Pub. 557 for more information about group exemption numbers.

Withholding agent. If you are a withholding agent required to file Form 1042, check the "Other" box and enter "Withholding agent."

Personal service corporation. Check this box if the entity is a personal service corporation. An entity is a personal service corporation for a tax year only if:

● The principal activity of the entity during the testing period (prior tax year) for the tax year is the performance of personal services substantially by employee-owners, and

● The employee-owners own at least 10% of the fair market value of the outstanding stock in the entity on the last day of the testing period.

Personal services include performance of services in such fields as health, law, accounting, or consulting. For more information about personal service corporations, see the **Instructions for Form 1120,** U.S. Corporation Income Tax Return, and **Pub. 542,** Corporations.

Limited liability company (LLC). See the definition of limited liability company in the **Instructions for Form 1065.** An LLC with two or more members can be a partnership or an association taxable as a corporation. An LLC with a single owner can be an association taxable as a corporation or an entity disregarded as an entity separate from its owner. See Form 8832 for more details.

● If the entity is classified as a partnership for Federal income tax purposes, check the "partnership" box.

● If the entity is classified as a corporation for Federal income tax purposes, mark the "Other corporation" box and write "limited liability co." in the space provided.

● If the entity is disregarded as an entity separate from its owner, check the "Other" box and write in "disregarded entity" in the space provided.

Plan administrator. If the plan administrator is an individual, enter the plan administrator's SSN in the space provided.

Other corporation. This box is for any corporation other than a personal service corporation. If you check this box, enter the type of corporation (such as insurance company) in the space provided.

Household employer. If you are an individual, check the "Other" box and enter "Household employer" and your SSN. If you are a state or local agency serving as a tax reporting agent for public assistance recipients who become household employers, check the "Other" box and enter "Household employer agent." If you are a trust that qualifies as a household employer, you do not need a separate EIN for reporting tax information relating to household employees; use the EIN of the trust.

QSSS. For a qualified subchapter S subsidiary (QSSS) check the "Other" box and specify "QSSS."

Line 9. Check only **one** box. Do not enter N/A.

Started new business. Check this box if you are starting a new business that requires an EIN. If you check this box, enter the type of business being started. **Do not** apply if you already have an EIN and are only adding another place of business.

Hired employees. Check this box if the existing business is requesting an EIN because it has hired or is hiring employees and is therefore required to file employment tax returns. **Do not** apply if you already have an EIN and are only hiring employees. For information on the applicable employment taxes for family members, see **Circular E,** Employer's Tax Guide (Publication 15).

Created a pension plan. Check this box if you have created a pension plan and need this number for reporting purposes. Also, enter the type of plan created.

Note: *Check this box if you are applying for a trust EIN when a new pension plan is established.*

Banking purpose. Check this box if you are requesting an EIN for banking purposes only, and enter the banking purpose (for example, a bowling league for depositing dues or an investment club for dividend and interest reporting).

Changed type of organization. Check this box if the business is changing its type of organization, for example, if the business was a sole proprietorship and has been incorporated or has become a partnership. If you check this box, specify in the space provided the type of change made, for example, "from sole proprietorship to partnership."

Purchased going business. Check this box if you purchased an existing business. **Do not** use the former owner's EIN. **Do not** apply for a new EIN if you already have one. Use your own EIN.

Created a trust. Check this box if you created a trust, and enter the type of trust created. For example, indicate if the trust is a nonexempt charitable trust or a split-interest trust.

Note: *Do not check this box if you are applying for a trust EIN when a new pension plan is established. Check "Created a pension plan."*

Exception. Do **not** file this form for certain grantor-type trusts. The trustee does not need an EIN for the trust if the trustee furnishes the name and TIN of the grantor/owner and the address of the trust to all payors. See the Instructions for Form 1041 for more information.

Other (specify). Check this box if you are requesting an EIN for any reason other than those for which there are checkboxes, and enter the reason.

Line 10. If you are starting a new business, enter the starting date of the business. If the business you acquired is already operating, enter the date you acquired the business. Trusts should enter the date the trust was legally created. Estates should enter the date of death of the decedent whose name appears on line 1 or the date when the estate was legally funded.

Line 11. Enter the last month of your accounting year or tax year. An accounting or tax year is usually 12 consecutive months, either a calendar year or a fiscal year (including a period of 52 or 53 weeks). A calendar year is 12 consecutive months ending on December 31. A fiscal year is either 12 consecutive months ending on the last day of any month other than December or a 52-53 week year. For more information on accounting periods, see **Pub. 538,** Accounting Periods and Methods.

Individuals. Your tax year generally will be a calendar year.

Partnerships. Partnerships generally must adopt one of the following tax years:

● The tax year of the majority of its partners,

● The tax year common to all of its principal partners,

● The tax year that results in the least aggregate deferral of income, or

● In certain cases, some other tax year.

See the **Instructions for Form 1065,** U.S. Partnership Return of Income, for more information.

REMIC. REMICs must have a calendar year as their tax year.

Personal service corporations. A personal service corporation generally must adopt a calendar year unless:

● It can establish a business purpose for having a different tax year, or

● It elects under section 444 to have a tax year other than a calendar year.

Trusts. Generally, a trust must adopt a calendar year except for the following:

● Tax-exempt trusts,

● Charitable trusts, and

● Grantor-owned trusts.

Line 12. If the business has or will have employees, enter the date on which the business began or will begin to pay wages. If the business does not plan to have employees, enter N/A.

Withholding agent. Enter the date you began or will begin to pay income to a nonresident alien. This also applies to individuals who are required to file Form 1042 to report alimony paid to a nonresident alien.

Line 13. For a definition of agricultural labor (farmwork), see **Circular A,** Agricultural Employer's Tax Guide (Publication 51).

Line 14. Generally, enter the exact type of business being operated (for example, advertising agency, farm, food or beverage establishment, labor union, real estate agency, steam laundry, rental of coin-operated vending machine, or investment club). Also state if the business will involve the sale or distribution of alcoholic beverages.

Governmental. Enter the type of organization (state, county, school district, municipality, etc.).

Nonprofit organization (other than governmental). Enter whether organized for religious, educational, or humane purposes, and the principal activity (for example, religious organization—hospital, charitable).

Mining and quarrying. Specify the process and the principal product (for example, mining bituminous coal, contract drilling for oil, or quarrying dimension stone).

Contract construction. Specify whether general contracting or special trade contracting. Also, show the type of work normally performed (for example, general contractor for residential buildings or electrical subcontractor).

Food or beverage establishments. Specify the type of establishment and state whether you employ workers who receive tips (for example, lounge—yes).

Trade. Specify the type of sales and the principal line of goods sold (for example, wholesale dairy products, manufacturer's representative for mining machinery, or retail hardware).

Manufacturing. Specify the type of establishment operated (for example, sawmill or vegetable cannery).

Signature. The application must be signed by (a) the individual, if the applicant is an individual, (b) the president, vice president, or other principal officer, if the applicant is a corporation, (c) a responsible and duly authorized member or officer having knowledge of its affairs, if the applicant is a partnership or other unincorporated organization, or (d) the fiduciary, if the applicant is a trust or an estate.

How To Get Forms and Publications

Phone. You can order forms, instructions, and publications by phone. Just call 1-800-TAX-FORM (1-800-829-3676). You should receive your order or notification of its status within 7 to 15 workdays.

Personal computer. With your personal computer and modem, you can get the forms and information you need using:

● IRS's Internet Web Site at **www.irs.ustreas.gov**

● Telnet at **iris.irs.ustreas.gov**

● File Transfer Protocol at **ftp.irs.ustreas.gov**

You can also dial direct (by modem) to the Internal Revenue Information Services (IRIS) at 703-321-8020. IRIS is an on-line information service on FedWorld.

For small businesses, return preparers, or others who may frequently need tax forms or publications, a CD-ROM containing over 2,000 tax products (including many prior year forms) can be purchased from the Government Printing Office.

CD-ROM. To order the CD-ROM call the Superintendent of Documents at 202-512-1800 or connect to **www.access.gpo.gov/su_docs**

Form W-4 (2000)

Purpose. Complete Form W-4 so your employer can withhold the correct Federal income tax from your pay. Because your tax situation may change, you may want to refigure your withholding each year.

Exemption from withholding. *If you are exempt, complete only lines 1, 2, 3, 4, and 7, and sign the form to validate it.* Your exemption for 2000 expires February 16, 2001.

Note: *You cannot claim exemption from withholding if (1) your income exceeds $700 and includes unearned income (e.g., interest and dividends) and (2) another person can claim you as a dependent on their tax return.*

Basic instructions. If you are not exempt, complete the Personal Allowances Worksheet. The worksheets on page 2 adjust your withholding allowances based on itemized deductions, adjustments to income, or two-earner/two-job situations. Complete all worksheets that apply. They will help you figure the number of withholding allowances you are entitled to claim. However, you may claim fewer allowances.

New—Child tax and higher education credits. For details on adjusting withholding for these and other credits, see **Pub. 919,** Is My Withholding Correct for 2000?

Head of household. Generally, you may claim head of household filing status on your tax return only if you are unmarried and pay more than 50% of the costs of keeping up a home for yourself and your dependent(s) or other qualifying individuals.

Nonwage income. If you have a large amount of nonwage income, such as interest or dividends, you should consider making estimated tax payments using Form 1040-ES. Otherwise, you may owe additional tax.

Two earners/two jobs. If you have a working spouse or more than one job, figure the total number of allowances you are entitled to claim on all jobs using worksheets from only one W-4. Your withholding will usually be most accurate when all allowances are claimed on the W-4 filed for the highest paying job and zero allowances are claimed for the others.

Check your withholding. After your W-4 takes effect, use Pub. 919 to see how the dollar amount you are having withheld compares to your estimated total annual tax. Get Pub. 919 especially if you used the Two-Earner/Two-Job Worksheet and your earnings exceed $150,000 (Single) or $200,000 (Married). To order Pub. 919, call 1-800-829-3676. Check your telephone directory for the IRS assistance number for further help.

Sign this form. Form W-4 is not valid unless you sign it.

Personal Allowances Worksheet

A	Enter "1" for **yourself** if no one else can claim you as a dependent	**A** __1__
B	Enter "1" if: { • You are single and have only one job; or • You are married, have only one job, and your spouse does not work; or • Your wages from a second job or your spouse's wages (or the total of both) are $1,000 or less. } . .	**B** _____
C	Enter "1" for your **spouse.** But, you may choose to enter -0- if you are married and have either a working spouse or more than one job. (This may help you avoid having too little tax withheld.).	**C** _____
D	Enter number of **dependents** (other than your spouse or yourself) you will claim on your tax return	**D** _____
E	Enter "1" if you will file as **head of household** on your tax return (see conditions under **Head of household** above)	**E** _____
F	Enter "1" if you have at least $1,500 of **child or dependent care expenses** for which you plan to claim a credit . .	**F** _____
G	**New—Child Tax Credit:** • If your total income will be between $16,500 and $47,000 ($21,000 and $60,000 if married), enter "1" for each eligible child. • If your total income will be between $47,000 and $80,000 ($60,000 and $115,000 if married), enter "1" if you have two or three eligible children, or enter "2" if you have four or more	**G** _____
H	Add lines A through G and enter total here. **Note:** This amount may be different from the number of exemptions you claim on your return. ▶	**H** __1__

For accuracy, complete all worksheets that apply.	• If you plan to **itemize or claim adjustments to income** and want to reduce your withholding, see the Deductions and Adjustments Worksheet on page 2. • If you are **single,** have **more than one job,** and your combined earnings from all jobs exceed $32,000 OR if you are **married** and have a **working spouse or more than one job,** and the combined earnings from all jobs exceed $55,000, see the Two-Earner/Two-Job Worksheet on page 2 to avoid having too little tax withheld. • If **neither** of the above situations applies, **stop here** and enter the number from line H on line 5 of Form W-4 below.

- - - - - - - - - - - - - - - **Cut here and give the certificate to your employer. Keep the top part for your records.** - - - - - - - - - - - - - - -

Form **W-4** Department of the Treasury Internal Revenue Service	## Employee's Withholding Allowance Certificate ▶ **For Privacy Act and Paperwork Reduction Act Notice, see page 2.**	OMB No. 1545-0010 **20**○○

1 Type or print your first name and middle initial Mary I.	Last name Poppins	**2** Your social security number 789 ¦ 10 ¦ 2345
Home address (number and street or rural route) 4569 George Street, Apt. 345	**3** ☒ Single ☐ Married ☐ Married, but withhold at higher Single rate. Note: *If married, but legally separated, or spouse is a nonresident alien, check the Single box.*	
City or town, state, and ZIP code Ocala, FL 00000	**4** If your last name differs from that on your social security card, check here and call 1-800-772-1213 for a new card . . . . . ▶ ☐	1

5	Total number of allowances you are claiming (from line H above or from the worksheets on page 2 if they apply) .	**5**	1
6	Additional amount, if any, you want withheld from each paycheck	**6** $	
7	I claim exemption from withholding for 2000, and I certify that I meet **BOTH** of the following conditions for exemption: • Last year I had a right to a refund of **ALL** Federal income tax withheld because I had **NO** tax liability **AND** • This year I expect a refund of **ALL** Federal income tax withheld because I expect to have **NO** tax liability. If you meet both conditions, enter "EXEMPT" here . . . . ▶	**7**	

Under penalties of perjury, I certify that I am entitled to the number of withholding allowances claimed on this certificate or entitled to claim exempt status.

Employee's signature ▶ *Merry I. Poppins*   Date ▶ *October 6, 2000*

8 Employer's name and address (Employer: Complete 8 and 10 only if sending to the IRS)	**9** Office code (optional)	**10** Employer identification number

Cat. No. 10220Q

Form W-4 (1998)   Page **2**

Deductions and Adjustments Worksheet

Note: *Use this worksheet only if you plan to itemize deductions or claim adjustments to income on your 1998 tax return.*

1	Enter an estimate of your 1998 itemized deductions. These include qualifying home mortgage interest, charitable contributions, state and local taxes (but not sales taxes), medical expenses in excess of 7.5% of your income, and miscellaneous deductions. (For 1998, you may have to reduce your itemized deductions if your income is over $124,500 ($62,250 if married filing separately). Get Pub. 919 for details.)	1	$_____
2	Enter: { $7,100 if married filing jointly or qualifying widow(er) / $6,250 if head of household / $4,250 if single / $3,550 if married filing separately }	2	$_____
3	**Subtract** line 2 from line 1. If line 2 is greater than line 1, enter -0-	3	$_____
4	Enter an estimate of your 1998 adjustments to income, including alimony, deductible IRA contributions, and education loan interest.	4	$_____
5	**Add** lines 3 and 4 and enter the total	5	$_____
6	Enter an estimate of your 1998 nonwage income (such as dividends or interest)	6	$_____
7	**Subtract** line 6 from line 5. Enter the result, but not less than -0-	7	$_____
8	**Divide** the amount on line 7 by $2,500 and enter the result here. Drop any fraction	8	_____
9	Enter the number from Personal Allowances Worksheet, line H, on page 1	9	_____
10	**Add** lines 8 and 9 and enter the total here. If you plan to use the Two-Earner/Two-Job Worksheet, also enter this total on line 1 below. Otherwise, **stop here** and enter this total on Form W-4, line 5, on page 1	10	_____

Two-Earner/Two-Job Worksheet

Note: *Use this worksheet only if the instructions for line H on page 1 direct you here.*

1	Enter the number from line H on page 1 (or from line 10 above if you used the Deductions and Adjustments Worksheet)	1	_____
2	Find the number in **Table 1** below that applies to the **LOWEST** paying job and enter it here	2	_____
3	If line 1 is **GREATER THAN OR EQUAL TO** line 2, subtract line 2 from line 1. Enter the result here (if zero, enter -0-) and on Form W-4, line 5, on page 1. **DO NOT** use the rest of this worksheet	3	_____

Note: *If line 1 is **LESS THAN** line 2, enter -0- on Form W-4, line 5, on page 1. Complete lines 4–9 to calculate the additional withholding amount necessary to avoid a year end tax bill.*

4	Enter the number from line 2 of this worksheet	4	_____
5	Enter the number from line 1 of this worksheet	5	_____
6	**Subtract** line 5 from line 4	6	_____
7	Find the amount in **Table 2** below that applies to the **HIGHEST** paying job and enter it here	7	$_____
8	**Multiply** line 7 by line 6 and enter the result here. This is the additional annual withholding amount needed	8	$_____
9	Divide line 8 by the number of pay periods remaining in 1998. (For example, divide by 26 if you are paid every other week and you complete this form in December 1997.) Enter the result here and on Form W-4, line 6, page 1. This is the additional amount to be withheld from each paycheck	9	$_____

Table 1: Two-Earner/Two-Job Worksheet

Married Filing Jointly				All Others			
If wages from LOWEST paying job are—	Enter on line 2 above	If wages from LOWEST paying job are—	Enter on line 2 above	If wages from LOWEST paying job are—	Enter on line 2 above	If wages from LOWEST paying job are—	Enter on line 2 above
0 - $4,000	0	38,001 - 43,000	8	0 - $5,000	0	70,001 - 85,000	8
4,001 - 7,000	1	43,001 - 54,000	9	5,001 - 11,000	1	85,001 - 100,000	9
7,001 - 12,000	2	54,001 - 62,000	10	11,001 - 16,000	2	100,001 and over	10
12,001 - 18,000	3	62,001 - 70,000	11	16,001 - 21,000	3		
18,001 - 24,000	4	70,001 - 85,000	12	21,001 - 25,000	4		
24,001 - 28,000	5	85,001 - 100,000	13	25,001 - 42,000	5		
28,001 - 33,000	6	100,001 - 110,000	14	42,001 - 55,000	6		
33,001 - 38,000	7	110,001 and over	15	55,001 - 70,000	7		

Table 2: Two-Earner/Two-Job Worksheet

Married Filing Jointly		All Others	
If wages from HIGHEST paying job are—	Enter on line 7 above	If wages from HIGHEST paying job are—	Enter on line 7 above
0 - $50,000	$400	0 - $30,000	$400
50,001 - 100,000	760	30,001 - 60,000	760
100,001 - 130,000	840	60,001 - 120,000	840
130,001 - 240,000	970	120,001 - 250,000	970
240,001 and over	1,070	250,001 and over	1,070

Paying Your Employees 4

Paying your employee involves keeping accurate records, understanding what work needs to be compensated and when you must issue paychecks, calculating gross income, deducting for room and board, and withholding the proper amounts for state and federal income taxes and social security. For an hourly employee, you must keep daily records of when she worked, meals you provided, expenses she incurred, and so forth. For a salaried employee, record keeping is considerably simpler.

Record Keeping

PAYROLL
SERVICES

If the paperwork involved seems too onerous, you may want to consider a commercial payroll service. They will take care of the paperwork and issuing paychecks for you (for a price, of course). Check under *Payroll Preparation Services* in the Yellow Pages. If you choose this option, consider putting your employee on a fixed salary so you do not have to track his or her hour worked.

DAILY RECORD
KEEPING FOR
HOURLY
EMPLOYEES

For an hourly employee, you will need a ledger to keep daily track of when she began and stopped work, any meals provided, and any expenses that need to be reimbursed. You will also need to do weekly calculations of regular and overtime pay, deductions, and reimbursements for purposes of issuing a paycheck. This same account book can serve both purposes.

Office supply stores sell "payroll books" designed for this purpose. They are set up on a week-by-week basis, and have columns for hours worked, regular and overtime pay, deductions, withheld taxes, and so forth. They are convenient, especially if you have several household employees.

However, if you have only one employee, we prefer using a standard eight-column account book because it is more flexible. Unlike a payroll book, the account book includes space for noting any job-related comments, such as reprimands, instructions, or descriptions of erratic behavior. Keeping daily track of employee performance is just as important as recording the hours worked. Your notes will be invaluable later for conducting performance reviews or for justifying why you had to fire the employee.

Eight-column account books are available at any office supply store. The columns are spread across two facing pages. You can label the columns anything you want, and adapt it to fit your needs. We suggest columns for the date, performance comments, hours worked, time off, meals provided, and expenses that need reimbursement. A typical week's entry might look like Figure 1 on the following page.

Figure 1

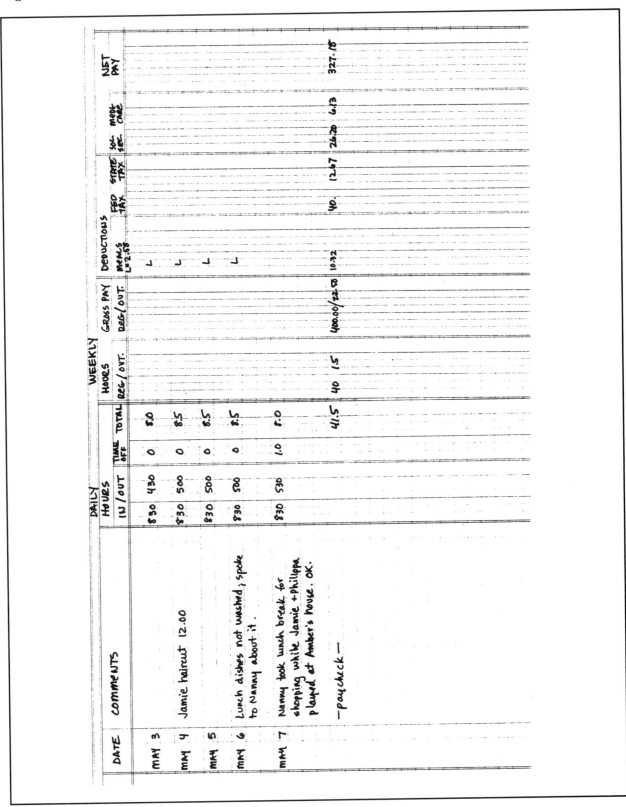

DAILY RECORD
KEEPING FOR
SALARIED
EMPLOYEES

For salaried employees who are paid substantially more than minimum wage, you do not need to keep a daily record of hours worked. Weekly or bi-weekly record-keeping should be sufficient. However, if you have a salaried employee whose total compensation is near minimum wage, you must keep track of her total hours worked each week to make sure her salary is above what she is entitled to under minimum wage and overtime laws. In this case, use the daily record-keeping system.

If you pay your employees once a week, you should keep weekly records; if you pay twice a month, you should keep semimonthly records. You will need to keep track of meals and lodging provided, expenses to be reimbursed, and your observations and comments on their work. You will also need to calculate gross pay, deductions, and reimbursements for purposes of issuing a paycheck.

Again, we recommend purchasing a standard eight-column account book, available at any office supply store. A typical month's entry might look like Figure 2 on the following page.

Figure 2

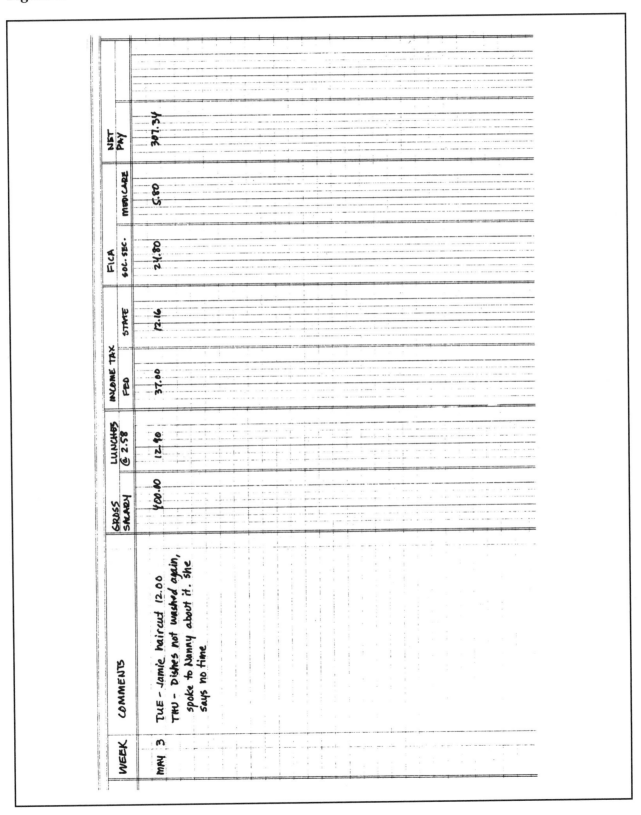

WEEK	COMMENTS	GROSS SALARY	LUNCHES @ 2.58	INCOME TAX FED	STATE	FICA SOC. SEC.	MEDICARE	NET PAY
MAY 3	TUE - Jamie haircut 12.00 THU - Dishes not washed again, spoke to Nanny about it. She says no time	400.00	12.90	37.00	12.16	24.80	5.80	307.34

PAYCHECK
RECORDS

You must keep a record of each paycheck. At the end of each pay period, when you go through the calculation of how much gross pay your employee has earned and the amount of each deduction, write down these amounts! We have previously suggested a simple bookkeeping method that includes space for these calculations. You will need this information when you file quarterly and year-end reports concerning your employee's wages, income taxes, social security, and unemployment taxes. Filing these periodic reports is covered in the next chapter, but you will not be able to do so if you have not kept records.

HOW LONG TO
KEEP RECORDS

We recommend that you keep your records for five years. Legally, you only need to keep them for four years for most employment law purposes, but the extra year won't hurt and might prevent you from inadvertently throwing away a record too soon because you've forgotten the legal time limit.

WHAT IS "WORK" THAT MUST BE COMPENSATED?

You must pay your domestic employees for all hours they work. If you pay your employee a salary for full-time work and it is high enough to avoid minimum wage problems, this will not be a problem.

If you pay an hourly rate or pay near the minimum wage, you will have to keep track of the hours your employees work. To do this, you must understand what is and is not considered "work time" that must be compensated.

Time that must be compensated includes:

- ☛ All regular hours as set by agreement or contract
- ☛ Coffee breaks
- ☛ Meals if the employee is supposed to stay on your property
- ☛ Stand-by or on-call periods, whether or not actually called

- Conferences, reviews, or discussing work with you outside regular hours
- Off duty errands run at your request
- Work at their own homes done at your request
- Time off to vote

The following kinds of activities do not have to be compensated:

- Vacations and days off unless your contract says otherwise
- Meals longer than thirty minutes if the employee is free to leave the premises
- Sleep time for live-ins if "off duty"
- Time off for jury duty
- Commuting time to and from work
- Work at their own homes when voluntary

ISSUING A PAYCHECK

The purpose of all this record keeping is to enable you to calculate your employee's paycheck and issue it correctly. You will have to know when you must pay your employees, how to calculate the value of meals or lodgings provided a live-in domestic employee, how to deduct for federal and state income taxes, and how much to withhold for social security taxes.

TIMELY AND COMPLETE PAYCHECKS

The Fair Labor Standards Act requires you to pay your employees on a *timely* basis for all work they have performed. If you fail to pay promptly, or decide to withhold some pay because she broke an expensive vase, your employee could bring a lawsuit against you for damages.

The definition of *timely* varies depending on the way your employee's wages are set. If your cook is paid an hourly wage, she must be paid at least once a week, including any overtime worked that week. If you are providing comp time instead of overtime pay, that is still compensation that must be "paid" within a week.

On the other hand, if your nanny is paid a salary (for example, $18,000 per year), you may pay her every week, twice a month, or once a month. The IRS booklet on calculating proper withholding taxes from her paycheck has separate tables for each of these pay periods.

CALCULATING
GROSS
COMPENSATION
FOR LIVE-IN
DOMESTICS

We previously calculated that the Banks family would have to pay Mary Poppins almost $30,000 per year to satisfy minimum wage rules. That does not mean they would have to pay it all in cash. If they supplied her with food, lodging, or other perks, they can include the fair value of these services as part of her compensation.

You cannot require nanny to accept goods and services instead of cash, but you can negotiate it. You may fairly state a hiring preference for a nanny willing to live with you and accept your room and board as part of her compensation because these are legitimate job-related qualifications. You can take a deduction from the nanny's cash wages for the reasonable cost or fair value of these goods and services if the nanny voluntarily accepts your food, lodging, and other items you provide for her (such as laundry or use of the family car); and these are customarily and reasonably furnished to nannies in similar positions.

This is not an area where you can evade minimum wage laws by inflating the value of meals and lodging. Under federal law, the maximum credits you are allowed to take include:

1. Up to 37.5% of the statutory minimum hourly wage for a breakfast (currently $1.93);

2. Up to 50% of the statutory minimum hourly wage for a lunch (currently $2.58);

3. Up to 62.5% of the statutory minimum hourly wage for a dinner (currently $3.22).

In other words, the total meal credits for one day cannot exceed 150% of the statutory minimum hourly wage. At the current minimum wage of $5.15 per hour, that's a maximum deduction of $7.73 for three meals a day. If your actual costs to feed nanny are less than $7.73 per day, you may use the actual costs instead if you keep complete records of them. However, even if your actual meal costs exceed $7.73 per day you cannot deduct the higher amount from the wages, so why bother? Just take the standard meal allowance per meal that you supply.

You can also take a deduction from the nanny's wages if you provide her with lodging. This credit can be figured one of two ways. The standard weekly lodging allowance is seven times the statutory minimum hourly wage or $38.63 per week at the current minimum wage. You may alternatively deduct the fair value of the lodging from her salary. However, to deduct actual value, you must first establish a market value and then keep records for three years for any variation from the guideline amount. Unlike meals, lodgings may be deducted at their true value even if that amount is more than the standard allowance.

You cannot inflate the value of lodgings as a way to defeat the minimum wage laws. If the nanny sleeps in a room adjacent to the nursery, has little privacy, and generally lives with the family, the fair value of that particular lodging arrangement is probably less than the standard allowance. Who would want to rent such a room next to babies that cry all night? You cannot use the average cost a one-room apartment in the area as an indication of value.

However, if the nanny lives in a separate apartment over the garage which has its own bathroom and is fairly private, you could realistically rent that apartment on the open market (if zoning laws permit). In that case, you may be able to deduct several hundred dollars a month for the apartment. Your problem probably will be establishing the value of such an apartment if you have never rented it before. The best case is if you previously rented the apartment to a non-employee at a mutually agreeable rate (e.g., $400 per month). Then you can safely "rent" that same apartment to the nanny at the same price. Bear in mind that she must voluntarily consent to this arrangement.

To continue our example of Mary Poppins, who lived with the Banks family six days a week in a small bedroom adjacent to the nursery and worked over eighty hours per week but received food and lodging, her minimum cash salary would be calculated as follows:

40 hours x $5.15 minimum wage:	$	206.00
+ 46 hours of overtime x $7.73:	+ $	355.58
Subtotal per week:	$	561.58
- standard meal allowance: $7.73 x 6 days:	- $	46.38
- standard lodging allowance per week:	- $	38.63
Minimum weekly cash salary:	$	476.57
x 52 weeks per year:	x	52
Minimum yearly salary in cash:		$24,781.64

CALCULATING
FEDERAL
INCOME TAX TO
BE WITHHELD

Note: The information below applies to withholding taxes on both U.S. citizens and resident aliens. If you are paying wages to a nonresident alien on a temporary visa, you will need to obtain and read IRS Publication 515, "Withholding of Tax on Nonresident Aliens."

You are not required to withhold federal income taxes from the paycheck of a household employee; however, as discussed in chapter 2, we recommend that you do so in most cases. If you withhold federal taxes, you will need your employee's W-4 form and the federal withholding tables which are contained in an IRS publication called "Circular E - Employer's Tax Guide." The tax guide is available at your local IRS office, online at www.irs.ustreas.gov, or by calling 1-800-829-3676. Use the tax withholding tables as follows:

1. Find the table that corresponds to both the filing status of your employee (single or married) and your pay period (weekly, biweekly, or semimonthly). There is a different table if you pay every two weeks (biweekly) or twice a month (semi-monthly).

2. Look down the left column to find the gross wages your employee earned this pay period. Gross wages are calculated before deductions for room and board and do not include reimbursements.

3. Scan across the page left to right to find the correct column for the number of allowances your employee claimed on her W-4. There you will find the dollar amount of income taxes to withhold.

Example: You hire a nanny for a salary of $18,000 per year, payable twice a month (24 times a year). Her gross salary each period is $750. She is married with no children and claimed 3 allowances on her W-4. As shown in Figure 3 below, you: (A) find the table labeled "Married Persons - Semimonthly Payroll Period," (B) locate the line for wages between $740-760, (C) move across to the column for 3 allowances, and (D) see that you must withhold $21 from each paycheck.

Figure 3

MARRIED Persons—SEMIMONTHLY Payroll Period
(For Wages Paid in 1999)

At least	But less than	0	1	2	3	4	5	6	7	8
$0	$270	0	0	0	0	0	0	0	0	0
270	280	1	0	0	0	0	0	0	0	0
280	290	2	0	0	0	0	0	0	0	0
290	300	4	0	0	0	0	0	0	0	0
300	310	5	0	0	0	0	0	0	0	0
310	320	7	0	0	0	0	0	0	0	0
320	330	8	0	0	0	0	0	0	0	0
330	340	10	0	0	0	0	0	0	0	0
340	350	11	0	0	0	0	0	0	0	0
350	360	13	0	0	0	0	0	0	0	0
360	370	14	0	0	0	0	0	0	0	0
370	380	16	0	0	0	0	0	0	0	0
380	390	17	0	0	0	0	0	0	0	0
390	400	19	2	0	0	0	0	0	0	0
400	410	20	3	0	0	0	0	0	0	0
410	420	22	5	0	0	0	0	0	0	0
420	430	23	6	0	0	0	0	0	0	0
430	440	25	8	0	0	0	0	0	0	0
440	450	26	9	0	0	0	0	0	0	0
450	460	28	11	0	0	0	0	0	0	0
460	470	29	12	0	0	0	0	0	0	0
470	480	31	14	0	0	0	0	0	0	0
480	490	32	15	0	0	0	0	0	0	0
490	500	34	17	0	0	0	0	0	0	0
500	520	36	19	2	0	0	0	0	0	0
520	540	39	22	5	0	0	0	0	0	0
540	560	42	25	8	0	0	0	0	0	0
560	580	45	28	11	0	0	0	0	0	0
580	600	48	31	14	0	0	0	0	0	0
600	620	51	34	17	0	0	0	0	0	0
620	640	54	37	20	3	0	0	0	0	0
640	660	57	40	23	6	0	0	0	0	0
660	680	60	43	26	9	0	0	0	0	0
680	700	63	46	29	12	0	0	0	0	0
700	720	66	49	32	15	0	0	0	0	0
720	740	69	52	35	18	0	0	0	0	0
740	760	72	55	38	21	3	0	0	0	0
760	780	75	58	41	24	6	0	0	0	0
780	800	78	61	44	27	9	0	0	0	0
800	820	81	64	47	30	12	0	0	0	0

CALCULATING
STATE AND
LOCAL TAXES TO
BE WITHHELD

State and local income taxes to be withheld are calculated in the same way. You obtain tax withholding tables from the state department of revenue, use the employee's W-4 form as a guide, find the correct table and determine how much to withhold. State withholding tables can be obtained from a local state revenue office or from the addresses listed in appendix A.

CALCULATING
SOCIAL SECURITY
TAXES TO BE
WITHHELD

Regardless of whether you withhold income taxes, you must withhold social security and medicare taxes, which you deduct from your employee's paycheck. This is a simple process, since social security and medicare taxes are a flat rate. For social security, you withhold 6.2% of gross income, and for medicare you withhold 1.45% of gross income. It doesn't matter whether your employee is single or married, nor how many allowances were claimed on his or her W-4, nor whether the pay period is paid weekly, biweekly, or semimonthly. You just multiply the gross pay (before any deductions) by .062 for social security withholding and by .0145 for medicare withholding. You deduct that amount from the paycheck.

Let's use the same example as we did for income tax withholding. You employ a nanny for $18,000 per year and pay her on a semimonthly basis. That makes her gross pay $750 per pay period. To calculate social security withholding, you multiply $750 x .062, which equals $46.50. To calculate medicare withholding, you multiply $750 x .0145, which equals $10.88. Both amounts are subtracted from her gross pay before you issue the check.

EXPENSE REIMBURSEMENT

It is common for some kinds of household employees to have reimbursable expenses. During the week, your nanny may have paid $12.00 for a child's haircut, $7.50 for lunch at McDonald's, and $25.00 to take your child and a friend to play at Discovery Zone. Your gardener may have picked up a $20.00 bag of fertilizer for the lawn. At the end of the week, you owe each of them for out-of-pocket expenses.

We suggest that reimbursements like these should be paid independently from the employee's wages. Write a separate check for the reimbursement amount rather than adding it to the paycheck. Otherwise, your records may be hopelessly confusing should you ever be involved in a tax audit.

You may reimburse your employees any way you see fit—daily, weekly, biweekly, or even monthly. You may give them cash or write checks. You do not have to keep records of cash reimbursements, although you may find it helpful to do so. Most people find it convenient to keep track of daily reimbursable expenses the same way you keep track of hours worked, and issue a reimbursement check at the same time you issue a paycheck. The regularity of it helps avoid disagreements between you and the employee over whether he or she was ever reimbursed for something.

GOVERNMENT REPORTING 5

USEFUL GOVERNMENT PUBLICATIONS

Three useful Internal Revenue Service publications are:

☞ Publication 503. *Child and Dependent Care Expenses*

☞ Publication 926. *Household Employer's Tax Guide*

☞ Circular E - *Employer's Tax Guide*, which will be mainly valuable to you for its tax withholding tables. It also contains other information, most of which does not apply to household employers.

These and other publications, and the forms and instructions mentioned in this chapter, are available online at www.irs.ustreas.gov, from your local IRS office, may be ordered by calling 1-800-829-3676, or can be requested by mail from any of the following three locations:

Western Area Distribution Center
Rancho Cordova, CA 95743-0001

Central Area Distribution Center
PO Box 8903
Bloomington IL, 61702-8903

Eastern Area Distribution Center
PO Box 85074
Richmond, VA 23261-5074

PERIODIC REPORTS DURING THE YEAR

FEDERAL TAXES
YOU WITHHELD

You have been withholding social security and medicare taxes from your employee's paychecks. If you have taken our advice, you have also been withholding income taxes. What do you do with the money?

Although you do not officially "pay" the government until you file your own tax return by April 15 of the following year, the government does not want to wait that long to get the money. If you were a big corporation, you would be depositing the withheld taxes into an account at the Federal Reserve Bank on at least a monthly basis. As a household employer, you are exempt from this requirement, but you still have to make periodic payments of the money you have been withholding.

The IRS requires that you pay the withheld amounts quarterly using "Estimated Tax" forms. If you are self-employed you are already familiar with these forms. Simply increase the amount you are paying by the amount of income taxes you have withheld from your employee's paychecks, and twice the amount of Social Security and Medicare taxes you have been withholding (you must make a matching contribution).

If you have not previously filed estimated tax payments, you will need to obtain a current Form 1040-ES, Estimated Tax for Individuals, which will contain four "payment vouchers." This form can be obtained from the IRS by any of the methods listed at the beginning of this chapter.

When you get the form, ignore all instructions and worksheets. They are for self-employed persons who need to calculate their own income taxes. All you do is go directly to the vouchers and select the one that covers the time period in which you first hired your employee.

The vouchers have the following due dates:

Voucher 1:	April 15
Voucher 2:	June 15
Voucher 3:	September 15
Voucher 4:	January 18

Select the one that is due next after you first withhold taxes. For example, if you hire a nanny in July, she starts work August 1, and receives her first paycheck August 15; you would use the voucher with the next closest due date: Voucher 3, due September 15.

You need not do any estimating—simply send them exactly what you owe, which is:

1. the amount you withheld in federal income taxes; plus

2. twice the amount you withheld in social security and medicare taxes.

Fill in your names, social security numbers, and address and write down the amount of your payment.

Figure 4

Form **1040-ES** Department of the Treasury Internal Revenue Service	**1999** Payment Voucher **3**		OMB No. 1545-0087

File only if you are making a payment of estimated tax. Return this voucher with check or money order payable to the "**United States Treasury.**" Please write your social security number and "1999 Form 1040-ES" on your check or money order. Do not send cash. Enclose, but do not staple or attach, your payment with this voucher. — **Calendar year—Due Sept. 15, 1999**

Amount of payment	Please type or print	Your first name and initial John Q.	Your last name Doe	Your social security number 100-10-1010
		If joint payment, complete for spouse		
		Spouse's first name and initial Suzanne L.	Spouse's last name Doe	Spouse's social security number 200-20-200
$ 407.28		Address (number, street, and apt. no.) 2000 Woodstock Ave.		
		City, state, and ZIP code (If a foreign address, enter city, province or state, postal code, and country.) Citytown, IN 46000		

For Privacy Act and Paperwork Reduction Act Notice, see instructions on page 5.

For all subsequent vouchers, you should send three months' worth of taxes. You can calculate, based on the first few weeks' withholding, what a three-month total will be. You should send in that three-month total, even though the reporting periods are not evenly spaced three months apart. Remember to double what you withheld for social security and medicare to account for your matching contribution. These are *estimated* tax payments, so it doesn't matter if you are off by a few dollars.

Example: You hire a nanny for $18,000 a year. She starts work on August 1, and is paid semimonthly. You withhold $21.00 per paycheck for income taxes, $46.50 in social security taxes, and $10.88 in Medicare taxes. When you send in her first voucher on September 15, she has received three paychecks (August 15, August 31, and September 15). You pay:

Income taxes:	3 x $21.00	=	$ 63.00
Withheld social security:	3 x $46.50	=	139.50
Your matching contribution		=	139.50
Withheld medicare	3 x $10.88	=	32.64
Your matching contribution		=	32.64
TOTAL			$407.28

When you send subsequent vouchers, you would base your three-month payment on six paychecks, even though she will actually have been paid fewer than six times when you send the June voucher, and more than six times when you send the January voucher. You pay:

Income taxes:	6 x $21.00	=	$ 126.00
Withheld social security:	6 x $46.50	=	279.00
Your matching contribution		=	279.00
Withheld medicare	6 x $10.88	=	65.28
Your matching contribution		=	65.28
TOTAL			$ 814.56

Your first voucher will be sent to a special IRS address, not the same one you used last year to file your Form 1040. This list of addresses is printed below. Thereafter, the IRS supposedly will send you your own customized and pre-printed vouchers with instructions on where to mail them. They sometimes don't, so you may need to send a follow-up letter. When you get your customized vouchers, throw out the plain ones, and use the pre-printed ones.

WHERE TO FILE YOUR PAYMENT VOUCHER

Note: Do not mail tax returns to these addresses. Also, only the U.S. Postal Service can deliver to P.O. boxes.

If you live in:	Use this address:
New Jersey, New York (New York City and counties of Nassau, Rockland, Suffolk, and Westchester)	P.O. Box 162 Newark, NJ 07101-0162
New York (all other counties), Connecticut, Maine, Massachusetts, New Hampshire,	P.O. Box 371999 Pittsburgh, PA 15250-7999
Delaware, District of Columbia, Maryland, Pennsylvania, Virginia	P.O. Box 8318 Philadelphia, PA 19162-8318
Florida, Georgia, South Carolina	P.O. Box 105900 Atlanta, GA 30348-5900
Indiana, Kentucky, Michigan, Ohio, West Virginia	P.O. Box 7422 Chicago, IL 60680-7422
Alabama, Arkansas, Louisiana, Mississippi, North Carolina, Tennessee	P.O. Box 1219 Charlotte, NC 28201-1219
Illinois, Iowa, Minnesota Missouri, Wisconsin	P.O. Box 970006 St. Louis, MO 63197-0006
Kansas, New Mexico, Oklahoma, Texas	P.O. Box 970001 St. Louis, MO 63197-0001
Alaska, Arizona, California (counties of Alpine, Amador, Butte, Calaveras, Colusa, Contra Costa, Del Norte, El Dorado, Glenn, Humboldt, Lake, Lassen, Marin, Mendocina, Modoc, Napa, Nevada, Placer, Plumas, Sacramento, San Joaquin, Shasta, Sierra, Siskiyou, Solano, Sonoma, Sutter, Tehema, Trinity, Yolo, and Yuba) Colorado, Idaho, Montana, Nebraska, Nevada, North Dakota, Oregon, South Dakota, Utah, Washington, Wyoming	P.O. Box 5100000 San Francisco, CA 94151-5100
California (all other counties), Hawaii	P.O. Box 54030 Los Angeles, CA 90054-0030
American Samoa; Commonwealth of Northern Mariana Islands; Puerto Rico; Guam (nonpermanent residents); Virgin Islands (nonpermanent residents); all APO and FPO addresses; U.S. citizens living in a foreign country and those filing Form 2555, Form 2555-EZ, or Form 4563; or if excluding income under section 933	P.O. Box 8318 Philadelphia, PA 19162-8318
Guam (permanent residents)*	Dept. of Revenue and Taxation Government of Guam P.O. Box 23607 GMF, GU 96921
Virgin Islands (permanent residents)*	V.I. Bureau of Internal Revenue 9601 Estate Thomas Charlotte Amalie St. Thomas, VI 00802

* Must send estimated income tax vouchers to the Guam or Virgin Islands address; and send self-employment tax vouchers to the Philadelphia address for nonpermanent residents.

You will need to keep track of exactly how much you send to the IRS in estimated payments. When you fill out your regular tax return next year, you will have to write down how much you paid in estimated taxes, so you will need to be able to find this amount.

STATE INCOME TAXES

In most states, you are not required to withhold state income taxes from your household employees' wages. If you do not withhold, there is nothing to send to the state, and no periodic reporting is required. See appendix A to find out if your state requires withholding. Bear in mind that even if you do not withhold, you still have to file an annual reconciliation form when you send in your employee's W-2 forms.

Each state that requires or allows withholding has its own rules on when and how often you must send in the withheld taxes. You will need to obtain state-specific information from the state revenue department listed in the appendix A. You can expect to have to make quarterly payments in most states, although many states are converting to annual reports similar to the federal Schedule H. After you have registered for tax withholding, the state revenue department will usually send you the necessary forms (usually called *coupons*) for paying state taxes, which will contain instructions for when to file.

UNEMPLOYMENT
TAXES

As long as you are properly registered with your state employment agency, you are not required to file periodic reports concerning unemployment taxes with the federal government. You will only owe about $50 per employee, and they are willing to wait until the end of the year when you file your 1040 return and Schedule H (discussed below).

You will, however, have to file quarterly *wage and contribution* state reports. Once you are properly registered with your state employment agency (see appendix A), they will send you quarterly forms on which you report the number of employees and calculate your unemployment tax rate.

Caution: You may not have to pay unemployment taxes on an employee's entire yearly wages. In most states, taxes are due only on the first $7,000 you pay to each employee. If you have full-time household help, you are probably paying them more than $7,000 per year. Once your employee's wages exceed $7,000, you need pay no more unemployment taxes.

Example: If you were paying a nanny $18,000 per year ($4,500 per quarter), she would exceed the $7,000 maximum in the second quarter. Applying the standard unemployment tax rate (2.7%), your quarterly payments would be:

1st quarter:	2.7% of full $4,500 = $121.50
2nd quarter:	2.7% of first $2,500 = $ 67.50
	(nothing owed on remaining $2,000 because you have reached her $7,000 limit)
3rd & 4th quarters:	nothing owed

END-OF-YEAR REPORTS

DUE BY JANUARY 31

During the month of January, you must prepare a W-2 Form for your household employee for the previous year. The first time you submit one, you will have to obtain an original form from your local IRS office or by calling 1-800-829-3676. You cannot use a photocopy or download one from the IRS web site because they use special ink and paper to make the forms machine-readable at the Social Security Administration. Packages of W-2 forms for future years will be sent to you automatically.

Filling out a W-2 is easy. You may hand-write them with a ball-point pen; they do not have to be typed. Just make sure the last copy is readable, so press hard! The following instructions will help you fill out the W-2 form (a sample completed W-2 is found on page 89):

1. Box a: Leave blank.

2. Box b: Fill in your employer identification number, not your social security number. See chapter 3 if you do not already have an employer identification number.

3. Box c: Fill in your own name and address.

4. Box d: Enter your employee's social security number.

5. Box e/f: Fill in your employee's full name above the dotted line; and his or her address below the dotted line.

6. Box 1: Fill in the total gross wages you paid your employee before any deductions for room and board or other reason.

7. Box 2: Enter the total amount you withheld from his or her paycheck for federal income tax purposes. If none, put zero.

8. Box 3: Fill in the total gross wages you paid your employee (the same as box 1).

9. Box 4: Enter the total amount you withheld from his or her paycheck for social security.

10. Box 5: Enter the total gross wages you paid your employee (same as box 1).

11. Box 6: Enter the total amount you withheld from his or her paycheck for medicare.

12. Boxes 7: through 15: Leave blank.

13. Box 16: Write in your state abbreviation and your state employer identification number (if any). If you have only one state employer number used for both unemployment and income tax purposes, use it. If you have two state identification numbers, use the one for state income tax withholding.

14. Box 17: Fill in the total gross wages you paid your employee (same as box 1).

15. Box 18: Write down the total state income tax withheld from your employee's paychecks, if any. If you did not withhold state taxes (or your state has no income tax), put zero.

16. Box 19: To fill in this box, you must find out what the state department of revenue considers your locality. In most states, it will be your county of residence, but you will need to check your state tax return to determine this.

17. Box 20: Enter the total gross wages you paid your employee (this is the same as box 1).

18. Box 21: Fill in the total local income tax withheld from your employee's paychecks, if any. If you did not withhold (or if there are no local taxes), put zero.

There are six copies of the W-2 form in each set. Each copy has a separate number (for state forms) or letter (federal forms) at the bottom. Give your employee copies B, C, and 2. You must deliver them by January 31, either in person or by mail. Keep copies A, D, and 1 for yourself. You will need them to complete the reports mentioned in the next section.

In some states, you must also file the state's copy of the W-2 along with your reconciliation form (W-3) by January 31st. Check your state's listing in appendix A for the due date.

Figure 5

a Control number	22222	Void ☐	For Official Use Only ▶ OMB No. 1545-0008		
b Employer identification number 21-2121212			1 Wages, tips, other compensation 18000.00		2 Federal income tax withheld 504.00
c Employer's name, address, and ZIP code John and Suzanne Doe 2000 Woodstock Ave. Citytown, IN 46000			3 Social security wages 18000.00		4 Social security tax withheld 1116.00
			5 Medicare wages and tips 18000.00		6 Medicare tax withheld 261.00
			7 Social security tips		8 Allocated tips
d Employee's social security number 300-30-300			9 Advance EIC payment		10 Dependent care benefits
e Employee's name (first, middle initial, last) Nanette N. Nanny			11 Nonqualified plans		12 Benefits included in box 1
123 Elm St. Anytown, IN 47000			13 See instrs. for box 13		14 Other

15 Statutory employee ☐	Deceased ☐	Pension plan ☐	Legal rep. ☐	Deferred compensation ☐

f Employee's address and ZIP code

16 State	Employer's state I.D. no.	17 State wages, tips, etc.	18 State income tax	19 Locality name	20 Local wages, tips, etc.	21 Local income tax

Form **W-2** **Wage and Tax Statement** 1999

Department of the Treasury—Internal Revenue Service

For Privacy Act and Paperwork Reduction Act Notice, see separate instructions.

Copy A For Social Security Administration—Send this entire page with Form W-3 to the Social Security Administration; photocopies are **not** acceptable.

Cat. No. 10134D

DUE BY
FEBRUARY 28

Before the end of February, you must file your copy of your employee's W-2 (copy A) with the Social Security Administration. You do this by attaching it (or them, if you have more than one household employee) to a W-3 form. Like the W-2, you must get an original W-3 form from the IRS local office or by calling 1-800-829-3676. You cannot use a photocopy or download one from the IRS web site because the Social Security Administration uses special ink and paper to make the forms machine-readable. After you have filed your first W-3, you will automatically be sent the correct forms in future years.

Filling out a W-3 form is easy. It looks remarkably like a W-2. The following instructions will help you complete the W-3 form (a sample completed W-3 may be found on page 92):

1. Box a: Leave blank.

2. Box b: Check the box marked "Hshld. emp."

3. Box c: Write in the total number of employees you had for which you filled out W-2 forms.

4. Box d: Leave blank.

5. Box e: Fill in your employer identification number, not your social security number. See chapter 3 if you do not already have an employer identification number.

6. Box f/g: Fill in your name above the dotted line, and your address below the line.

7. Box h: Leave blank unless you had a second employer identification number for some bizarre reason.

8. Box i: Write in your state abbreviation and state employer identification number (if any). If you have one state employer number for both unemployment and income tax purposes, use it. If you have two state identification numbers, use the one for state income tax withholding. Fill in the same number here as you put in box 16 of your employee's W-2.

9. Box 1: Fill in the total gross wages you paid your employee before any deductions. If you have more than one household employee, combine all their wages and enter the grand total.

10. Box 2: Enter the total amount you withheld from your employee's paycheck for federal income tax purposes. If none, fill in zero. If you have more than one household employee, combine all their withheld taxes and enter the grand total.

11. Box 3: Fill in the total gross wages you paid your employees (this will be the same as box 1).

12. Box 4: Enter the total amount you withheld from their paychecks for social security.

13. Box 5: Fill in the total gross wages you paid your employees (this will be the same as box 1).

14. Box 6: Enter the total amount you withheld from their paychecks for medicare.

15. Boxes 7 through 15: Leave blank.

16. Fill in your own name, telephone number, fax number, and e-mail address at the bottom as the "contact person." Be sure to sign and date the form, but leave the "title" space blank. Make a photocopy of this form before you send it off. There is no carbon copy for you.

Find Copy A of your employee's W-2 form, and send it and the W-3 to the Social Security Administration (not the IRS) at the address on the form. If you had more than one employee, include a W-2, Copy A, for each. Mail them by ordinary first-class mail.

Figure 6

```
DO NOT STAPLE

a  Control number        33333        For Official Use Only ▶
                                      OMB No. 1545-0008

b                    941    Military    943   │ 1  Wages, tips, other compensation │ 2  Federal income tax withheld
    Kind              ☐       ☐        ☐     │      18000.00                      │      504.00
    of                                        ├───────────────────────────────────┼──────────────────────────────
    Payer  ▶         CT-1   Hshld.   Medicare │ 3  Social security wages          │ 4  Social security tax withheld
                      ☐     emp. ☑   govt. emp.│     18000.00                      │     1116.00
                                        ☐      │
c  Total number of Forms W-2 │ d  Establishment number │ 5  Medicare wages and tips │ 6  Medicare tax withheld
                                                        │     18000.00              │     261.00

e  Employer identification number                │ 7  Social security tips   │ 8  Allocated tips
     21-2121212

f  Employer's name                               │ 9  Advance EIC payments   │ 10  Dependent care benefits

                                                 │ 11  Nonqualified plans    │ 12  Deferred compensation
    2000 Woodstock Ave.
    Citytown, IN 46000                           │ 13

                                                 │ 14

g  Employer's address and ZIP code
h  Other EIN used this year                      │ 15  Income tax withheld by third-party payer

i  Employer's state I.D. no.
     31426

Contact person      │ Telephone number  │ Fax number        │ E-mail address
John Q. Doe         │ (812) 555-5555    │ (812) 555-5556    │

Under penalties of perjury, I declare that I have examined this return and accompanying documents, and, to the best of my knowledge and belief,
they are true, correct, and complete.

Signature ▶ John Q. Doe          Title ▶                      Date ▶ 2/15/00

Form W-3 Transmittal of Wage and Tax Statements 1999    Department of the Treasury
                                                        Internal Revenue Service

Send this entire page with the entire Copy A page of Forms W-2 to the Social Security Administration. Photocopies are NOT acceptable.
Do not send any remittance (cash, checks, money orders, etc.) with FORMS W-2 and W-3.
```

STATE TAX REPORTING

If you withheld state or local income taxes, at some point in February or March, you will have to send the state revenue department its copy of the W-2 forms for each of your employees. Dates and procedures vary from state to state, so you will need to obtain the necessary information from your state revenue department (see appendix A). If you have properly registered as an employer, the state revenue department will mail you the forms and instructions you need.

The basic procedure will be the same as sending the W-2s to the Social Security Administration. You will fill out a state equivalent of a W-3, summarizing state and local taxes you withheld, and you send it to the state revenue department along with Copy 1 of each employee's W-2.

YOUR FEDERAL INCOME TAX RETURN

FORM 1040

If you employ household help, you must file your personal income tax return using IRS Form 1040, which is the long form for itemizing deductions and reporting your own income. You cannot use the 1040A or 1040EZ short forms. Most people employing household help already itemize deductions and file a Form 1040; however, if you have been filing the abbreviated 1040A or 1040EZ form, you will have to switch to the long form.

SCHEDULE H

In an extraordinary event, Congress, in 1996, actually simplified one small aspect of the tax system. It created Schedule H, a simple and easy way for household employers to report the income taxes they have withheld, pay social security and medicare taxes, and determine if they need to pay additional unemployment taxes. If you employ household help, you will need to file a Schedule H form along with Form 1040. You will need to obtain a Schedule H form for the current year at the same time that you get the rest of your tax forms.

We strongly recommend using one of the computer tax programs. They provide excellent results, print out all the necessary forms, and do all the calculations for you. They can even file your taxes for you electronically. A current list of the computer tax programs that cooperate with the IRS in electronic tax preparation and filing can be found on the IRS web site: www.irs.ustreas.gov.

A sample 1998 Schedule H for a nanny paid $18,000 a year is included on pages 100 and 101. You may report in whole dollars without worrying about cents. To complete Schedule H:

1. In the box at the top, fill in your own name, social security number, and employer identification number. See chapter 3 on obtaining an employer identification number of you do not already have one.

2. Check the "Yes" box after question A. You can skip the other two questions. We feel certain that if you bothered to buy this book, you undoubtedly are paying some employee more than $1,100 a year.

3. Line 1: Enter the total wages for all your employees in one lump sum. Don't worry about the social security cap—it's more than $72,000 per employee. If you're paying that much to your household employees, let us know and we'll come work for you.

4. Line 2: Multiply the amount on line 1 by .124 (12.4%) and enter the total on line 2. You may have noticed that this amount is twice as much as the 6.2% social security taxes you withheld from your employee's paycheck. That's because all employers are required to make a matching contribution equal to the amounts paid by (withheld from) their employees. Therefore, do not put the amount withheld into line 2. You actually owe twice what you withheld.

5. Line 3: Fill in the total wages for all employees in one lump sum. It is all subject to Medicare taxes.

6. Line 4: Multiply line 3 by .029 (2.9%) and put the total on line 4. Like social security taxes, this amount is twice as much as the 1.45% for medicare taxes you withheld from your employee's paycheck because you are required to make a matching contribution.

7. Line 5: If you are withholding federal income tax, fill in the amount here. In this case, write down the exact amount you actually withheld throughout the year. In our previous example, we calculated that we should be withholding $21 each paycheck based on semi-monthly pay periods. This is $21 in each of her 24 pay periods, or $504 for the year.

8. Line 6: Add the amounts on lines 2, 4, and 5, and fill in the total.

9. Line 7: Skip this line.

10. Line 8: Enter the same amount as on line 6.

11. Line 9: In most cases, you will check "Yes" and proceed to the back of the form.

12. Lines 10-11: Your answers will almost certainly be "Yes."

13. Line 12: FUTA taxes only the first $7,000 of each employee's wages. Every state taxes at least that much; some states tax more. Therefore, you should check the "Yes" box for this line also.

14. Line 13: Fill in the postal abbreviation for your state.

15. Line 14: You will need the account number from your state unemployment tax return. See the instructions for registering as a new employer in chapter 3 if you have not already opened a state unemployment account.

16. Line 15: Skip this line; it doesn't apply to you.

17. Line 16: In 1999, the total cash wages subject to FUTA were the first $7,000 of each employee's wages. This amount has remained stable over the last few years. If you have a full-time nanny who was paid $18,000 a year and a part-time yardworker who was paid $4,000 last year, your total FUTA wages would be $11,000—the first $7,000 of the nanny's salary and all of the yardworker's because he earned less than $7,000.

18. Line 17: Multiply line 16 by .008 and enter that total on line 17.

19. Lines 18-25: Skip these lines.

20. Line 26: Get this number from line 8 on front of form.

21. Line 27: Add the amount from line 17 to the amount from line 26, and fill in the total on line 27.

22. Line 28: Check "yes" and enter the amount from line 27 on line 55 on the back of Form 1040.

TAX CREDITS
FOR CHILD CARE
(FORM 2441)

If your household employee is a nanny for your children or a caregiver for a disabled adult, you may be entitled to some form of tax relief for the first $5,000 you spend. We already discussed, in chapter 3, the tax value of using a deferred compensation plan at your own workplace to pay for childcare if such a plan is available. If you use this system, your own W-2 will show an amount up to $5,000 in box 10, and "deferred compensation" will be checked in box 15. If you are self-employed or no such deferred compensation plan is available, you may be able to claim a tax credit for a portion of your expenses. In either event, you will need to fill out a Form 2441 for "Child and Dependent care Expenses."

As with Schedule H, if you use a computer-based tax system, it will do the calculations and prepare the necessary forms for you, so you can be doing something more productive than filling out tax forms—like taking your children to the park. On pages 102 and 103 we have included a sample completed 1998 Form 2441 so you can see what it looks like, but you will need the current year's form to coordinate with your 1040. The following instructions will help you fill in Form 2441:

1. Line 1: Fill in the nanny's name, address, social security number, and total amount paid, regardless of whether it was reimbursed by your employer's deferred compensation plan.

2. For the rest of the form:

   - If you took maximum advantage of your employer's deferred compensation plan, you probably had your company withhold $5,000 from your salary to be used exclusively for child care. If so, then you will fill out only lines 10-22 on the back of the form, because you are not eligible for any further child care tax credit.

   - If you did not participate in a deferred compensation plan covering child care, you will fill out only lines 2-9 on the front of the form.

   - Only in the unusual event that you elected to take a small portion of the available deferred compensation but had large child care costs would you fill out both sections, starting with the back of the form first.

If You Did Not Receive Deferred Dependent Care Benefits. If you did not participate in a deferred compensation plan covering child care, you will fill out only lines 2-9 on the front of the form. We will continue to use our example of the nanny who is paid $18,000 per year.

1. Line 2. Write the names and social security numbers of your children who received the care. The child must have been under age thirteen (or disabled), lived with you for most of the year, and been claimed as a dependent on your tax return. If you are divorced, separated, or have joint custody of a child and are not certain

whether you can claim the child as a dependent, you will probably need to consult a tax adviser. Put down in column (c) what you spent, up to a maximum of $2,400 per child.

2. Line 3. The most you can enter in this line is $4,800, regardless of how much you really spent.

3. Line 4: Look at your own W-2, Box 1, for the amount of "wages, tips, other compensation," and write this number down here. For our example, we made up a number.

4. Line 5: If your spouse received a W-2, enter his or her total wages from Box 1. If not, repeat whatever you put in line 4 (We know this makes no sense; but do it anyway). If you are married but filing a separate return, you need a tax adviser. Let him or her figure out how to fill in this line. Again, we made up a number.

5. Line 6: Usually you will enter $4,800.

6. Line 7: You have to go back to your Form 1040 to find your adjusted gross income.

7. Line 8. If you have hired a nanny, you will almost certainly enter the lowest number: .20

8. Line 9: Multiply line 6 by line 8, and enter the result, which will usually be $960.

9. Take the amount from line 9 (usually $960), and write it in line 41 of your Form 1040.

If You Received Deferred Dependent Care Benefits from Your Employer. If you participated in a deferred compensation plan at your place of work that reimbursed you for child care, you will fill out only lines 10-22 on the back of the form, ignoring the front.

1. Line 10: Look at your W-2, Box 10, for the amount of "dependent care benefits" (usually $5,000) and write this number in here.

2. Line 11: Usually zero. If for some unusual reason you forfeited some of the deferred compensation, enter the forfeited amount here.

3. Line 12: Usually the same as line 10: $5,000.

4. Line 13: Fill in the total wages you paid your nanny for the year.

5. Line 14: You will usually enter the line 12 amount: $5,000.

6. Line 15: Look at your W-2, Box 1, for the amount of "wages, tips, other compensation," and write this number in here.

7. Line 16: If your spouse received a W-2, enter your spouse's income here. If not, repeat whatever you put in line 15. (We know this makes no sense, but do it anyway.) If you are married but filing a separate return, you need a tax accountant, so let him or her figure out how to fill in this line.

8. Line 17: Usually the same as line 10: $5,000.

9. Line 18: Usually the same as line 10: $5,000.

10. Line 19: Usually zero.

11. Line 20: Write down $2,400 if you have one child under age thirteen; $4,800 if you have more than one child under age thirteen. The child must live with you and be claimed as a dependent on your tax return. If you are divorced, separated, or have joint custody of a child and are not certain whether you can claim the child as a dependent, you will probably need to consult a tax adviser.

12. Line 21: Usually the same as line 10: $5,000.

13. Line 22: You will usually stop here, because most corporate deferred compensation plans withhold the maximum $5,000 for you. Enter zero.

In unusual situations, your employer may have provided less than the maximum $5,000 in deferred compensation, so you will be entitled to a small Child Care tax credit in addition to the deferred compensation. If so, follow the instructions on the form (and above) for filling out lines 2-9 for your expenses between the amount you received in deferred compensation and the maximum of $4,800.

IF YOU MOVE

As an employer, you must notify various government agencies if you move.

☛ File Form 8822 with the IRS. A sample filled-in copy, along with instructions, may be found on the following two pages. A blank copy is form 13 in appendix B.

☛ Contact your state department of revenue (see appendix A) to see if they have a similar required report.

☛ For state unemployment tax purposes, there will be a "change of status" form included with your quarterly reporting form. Simply fill in your new address.

SCHEDULE H (Form 1040)	Household Employment Taxes	OMB No. 1545-0074

SCHEDULE H
(Form 1040)

Department of the Treasury
Internal Revenue Service (99)

Household Employment Taxes
(For Social Security, Medicare, Withheld Income, and Federal Unemployment (FUTA) Taxes)
▶ Attach to Form 1040, 1040NR, 1040NR-EZ, 1040-SS, or 1041.
▶ See separate instructions.

OMB No. 1545-0074
1998
Attachment
Sequence No. **44**

Name of employer

John and Suzanne Doe

Social security number
100 10 1010

Employer identification number

Caution: *The $1,100 per year test applies only to line A. The $1,000 per quarter test applies only to line C and line 9.*

A Did you pay **any one** household employee cash wages of $1,100 or more in 1998? (If any household employee was your spouse, your child under age 21, your parent, or anyone under age 18, see the line A instructions on page 3 before you answer this question.)

☑ **Yes.** Skip lines B and C and go to line 1.
☐ **No.** Go to line B.

B Did you withhold Federal income tax during 1998 for any household employee?

☐ **Yes.** Skip line C and go to line 5.
☐ **No.** Go to line C.

C Did you pay **total** cash wages of $1,000 or more in **any** calendar **quarter** of 1997 or 1998 to household employees? (**Do not** count cash wages paid in 1997 or 1998 to your spouse, your child under age 21, or your parent.)

☐ **No. Stop.** Do not file this schedule.
☐ **Yes.** Skip lines 1-9 and go to line 10 on the back.

Social Security, Medicare, and Income Taxes

1	Total cash wages subject to social security taxes (see page 3) . . **1** 18000	
2	Social security taxes. Multiply line 1 by 12.4% (.124)	**2** 2232
3	Total cash wages subject to Medicare taxes (see page 3) **3** 18000	
4	Medicare taxes. Multiply line 3 by 2.9% (.029)	**4** 522
5	Federal income tax withheld, if any	**5** 504
6	Add lines 2, 4, and 5	**6** 3258
7	Advance earned income credit (EIC) payments, if any	**7** 0
8	**Total social security, Medicare, and income taxes.** Subtract line 7 from line 6	**8** 3258

9 Did you pay **total** cash wages of $1,000 or more in **any** calendar **quarter** of 1997 or 1998 to household employees? (**Do not** count cash wages paid in 1997 or 1998 to your spouse, your child under age 21, or your parent.)

☐ **No. Stop.** Enter the amount from line 8 above on Form 1040, line 55. If you are not required to file Form 1040, see the line 9 instructions on page 4.

☐ **Yes.** Go to line 10 on the back.

For Paperwork Reduction Act Notice, see Form 1040 instructions. Cat. No. 12187K **Schedule H (Form 1040) 1998**

Schedule H (Form 1040) 1998   Page **2**

Federal Unemployment (FUTA) Tax

		Yes	No
10	Did you pay unemployment contributions to only one state? **10**	✓	
11	Did you pay all state unemployment contributions for 1998 by April 15, 1999? Fiscal year filers, see page 4 **11**	✓	
12	Were all wages that are taxable for FUTA tax also taxable for your state's unemployment tax? . . . **12**	✓	

Next: If you checked the **"Yes"** box on **all** the lines above, complete Section A.

If you checked the **"No"** box on **any** of the lines above, skip Section A and complete Section B.

Section A

13	Name of the state where you paid unemployment contributions ▶	In	
14	State reporting number as shown on state unemployment tax return ▶	32123	
15	Contributions paid to your state unemployment fund (see page 4) .	**15**	
16	Total cash wages subject to FUTA tax (see page 4)	**16**	7000
17	**FUTA tax.** Multiply line 16 by .008. Enter the result here, skip Section B, and go to line 26 . .	**17**	56

Section B

18   Complete all columns below that apply (if you need more space, see page 4):

(a) Name of state	(b) State reporting number as shown on state unemployment tax return	(c) Taxable wages (as defined in state act)	(d) State experience rate period		(e) State experience rate	(f) Multiply col. (c) by .054	(g) Multiply col. (c) by col. (e)	(h) Subtract col. (g) from col. (f). If zero or less, enter -0-.	(i) Contributions paid to state unemployment fund
			From	To					

19	Totals	**19**	
20	Add columns (h) and (i) of line 19	**20**	
21	Total cash wages subject to FUTA tax (see the line 16 instructions on page 4)	**21**	
22	Multiply line 21 by 6.2% (.062)	**22**	
23	Multiply line 21 by 5.4% (.054)	**23**	
24	Enter the **smaller** of line 20 or line 23	**24**	
25	**FUTA tax.** Subtract line 24 from line 22. Enter the result here and go to line 26	**25**	

Total Household Employment Taxes

26	Enter the amount from line 8	**26**	3258
27	Add line 17 (or line 25) and line 26	**27**	3314
28	Are you required to file Form 1040?		

       ☐ **Yes.**   **Stop.** Enter the amount from line 27 above on Form 1040, line 55. **Do not** complete Part IV below.

       ☐ **No.**   You may have to complete Part IV. See page 4 for details.

Address and Signature—Complete this part **only** if required. See the line 28 instructions on page 4.

Address (number and street) or P.O. box if mail is not delivered to street address	Apt., room, or suite no.

City, town or post office, state, and ZIP code

Under penalties of perjury, I declare that I have examined this schedule, including accompanying statements, and to the best of my knowledge and belief, it is true, correct, and complete. No part of any payment made to a state unemployment fund claimed as a credit was, or is to be, deducted from the payments to employees.

▶ _____   ▶ _____
     Employer's signature   Date

Form **2441**	**Child and Dependent Care Expenses**	OMB No 1545-0068
Department of the Treasury Internal Revenue Service (99)	▶ Attach to Form 1040. ▶ See separate instructions.	**1998** Attachment Sequence No. **21**

Name(s) shown on Form 1040	Your social security number
John and Suzanne Doe	100 10 1010

Before you begin, you need to understand the following terms. See **Definitions** on page 1 of the instructions.

- **Dependent Care Benefits**
- **Qualifying Person(s)**
- **Qualified Expenses**
- **Earned Income**

Persons or Organizations Who Provided the Care—You **must** complete this part.
(If you need more space, use the bottom of page 2.)

1	(a) Care provider's name	(b) Address (number, street, apt. no., city, state, and ZIP code)	(c) Identifying number (SSN or EIN)	(d) Amount paid (see instructions)
	Nanette Nanny	123 Elm St. Anytown IN 47000		

Did you receive **dependent care benefits?**	**No** ⟶ Complete only Part II below.
	Yes ⟶ Complete Part III on the back next.

Caution: *If the care was provided in your home, you may owe employment taxes. See the instructions for Form 1040, line 55.*

Credit for Child and Dependent Care Expenses

2 Information about your **qualifying person(s).** If you have more than two qualifying persons, see the instructions.

(a) Qualifying person's name		(b) Qualifying person's social security number	(c) Qualified expenses you incurred and paid in 1998 for the person listed in column (a)
First	Last		
Philippa	Doe	400 40 4000	2400
James	Doe	500 50 500	2400

3	Add the amounts in column (c) of line 2. DO NOT enter more than $2,400 for one qualifying person or $4,800 for two or more persons. If you completed Part III, enter the amount from line 24	3	4800
4	Enter YOUR **earned income**	4	102000
5	If married filing a joint return, enter YOUR SPOUSE'S earned income (if your spouse was a student or was disabled, see the instructions); **all others,** enter the amount from line 4	5	44000
6	Enter the **smallest** of line 3, 4, or 5	6	4800
7	Enter the amount from Form 1040, line 34 **7**		
8	Enter on line 8 the decimal amount shown below that applies to the amount on line 7		

If line 7 is—		Decimal amount is	If line 7 is—		Decimal amount is
Over	But not over		Over	But not over	
$0—	10,000	.30	$20,000—	22,000	.24
10,000—	12,000	.29	22,000—	24,000	.23
12,000—	14,000	.28	24,000—	26,000	.22
14,000—	16,000	.27	26,000—	28,000	.21
16,000—	18,000	.26	28,000—	No limit	.20
18,000—	20,000	.25			

		8	×.20

9	Multiply **line 6** by the decimal amount on line 8. Enter the result. Then, see the instructions for the amount of credit to enter on Form 1040, line 41	9	960

For Paperwork Reduction Act Notice, see page 3 of the instructions.   Cat. No. 11862M   Form **2441** (1998)

Form 2441 (1998)   Page **2**

	Dependent Care Benefits			

10 Enter the total amount of **dependent care benefits** you received for 1998. This amount should be shown in box 10 of your W-2 form(s). DO NOT include amounts that were reported to you as wages in box 1 of Form(s) W-2 . . . . **10** | 5000

11 Enter the amount forfeited, if any. See the instructions . . . . **11** | 0

12 Subtract line 11 from line 10 . . . . **12** | 5000

13 Enter the total amount of **qualified expenses** incurred in 1998 for the care of the **qualifying person(s)** . . . **13**

14 Enter the **smaller** of line 12 or 13 . . . . **14**

15 Enter YOUR **earned income** **15**

16 If married filing a joint return, enter YOUR SPOUSE'S earned income (if your spouse was a student or was disabled, see the instructions for line 5); if married filing a separate return, see the instructions for the amount to enter; **all others,** enter the amount from line 15 . . . **16**

17 Enter the **smallest** of line 14, 15, or 16 . . . . . . **17**

18 **Excluded benefits.** Enter here the **smaller** of the following:

   - The amount from line 17, or
   - $5,000 ($2,500 if married filing a separate return **and** you were required to enter your spouse's earned income on line 16). } . . . . **18** | 5000

19 **Taxable benefits.** Subtract line 18 from line 12. Also, include this amount on Form 1040, line 7. On the dotted line next to line 7, enter "DCB" . . . . **19** | 0

To claim the child and dependent care
credit, complete lines 20–24 below.

20 Enter $2,400 ($4,800 if two or more qualifying persons) . . . . **20** | 4800

21 Enter the amount from line 18 . . . . **21** | 5000

22 Subtract line 21 from line 20. If zero or less, **STOP.** You cannot take the credit. **Exception.** If you paid 1997 expenses in 1998, see the instructions for line 9 . . . . . **22** | 0

23 Complete line 2 on the front of this form. DO NOT include in column (c) any excluded benefits shown on line 18 above. Then, add the amounts in column (c) and enter the total here **23**

24 Enter the **smaller** of line 22 or 23. Also, enter this amount on line 3 on the front of this form and complete lines 4–9 . . . . **24**

Form **8822** (Rev. Oct. 1997) Department of the Treasury Internal Revenue Service	**Change of Address** ▶ **Please type or print.** ▶ **See instructions on back.** ▶ **Do not attach this form to your return.**	OMB No. 1545-1163

Complete This Part To Change Your Home Mailing Address

Check **ALL** boxes this change affects:

1 ☐ Individual income tax returns (Forms 1040, 1040A, 1040EZ, 1040NR, etc.)

  ▶ If your last return was a joint return and you are now establishing a residence separate from the spouse with whom you filed that return, check here . . . . ▶ ☐

2 ☐ Gift, estate, or generation-skipping transfer tax returns (Forms 706, 709, etc.)

  ▶ For Forms 706 and 706-NA, enter the decedent's name and social security number below.

  ▶ Decedent's name   ▶ Social security number

3a Your name (first name, initial, and last name)	**3b** Your social security number
4a Spouse's name (first name, initial, and last name)	**4b** Spouse's social security number

5 Prior name(s). See instructions.

6a Old address (no., street, city or town, state, and ZIP code). If a P.O. box or foreign address, see instructions.	Apt. no.
6b Spouse's old address, if different from line 6a (no., street, city or town, state, and ZIP code). If a P.O. box or foreign address, see instructions.	Apt. no.
7 New address (no., street, city or town, state, and ZIP code). If a P.O. box or foreign address, see instructions.	Apt. no.

Complete This Part To Change Your Business Mailing Address or Business Location

Check **ALL** boxes this change affects:

8 ☑ Employment, excise, and other business returns (Forms 720, 940, 940-EZ, 941, 990, 1041, 1065, 1120, etc.)
9 ☐ Employee plan returns (Forms 5500, 5500-C/R, and 5500-EZ). See instructions.
10 ☐ Business location

11a Business name	**11b** Employer identification number
John Q. Doe	21 2121212

12 Old mailing address (no., street, city or town, state, and ZIP code). If a P.O. box or foreign address, see instructions.	Room or suite no.

13 New mailing address (no., street, city or town, state, and ZIP code). If a P.O. box or foreign address, see instructions.	Room or suite no.
2000 Woodstock Ave., Citytown, IN 46000	

14 New business location (no., street, city or town, state, and ZIP code). If a foreign address, see instructions.	Room or suite no.

Signature *John Q. Doe*

Daytime telephone number of person to contact (optional) ▶ (812) 555-5555

Please Sign Here

▶ _____
Your signature   Date

▶ _____
If joint return, spouse's signature   Date

▶ *John Q. Doe* | 2/15/00
If Part II completed, signature of owner, officer, or representative   Date

▶ owner
Title

For Privacy Act and Paperwork Reduction Act Notice, see back of form.   Cat. No. 12081V   Form **8822** (Rev. 10-97)

Form 8822 (Rev. 10-97)   Page **2**

Purpose of Form

You may use Form 8822 to notify the Internal Revenue Service if you changed your home or business mailing address or your business location. Generally, complete only one Form 8822 to change your home and business addresses. If this change also affects the mailing address for your children who filed income tax returns, complete and file a separate Form 8822 for each child. If you are a representative signing for the taxpayer, attach to Form 8822 a copy of your power of attorney.

Note: *If you moved after you filed your return and you are expecting a refund, also notify the post office serving your old address. This will help forward your check to your new address.*

Prior Name(s)

If you or your spouse changed your name because of marriage, divorce, etc., complete line 5. Also, be sure to notify the **Social Security Administration** of your new name so that it has the same name in its records that you have on your tax return. This prevents delays in processing your return and issuing refunds. It also safeguards your future social security benefits.

Addresses

Be sure to include any apartment, room, or suite number in the space provided.

P.O. Box

If your post office does not deliver mail to your street address, show your P.O. box number instead of your street address.

Foreign Address

If your address is outside the United States or its possessions or territories, enter the information in the following order: city, province or state, and country. Follow the country's practice for entering the postal code. Please **do not** abbreviate the country name.

Employee Plan Returns

A change in the mailing address for employee plan returns must be shown on a separate Form 8822 unless the **Exception** below applies.

Exception. If the employee plan returns were filed with the same service center as your other returns (individual, business, employment, gift, estate, etc.), you do not have to use a separate Form 8822. See **Where To File** on this page.

Signature

If you are completing Part II, the owner, an officer, or a representative must sign. An officer is the president, vice president, treasurer, chief accounting officer, etc. A representative is a person who has a valid power of attorney to handle tax matters.

Where To File

Send this form to the **Internal Revenue Service Center** shown below for your old mailing address. But if you checked the box on line 9 (employee plan returns), send it to the address shown in the far right column.

IF your old mailing address was in . . .	THEN use this address. . .
Florida, Georgia, South Carolina	Atlanta, GA 39901
New Jersey, New York (New York City and counties of Nassau, Rockland, Suffolk, and Westchester)	Holtsville, NY 00501
New York (all other counties), Connecticut, Maine, Massachusetts, New Hampshire, Rhode Island, Vermont	Andover, MA 05501
Alaska, Arizona, California (counties of Alpine, Amador, Butte, Calaveras, Colusa, Contra Costa, Del Norte, El Dorado, Glenn, Humboldt, Lake, Lassen, Marin, Mendocino, Modoc, Napa, Nevada, Placer, Plumas, Sacramento, San Joaquin, Shasta, Sierra, Siskiyou, Solano, Sonoma, Sutter, Tehama, Trinity, Yolo, and Yuba), Colorado, Idaho, Montana, Nebraska, Nevada, North Dakota, Oregon, South Dakota, Utah, Washington, Wyoming	Ogden, UT 84201
California (all other counties), Hawaii	Fresno, CA 93888
Indiana, Kentucky, Michigan, Ohio, West Virginia	Cincinnati, OH 45999
Kansas, New Mexico, Oklahoma, Texas	Austin, TX 73301
Delaware, District of Columbia, Maryland, Pennsylvania, Virginia	Philadelphia, PA 19255
Alabama, Arkansas, Louisiana, Mississippi, North Carolina, Tennessee	Memphis, TN 37501
Illinois, Iowa, Minnesota, Missouri, Wisconsin	Kansas City, MO 64999
American Samoa	Philadelphia, PA 19255
Guam: Permanent residents	Department of Revenue and Taxation Government of Guam P.O. Box 23607 GMF, GU 96921
Guam: Nonpermanent residents Puerto Rico (or if excluding income under Internal Revenue Code section 933) Virgin Islands: Nonpermanent residents	Philadelphia, PA 19255
Virgin Islands: Permanent residents	V. I. Bureau of Internal Revenue 9601 Estate Thomas Charlotte Amalie St. Thomas, VI 00802
Foreign country: U.S. citizens and those filing Form 2555, Form 2555-EZ, or Form 4563	Philadelphia, PA 19255
All APO and FPO addresses	

Employee Plan Returns ONLY (Form 5500 series)

IF the principal office of the plan sponsor or the plan administrator was in . . .	THEN use this address . . .
Connecticut, Delaware, District of Columbia, Maine, Maryland, Massachusetts, New Hampshire, New Jersey, New York, Pennsylvania, Puerto Rico, Rhode Island, Vermont, Virginia	Holtsville, NY 00501
Alabama, Alaska, Arkansas, California, Florida, Georgia, Hawaii, Idaho, Louisiana, Mississippi, Nevada, North Carolina, Oregon, South Carolina, Tennessee, Washington	Atlanta, GA 39901
Arizona, Colorado, Illinois, Indiana, Iowa, Kansas, Kentucky, Michigan, Minnesota, Missouri, Montana, Nebraska, New Mexico, North Dakota, Ohio, Oklahoma, South Dakota, Texas, Utah, West Virginia, Wisconsin, Wyoming	Memphis, TN 37501
Foreign country	Holtsville, NY 00501
All Form 5500-EZ filers	Memphis, TN 37501

Privacy Act and Paperwork Reduction Act Notice. We ask for the information on this form to carry out the Internal Revenue laws of the United States. We may give the information to the Department of Justice and to other Federal agencies, as provided by law. We may also give it to cities, states, the District of Columbia, and U.S. commonwealths or possessions to carry out their tax laws. And we may give it to foreign governments because of tax treaties they have with the United States.

You are not required to provide the information requested on a form that is subject to the Paperwork Reduction Act unless the form displays a valid OMB control number. Books or records relating to a form or its instructions must be retained as long as their contents may become material in the administration of any Internal Revenue law. Generally, tax returns and return information are confidential, as required by Internal Revenue Code section 6103.

If you fail to provide the Internal Revenue Service with your current mailing address, you may not receive a notice of deficiency or a notice and demand for tax. Despite the failure to receive such notices, penalties and interest will continue to accrue on the tax deficiencies.

The time needed to complete and file this form will vary depending on individual circumstances. The estimated average time is 16 minutes.

If you have comments concerning the accuracy of this time estimate or suggestions for making this form simpler, we would be happy to hear from you. You can write to the Tax Forms Committee, Western Area Distribution Center, Rancho Cordova, CA 95743-0001. **DO NOT** send the form to this address. Instead, see **Where To File** on this page.

TERMINATION OF EMPLOYMENT 6

Some employees quit for no apparent reason. Others have to be fired. This chapter describes the legal considerations that arise at the end of the employment relationship.

Before you proceed any farther into this chapter, review the written contract you entered into with your employee. Does it say anything about the conditions under which the employee can be fired or quit? Does it require two weeks' notice, or a warning, or severance pay? If you and your employee agreed to something concerning her discharge (we agreed with our nanny that we would give her a month's notice so she could take advantage of accumulated vacation time and look for a new job; she agreed to give us the same notice), you and she must abide by it when the time comes to end the employment relationship. Specific terms in a contract can override most of the general legal principles discussed below.

FIRING AN EMPLOYEE

EMPLOYMENT AT WILL
If you are contemplating firing a household employee, the first step is to check the listing for your state in appendix A to determine whether you live in an employment-at-will state, a quasi-employment-at-will-state, or a state that limits firing to *cause*. Most states follow a law

known as *employment at will,* which means that you may fire an employee at any time and for any reason other than their race. You do not have to give notice or prove good cause.

Some states have modified this law and are classified as *quasi-employment-at-will* jurisdictions. If you live in one of them, you may still fire your employee for almost any reason. However, your state anti-discrimination laws may make it illegal to fire someone for a list of reasons that include their race, gender, age, use of tobacco, religion, ethnicity and (in a few states) sexual orientation. If your employee thinks you fired her for one of the prohibited reasons, she may file an administrative claim or even a lawsuit against you regardless of whether you really fired her for a prohibited reason. In that circumstance, you will probably be asked to explain or justify your decision to fire her. We will discuss later the process of documenting poor job performance, and how documentation will give you substantial protection against a groundless complaint.

Montana is currently the only state that requires you to have "good cause" for firing an employee. You have good cause if your reason for firing her is related exclusively to job performance—failure to perform her duties satisfactorily, disruption of your household routine, refusal to follow your instructions, conduct that endangers your property or family, or other legitimate reason connected to the nature of household employment.

PUBLIC POLICY EXCEPTION

Just because you live in an employment-at-will state does not automatically protect you from a wrongful discharge lawsuit. Even though household employers are exempt from most state anti-discrimination laws, a court could invoke a "public policy" principle and rule that it is against public policy to permit employees to be fired for reasons unrelated to job performance and related solely to gender, age, ethnicity, religion, or sexual orientation.

Why would you ever want to fire an employee for reasons unrelated to the job? Usually, you wouldn't. But suppose you discover after she has been working for you for six months that your nanny is a lesbian, a member of a religious cult, or advocates the legalization of marijuana; and this makes you uncomfortable. Can you fire her for these non-job-related reasons in an employment-at-will state? Yes, unless the courts in your state have found such grounds to be a violation of public policy. This is an area where you should definitely check with a local attorney who specializes in employment law before you fire an employee for such non-job-related reasons.

Another common public policy exception is a "bad faith" firing done in such a way as to prevent your employee from taking advantage of a job benefit. For example, if your contract calls for two weeks' paid vacation per year for your nanny, and you knew she planned to take that time the first two weeks of October, you could not fire her on September 30. That would deprive her of her earned paid vacation, and would constitute a bad faith firing on your part, unless you could prove good cause related to her job performance. Those states that are known to invoke this bad faith policy are listed in appendix A.

GIVING NOTICE

Do you have to give notice? Unless you promised to give notice in your contract, no notice is required.

GIVING A
WARNING

Do you have to give a warning? Maybe. This is another way of asking whether you can fire an employee for a "first offense." Unfortunately, there is no universal answer.

In true employment-at-will states, you do not need to give any warnings because you can fire an employee any time for any reason (or no reason) at all. The problem is that even in most employment-at-will states, there is at least one illegal reason for firing an employee—her race—that could lead to a wrongful discharge lawsuit. If you fire your African-American nanny for smoking in front of your children and two weeks later hire a white nanny to replace her, she may claim you fired her because of her race. If she files a claim against you, you would have to prove you fired her for legitimate job-related reasons.

You may genuinely have fired the nanny for smoking in front of the children, but the judge may believe it is unreasonable to fire someone the first time they are caught smoking in the house. To the judge, your reason may look like a pretext to cover the fact that you fired the nanny because of her race. Although you were never required to give the nanny a warning, if you can show that you gave her two warnings and an opportunity to stop the offending conduct but she continued to smoke, your conduct now looks reasonable and is more likely to convince a judge that you did not fire her because of her race.

It is generally good practice to give a written warning (keeping a copy) before firing an employee for what may be viewed as a trivial reason. What is important to you may seem inconsequential to an observer. For example, one of our children was a notoriously picky eater. His diet consisted almost entirely of hot dogs, French fries, and Fruit Loops. We thought our nanny was giving in to him too easily and we wanted her to try harder to make him eat healthy food for lunch. She would try for a couple of days, but our son wouldn't eat new foods and would get hungry and difficult, so she would give in and go back to serving him hot dogs every day. It got to the point where we were ready to fire her over this one issue of diet, despite the fact that she was in all other respects a wonderful nanny. Had we done so, it would undoubtedly have seemed reasonable to us, but trivial to a judge.

DOCUMENTING POOR PERFORMANCE

The best way to protect yourself against frivolous claims of wrongful discharge is to document an employee's job performance. In addition to keeping a copy of any warning letters you give your employee, you should keep a written record of your own observations about job performance and any informal discussions you have had with an employee. These records are important court documents if the employee ever sues you for illegal discharge.

These records need not be in any particular form. You can keep a diary, make entries into a computer file, or stick scraps of paper into a file folder. We previously suggested, in chapter 4, that you create a column for "comments" in your account book in which you keep track of your employee's hours. For each "incident" you record, you should include the following information:

1. The date

2. A description of the incident of poor judgment, poor performance, or violation of household rules

3. Whether you discussed it with your employee

4. Whether you set any specific conditions for improvement

5. What the employee said in response

6. If the incident is serious, whether there were any witnesses

In addition, it is a good idea to give periodic written reviews of job performance, where you mention any incidents over the last six months or so and set forth in writing those areas in which you expect improvement. Employee evaluations should be factual and summarize both positive and negative aspects of job performance. If you are going to provide written reviews, take this step seriously. Do not just write a nice paragraph saying what a wonderful job your nanny is doing if in fact you are having some problems. Your employee can use such a favorable evaluation as evidence that your recent claim that you fired her for poor job performance is merely a pretext, and you really fired her for some more sinister reason. After all, if her job performance was poor, as you claim, why did you write such a glowing evaluation? Your explanation that you didn't want to hurt nanny's feelings or inject a sour note into an otherwise good working relationship may be unconvincing.

SEVERANCE PAY

Do you have to give severance pay? No. Unless you promised it in your contract, you do not have to pay severance pay, whether your employee quits or you fire her. However, you do have to pay your employee for all work done up to the point at which they quit or were fired, since termination will rarely take place exactly at the end of a pay period.

If your employee was entitled to paid vacation at the time she is fired, you generally should pay her for the week or two to which she would otherwise have been entitled. This avoids a charge that you have fired her in bad faith. You do not have to give her paid vacation time if she quits.

WHEN AN EMPLOYEE QUITS

Unless your contract requires that she give you notice, your nanny or cook can quit any time and walk off the job. You cannot legally force him to work (nor would you want to entrust your children to an angry nanny or your digestive system to an angry cook who was being forced to work against his will).

Even if your contract calls for thirty day's notice, as a practical matter you cannot prevent an employee from quitting without notice. What are you going to do, have him arrested and brought back in chains? All you can do is sue him later for damages for breach of contract, and you probably have no out-of-pocket damages for which to sue (your inconvenience is generally not compensable). Besides, your former employee probably has no assets to pay a judgment so there is nothing you can do. A nanny can quit any time.

Just because an employee quits does not necessarily mean she cannot sue for wrongful discharge. In a state whose laws against sexual discrimination apply to household employers, if a young female nanny quits after being sexually propositioned by her male employer, the courts will treat it as *constructive discharge* and the employer will still be liable for damages just as if he had fired her for refusing his sexual advances (an illegal reason).

"GOING OUT OF BUSINESS"

We employed a nanny. When our children were old enough to start attending school full-time, we no longer needed her as a household employee and did not plan to hire any other household help. There will come a time when you also have no more household employees and do not expect to hire any more. Your children may be in school, or you may be retiring and moving to a planned community where housekeeping and yardwork are provided to you. When this happens, you can be said to be "going out of business" as a household employer.

Just as you had to register with your state labor and tax departments as a new employer (see chapter 3), you will have to inform them that you have gone out of business. The information on your state in appendix A gives you the current requirements for notifying the state that you are no longer an employer, but this information may be outdated by the time you need it. We suggest trying the telephone numbers listed in appendix A for the relevant state agency to seek information. Also check the quarterly or yearly reporting form used to pay your state unemployment taxes. There may be a place on it to indicate that you have closed your "business." You will probably have to notify both the state department of revenue and the state unemployment compensation agency.

What if you cannot find the information you need? This happened to us in Indiana when our children started school and we no longer needed to employ a nanny. The quarterly unemployment tax reporting form said to notify the department of workforce development if the business had been closed. We made several telephone calls, but could not find anyone who knew exactly what we were supposed to do. Finally, the assistant director of something-or-other told us just to write "Gone out of business" across the front of the form and send it in as usual. We did, and have heard nothing since. If you cannot easily find out what to do to close your household "business," we suggest you do the same. Simply write it on the form or attach a separate letter explaining that you have gone out of business (keep a copy). The state will get in touch with you if they want you to do anything else.

PROVIDING REFERENCES

Whether your employee quits or is fired, you may anticipate that some-day you will be called and asked about her job performance. For the same reasons that you checked her references when she applied for a job with you, the next person she applies to will probably call you. You may be worried about how to respond—if you give a bad reference, can your former nanny sue you for defamation? If you give an unjustified good reference to avoid being sued by your former nanny, can her new employer sue you for fraud? Should you tell the truth, lie, or simply refuse to give a reference?

In many states, you cannot refuse to give a reference. State law may require an employer to provide a "service letter" stating the dates of employment, the job description, and the reasons the employee quit or was fired. Luckily, if your state requires you to provide such a reference, it generally insulates you from being sued for giving a truthful one. Brief summaries of state laws concerning references can be found in appendix A.

In the absence of a state law requiring a service letter, whether you give a reference is up to you. If you decide to talk to a prospective employer about your former employee, you should follow these guidelines:

☛ Be truthful.

☛ Talk only about job-related performance, making no comments about your former employee's personal life, or off-the-job issues.

☛ Make it clear you are giving the information to them only for the purposes of making a hiring decision.

If you give your former employee a bad reference because she was not very good at her job, what happens if she sues you for defamation? Probably nothing more than a little irritation. Defamation is the act of saying or writing a false statement about your employee which harms her reputation. To constitute defamation, you must say bad things that are not true. If you only tell a prospective employer truthful negative things about the employee, you should prevail.

The problem, of course, is that the employee may claim what you are saying is false. You tell someone your former nanny smoked on the job, invited her boyfriend over to the house when on duty, and let the children watch too much TV, so you fired her. The nanny claims these accusations are false—she says she never smoked, never had her boyfriend over, and never let the kids watch TV. If the case were to go to court, it would be your word against hers, and there is no guarantee that the judge will believe you even if you are telling the truth.

This is another reason for keeping written records of your employee's performance. If you are able to produce written records, copies of warning notices, and the names of witnesses, you have a much greater chance of being believed.

In states that require or encourage references, you are further protected by something called *qualified immunity*. Qualified immunity allows you to tell a prospective employer harmful information about a former employee as long as you act in good faith and the information is job-related. For example, you may tell the next prospective employer that your maid stole your credit cards and went on a shopping spree. The information is directly job-related. However, if you inform him that you heard that she stole a credit card from her uncle and went on a shopping spree, you may not be able to claim immunity from suit because the information concerns her private life, not her job performance. About half the states have immunity laws for references. See the listing for your state in appendix A.

Are you safe from being sued if you give a former employee a positive reference? No. This is America, after all, and no one is safe from being sued. Potential employers who rely on your reference to their detriment can theoretically sue you if you made the employee sound better than she really is. For example, if you withhold the information that the nanny hit your children in anger a few times, and the Smith family hires her, and she hits and injures one of their children, they may have a potential lawsuit against you (if they can find out about and prove the incident in your home).

This puts you on the horns of a dilemma. If you say negative things about a former employee, he or she may sue you. If you withhold negative information, the new employer might sue you. This is why some people panic and refuse to give any reference at all. Realistically, of course, the chances of anyone suing you over a letter of reference are very small. But why run even a small risk? There are four things you can do to reduce your potential legal liability:

1. Keep good records of your employee's job performance, and only talk about negative information you can document.

2. Tell anyone who calls you that you will supply them with a written reference but prefer not to talk about it on the telephone. Prepare a written reference that includes dates of employment, job description, and the reasons she was fired or quit. If you have records to support poor job performance, you may mention them as well. Ask a lawyer who specializes in employment law to look over the letter before you send it.

3. When you fire an employee or she quits, ask her about whether she will want a future reference from you. Be honest with her about what it will say. If she wants you to supply references, have her sign the Employment Reference Release (form 7).

4. When you get a call from someone who says they are considering your former employee for a job and want a reference, ask them to send you a consent form signed by your former employee (recall that you asked him or her to sign such a form when he or she applied to work for you).

CIVIL AND CRIMINAL LIABILITY 7

YOUR LIABILITY FOR THE ACTS OF YOUR EMPLOYEES

If a sixteen-year-old kid working for a supermarket spills soap on the floor while mopping and someone slips and falls on it, who is legally responsible for their injuries? The sixteen-year-old kid? Of course not. It is the employer's legal headache. This is because of the legal principle known as *respondeat superior*—the boss is responsible. Well, you are now a "boss" with an employee, and you are similarly responsible for the negligent conduct of that employee. However, you are only liable to the extent that your employee's conduct was intentional or negligent and was the cause of someone else's injuries.

Negligence is measured against a standard of a reasonable careful and prudent person in that situation. Thus, if your nanny is five minutes late to pick up Junior from Pee-Wee Soccer practice, so she is speeding forty-five mph in a thirty mph zone and hits a car pulling out of a driveway, whether she has been "negligent" will depend on whether a reasonably careful and prudent person in her position (late to pick up a child) would drive that fast. Some people probably would and others would not, so the question of liability is not always easy.

You are not liable for the acts of your employees if they accidentally cause harm. If your nanny is driving to soccer practice and a dog runs out in front of her car, so she instinctively swerves to avoid it and hits an oncoming car, it probably will be classified as a simple accident. Most people would behave the way the nanny did, so it is not negligent to try to avoid a dog who has run out in the road. Here again, there may be a difference of opinion on whether she was driving reasonably safely. Was she keeping a watchful eye out for dogs (or people) suddenly running into the street? Why didn't she just slam on the brakes? Some people might believe that a careful and prudent person would hit the dog rather than swerve into the wrong lane.

You can see why lawsuits for damages are complicated events. There is no clear dividing line between lawful and unlawful behavior.

If your employee causes an auto accident while on the job, your car insurance will usually cover it. Insurance will pay damages assessed by a jury (or settled without trial) up to the limit of your policy (typically $300,000), and will also pay for a lawyer to defend you if you get sued. There are two conditions—you must have informed your insurance company that the employee was going to be a regular driver of your car, and you must promptly notify them about the accident. Under some circumstances, failure to give these notices to your insurance company can void your policy.

If an employee causes other kinds of harm, whether your insurance will pay for it is unclear. Suppose your gardener inexplicably attacks some children on their way home from school with a shovel, injuring one of them severely. What if your maid takes your handgun home one day and shoots her boyfriend? What if you give your nanny a blank check to buy groceries but she uses it to buy a $3,000 large screen TV? Do you have liability for these acts? Probably. Will your insurance cover you? The answer varies with the type of policy and its terms. Some homeowner's policies cover you for your employees' acts, some do not. Most so-called *umbrella* policies will cover you in case your homeowner's policy does not. This is why you need to go over the issue of insurance coverage with your agent before you hire household help.

INJURIES TO AN EMPLOYEE

If your employee is injured on the job, what are your obligations and potential legal liability? The answer depends on whether you live in a state that requires household employers to carry workers' compensation insurance. See the listing for your state in appendix A.

In a workers' compensation state, your employee must file a claim with the state workers' compensation board supplying proof of injury, proof that it happened on the job, and statements from doctors showing diagnosis and treatment. Workers' compensation pays claims regardless of whether the injury was your fault, and the whole thing is paid for by insurance.

If you are not in a workers' compensation state, you are personally liable for an employee's injuries if you were negligent. She is in the same position as anyone else. This kind of liability for injuries on your premises may be covered by homeowner's insurance, but some policies exclude employees. You must check with your own insurance agent.

WHAT IF YOU ARE THE VICTIM?

IN GENERAL
Your employee may cause harm to others. She may also cause harm to you. A nanny may harm the children. A maid may steal. A cook may set fire to the house. What are your legal options in these cases?

You have several options. You can sue the offender, of course, but the likelihood that someone working as a domestic servant will have much money is slim. If someone you called as a reference withheld relevant information from you, you could try suing them, but such cases are costly and difficult to prove. You can press criminal charges for assault and battery or theft, but this will not necessarily help you get your money back or your damages paid. A judge might order "restitution" as part of a sentence, but again, the offender is not likely to have much money to pay you back. Some states have crime victim compensation funds that may be able to provide some payments to you.

Your best chance of getting reimbursed is through your own insurance. However, some policies may not cover you if you are harmed by one of your own employees. This is another reason why you should check with your insurance agent when you first hire someone. Note also that insurance companies generally require two things: 1) prompt notice (within as few as ten days) that you have suffered a loss, injury, or theft; and 2) that you have called the police if your employee's conduct was potentially criminal, filed a criminal complaint against the person, and agreed to prosecute it.

We have a friend whose nanny stole some checks and wrote the checks out for several hundreds of dollars. When they confronted her, she explained that she was trying to help her brother who was in big trouble and deeply in debt. She pleaded with them not to call the police, and promised that she would pay them back. They agreed. Three months later, she quit. Nothing had been paid back, so our friends went to their insurance company. Because they had neither notified the company nor filed a criminal complaint, their insurance would not cover it.

You may consider using surveillance cameras to gather evidence against an employee you think is stealing, or a nanny you think is hitting the children. Small surveillance cameras and security recording equipment is readily available at electronics stores. The equipment is expensive, detects only what happens directly in front of the camera, and is time-consuming to use (someone has to look through all those hours of videotape). Therefore, surveillance may not be worth the cost and trouble. If you do think surveillance is necessary, video recording in your own home is legal in most states. However, you should not use any sound recording devices that may record telephone calls without first consulting an attorney or detective agency because the privacy of telephone calls is protected by federal law. Also, in a few states (such as Florida), it is illegal to tape record any conversation without the consent of all parties to the conversation.

IF A NANNY
INJURES YOUR
CHILD

Perhaps the most frightening prospect is that your nanny will harm your child, either accidentally or intentionally. When Louise Woodward was charged with homicide in the death of a child in her care, it sent shivers down the spines of every parent.

The most common situation posing a risk of harm to your child is discipline. Every person who has had the care of children for any length of time has felt the urge to whack them. Many of us have indeed spanked our children. The problem is that excessive physical discipline, or corporal punishment, may injure the child. Excessive physical discipline is so common, especially among frustrated inexperienced care givers, that it has a name: shaken baby syndrome.

If your nanny harms your children by excessive corporal punishment, do you have any legal recourse? That depends on whether she has done anything "wrong." This analysis starts with the employment contract. Each of us has different views on how to discipline children and where to draw the line between a spanking and a felonious assault. If you have given your nanny permission to hit and spank your children in order to discipline them, it is very hard to prove that she was wrong or unreasonable in following your instructions, even if she hits a child too hard and causes injury.

Your safest position is to prohibit all physical discipline, including spanking and shaking your children, and to put this into the contract. That gives you the right to fire her or sue her for excessive discipline, and increases the likelihood that you can get some compensation from insurance to pay for any medical expenses. You can even write into the contract that a "time out" system is to be the exclusive method of punishment without explicit approval by you. Qualified child development experts agree that this is the better method of discipline anyway. Physical punishment merely teaches children that violence is acceptable and does not tend to affect their underlying misbehavior.

Despite the expert consensus that corporal punishment is ineffective, some people believe that prompt, mild physical punishment (spanking) works in some situations. If you want to permit your nanny to be able to spank misbehaving children, it is especially important that you try to carefully define limits in the employment contract. If the contract merely states that this kind of punishment should be used only when reasonable and not to excess, it is not very helpful. "Excessive" punishment has many interpretations and you must realize that what you believe to be excessive and what the nanny believes to be excessive may be two different things. Instead, you probably should specifically limit her to a particular form of discipline, such as spanking on the bottom with a padded ping-pong paddle, and a particular frequency, such as no more than three spanks. This may sound silly, but it will help avoid problems later.

Regardless of whether you authorize your nanny to use corporal punishment, you should be aware that she will not automatically be subject to criminal or civil charges of assault and battery for using this form of discipline. Instead, if you believe the nanny has used excessive discipline, you must press charges against her by contacting the police. The police and the prosecutor will then conduct an investigation. If the investigators believe that the nanny has committed a battery or assault upon your child, she will have to go to court to answer for her actions. At that time, in determining whether an assault or battery has been committed, the court will consider the following:

☛ Whether the corporal punishment caused permanent injury to your child

☛ What your child did to provoke the nanny into using corporal punishment

☛ What the nanny was thinking when she used corporal punishment on your child

Your child may have to appear in court and be cross-examined. There is no doubt that this process will cause great trauma and distress to you and your child. Many people who have been through the criminal justice system say that the experience was not worth it. You don't actually get much satisfaction, and very little will happen to nanny if she is a first offender and the harm to your child was minor.

THEFT BY AN EMPLOYEE

Perhaps the most common crime committed against employers is theft. An employee may steal small items of value from your home and pawn them. Your maid may steal a blank check and pass it off as yours to buy merchandise. Your cook may use your phone to call her brother in Poland. Your nanny may obtain your credit card number and pass it on to a friend who uses it to order stuff from catalogues. Legitimate credit card numbers are easily sold to professional criminals. We even have a friend whose housekeeper gave her copy of our friend's front door key to her drug addict son, so he could break into the house and loot it.

Stolen credit cards. Theft and unauthorized use of credit cards will be a headache, but you are not liable for the charges if you act promptly. As soon as you discover that your card is missing or see unauthorized charges on your bill, notify the credit card company (not your bank). There will be a toll-free phone number listed on the back of your monthly statement for reporting theft. You should also report the theft to your police department and get a police report number.

If your employee has run up unauthorized charges, you will also have to dispute them in writing. An oral report over the telephone is not enough. On the back of your monthly statement will be a form for disputing charges or a procedure to follow. The credit card company will then have to supply you with evidence of the transaction (usually a copy of the charge slip). This may take up to sixty days, since they will have to get this from the merchant.

Once you get the evidence of the transaction, you will have to contact the company again (in writing), explaining why you think you are not responsible for the charge. You can point out that it is not your signature, that a mail order was placed in someone else's name and mailed to a different address, or attach a copy of a police report showing the card was stolen. However, you have to convince the company that it is not your charge, and they may not believe you. You may previously have allowed your employee to use the card, so the company will claim you authorized its use. Your employee may have used your card to order merchandise and had it sent to your address in your name —after all, she may be there all day while you are at work, so it is easy for her to intercept the shipment when it arrives. It will be hard for you to convince anyone that you did not make the charge.

If an employee steals a debit or ATM card and uses it, the law is very complicated. You should report the matter to your bank and the police, and cooperate with them in investigating the matter. You may have difficulty convincing the bank you did not make the transaction because there is no paper trail, no signature, and no address used in ATM/debit card transactions.

Stolen and forged checks. If you discover that an employee has stolen and forged your checks, you are protected from liability by banking law and practice if you act promptly. You are obligated to check your monthly bank statement for unauthorized withdrawals, and report them promptly to the bank. If you do, you are not financially responsible for them, even if they have already been cashed. The bank is supposed to return the money to your account. After all, you filled out a signature card when you opened the account, and it is the bank's responsibility not to pay a check without verifying the signature. Banks do not actually do this for small checks because it would simply cost too much to verify the signatures on the thousands of checks processed by computer each day. Each bank has a policy setting a dollar amount (for example, every check issued for more than $2,000) over which the signatures will in fact be verified. They simply absorb the occasional small bad check as a cost of doing business.

If you find missing checks or suspect that some have been stolen, notify your bank and the police immediately. You will need to tell them the name of the suspect, and you may have to close the account and open a new one. If a number of checks are missing but not yet cashed, it is generally better to close that account and open a new one than to obtain "stop payment" orders on the missing checks. Such orders can cost $25 or more for each check.

Other stolen property. If an employee steals other property, you must report it to the police. If it turns up at a pawn shop or in the home of a "fence," you are entitled to get it back. However, you will have to prove the item is yours and that it was stolen (a police report will usually suffice). You can't just walk into a pawn shop and claim that the recently pawned $5,000 diamond necklace is yours!

The chances of recovering stolen property are slim. Small stuff may be pawned locally and can sometimes be recovered. Generally, pawn shops are required to hold all pawned items for at least thirty days, so if you act promptly, you might find it. Be aware, the police do not go around to the pawn shops and look for your property. They just issue a weekly stolen property list which is sent to the pawn shops, where the owner is supposed to check it against recently pawned merchandise. You have a greater chance of getting things returned if (after you report it to the police) you prepare a list which describes the stolen items, and hand deliver it to all local pawn shops and auction houses yourself.

If the thief pawns the items out of town, sells them on the street, or uses a "fence," your chances of getting them back are virtually nil. However, your homeowner's insurance will probably cover stolen property if you can prove its value and if it is the kind of property everyone has—televisions, stereo equipment, microwave ovens, etc. If it is unique property —silver, china, jewelry, or antiques, you must have purchased a special *rider* to your homeowner's insurance specifically covering those items.

LIABILITY OF THIRD PARTIES

EMPLOYMENT
AGENCIES

What if you hired a nanny through a commercial agency? If she turns out to be a thief or harms your children, is the agency liable? Probably not. Agencies are not automatically liable for the harm caused by a nanny. We have previously discussed the concept of *respondeat superior*, which says that businesses are liable for acts of their employees; and the nanny is your employee, not theirs.

A placement agency has liability for its own negligence in the process of placing people. For you to have legal recourse against it, the agency must have done something intentionally wrong or negligent. If you hired the nanny through the Acme Agency, and she steals your credit cards, Acme is liable only if they knew she had a history of theft and did not tell you, or if they completely failed to do any background investigation despite some indication that there might be a problem (such as a letter of reference stating she was suspected of theft). In addition, some courts have decided that if an agency knows an employee is to be placed in a private home, they have a duty to conduct a background investigation. Failure to conduct such an investigation is negligence, but the agency need only conduct a reasonable background check.

If you suffered significant harm from an employee you hired through an agency, you should contact a local attorney who specializes in personal injury work. They can often be identified in the Yellow Pages by their membership in the American Trial Lawyer's Association (ATLA).

REFERENCES
WHO LIED

Theoretically, you could sue a reference who deliberately misled you by withholding critical information about their former employee. Like an employment agency, the reference must do something wrong. You cannot generally sue a reference just because they gave you incomplete or misleading information. In many states, references acting in good faith are protected against lawsuits even if they fail to give complete information. Winning a case against a reference is difficult, and you would need to consult an attorney who specializes in personal injury lawsuits.

APPENDIX A
STATE LAWS

This appendix contains a state-by-state listing, which provides important resources and a summary of each state's laws relating to domestic employees. While every effort has been made to provide up-to-date information, you need to be aware that the law (as well as the addresses, phone numbers, web sites, and e-mail addresses of government agencies) can change at any time.

ALABAMA

Registering as a new employer:
- ☛ Tax withholding: Not required (optional). If you plan to withhold state income taxes, obtain *Form COM:101, Combined Registration Application*, and withholding tables from:
  > Department of Revenue, Tax Division
  > P.O. Box 327480
  > Montgomery, AL 36132
  > (334) 242-1300 (general), 242-1303 (withholding)
  > www.ador.state.al.us
  > Forms by fax: (334) 242-0112
- ☛ Unemployment insurance: *Form SR2 - Report to Determine Liability*, available from:
  > Dept. of Industrial Relations, Unemployment Compensation Agency
  > 649 Monroe Street
  > Montgomery, AL 36131
  > (334) 242-8830, 242-8467
  > www.dir.state.al.us

Reporting new hires. For assistance call (334) 353-8491
- ☛ Forms: You can file a copy of the federal W-4 form if you write on it the date your employee starts work. Special "report of hire" cards are also available from the New Hire Unit, Department of Industrial Relations. Call (334) 353-8491.
- ☛ Filing: Within 7 days
  > Mail to: New-Hire Unit
  >   Department of Industrial Relations
  >   649 Monroe Street
  >   Montgomery, AL 36131
  > Fax to: (334) 242-8956.

Periodic reports
- ☛ Tax withholding: Quarterly on *Form A-1*, due end of April, July, October, and January; annual reconciliation (*Form A-3*) due end of February.
- ☛ Unemployment tax: Quarterly wage and contribution reports due end of April, July, October, and January.

When you have no more employees: Write to tax department and unemployment agency.

Employment at will state? Yes
Restrictions: cannot fire for serving on jury or filing worker's compensation claim.

State minimum wage: None

Are you required to carry workers' compensation insurance? No

State anti-discrimination laws: None

Laws concerning references: None

Sex offender registry: www.gsiweb.net; or call (334) 260-1135 or 260-1170

ALASKA

Registering as a new employer
- ☞ Tax withholding: Not required; no state income tax.
- ☞ Unemployment insurance: Obtain an *Employer Registration Form* from:
  > Department of Labor
  > Employment Security
  > P.O. Box 25509
  > Juneau, AK 99802
  > www.labor.state.ak.us
  > Statewide: 1-888-448-2937; or (907) 465-2757
  > Anchorage: 269-4850;
  > Fairbanks: 451-2876
  > Juneau: 465-4478
  > Kenai: 283-4478

Reporting new hires. For assistance call (907) 269-6685, 269-6089, or 269-6776; www.revenue.state.ak.us/csed
- ☞ Forms: W-4
- ☞ Filing: Within 20 days

Mail to:	Child Support Enforcement Division
	550 W. 7th Avenue
	Anchorage, AK 99501-6699
Fax to:	(907) 787-3197 or 787-3181

Periodic reports: Quarterly wage and contribution reports due end of April, July, October, and January

When you have no more employees: Call Department of Labor for instructions.

Employment at will state? Quasi employment at will; i.e., cannot fire an employee in "bad faith."

State minimum wage: $5.65 for people who work more than 30 hrs./wk.

Are you required to carry workers' compensation insurance? Yes

State anti-discrimination laws: Unlawful to discriminate based on race, religion, ethnicity, age, disability, marital status, pregnancy, or parenthood unless reasonably related to ability to perform job.

Laws concerning references: Employer immune from suit for giving reference on job performance.

Other relevant laws: Must allow employees time off to vote.

Sex offender registry: www.dps.state.ak.us/Sorcr/; or call (907) 269-0396

ARIZONA

Registering as a new employer:
- ☛ Combined registration for tax withholding and unemployment insurance: Obtain *Form UC-001, Joint Tax Application Form*; and a booklet called *Employment Tax Requirements Guide* from:
  > Department of Revenue
  > License & Regis Div.
  > P.O. Box 29069
  > Phoenix, AZ 85038
  > 1-800-634-6494; (602) 542-4576; or (602) 542-4260
  > www.revenue.state.az.us
- ☛ Unemployment insurance: Obtain quarterly wage reporting form from:
  > Department of Economic Security
  > P.O. Box 6028
  > Phoenix, AZ 85005
  > (602) 248-9354 or 248-9394
  > www.de.state.az.us

Reporting new hires. For assistance call (602) 340-0555; or online at www.az-newhire.com
- ☛ Forms: Copy of W-4
- ☛ Filing: Within 20 days
  > Mail to: New Hire Reporting Center
  > P.O. Box 25638
  > Phoenix, AZ 85002
  > Online: www.az-newhire.com

Periodic reports
- ☛ Tax withholding: Quarterly on forms *A1-QRT* and *A1-WP*, due end of April, July, October, and January.
- ☛ Unemployment tax: Quarterly wage and contribution reports due end of April, July, October, and January.

When you have no more employees: You will need to file *Form UC-018, Report of Changes,* available from from Department of Employment Security

Employment at will state? Quasi employment at will; i.e., cannot fire an employee in "bad faith."

State minimum wage: None

Are you required to carry workers' compensation insurance? No

State anti-discrimination laws: None

Laws concerning references: Employer immune from suit for giving reference on job performance and reason for termination.

Sex offender registry: (602) 223-2416

ARKANSAS

Registering as a new employer

- ☛ Tax withholding: Obtain the booklet *Income Tax Withholding Tables and Instructions for Employers,* and an *AR4ER Withholding Registration Form* from:

  Department of Finance
  P.O. Box 8055
  Little Rock, AR 72203
  1-800-882-9275; (501) 682-2212 (withholding tax unit); 682-7290 (general)
  www.state.ar.us/dfa/

- ☛ Unemployment insurance: Obtain a *Status Report (Form 201)* from:

  Department of Employment Security
  P.O. Box 2981
  Little Rock, AR 72203
  (501) 682-3100 or 682-3253
  www.state.ar.us/esd/employers.html

Reporting new hires. For assistance call 1-800-259-2095 or (502) 376-2125

- ☛ Forms: W-4 or State New hire form
- ☛ Filing: Within 20 days

Mail to:	New Hire Reporting Center
	P.O. Box 2540
	Little Rock, AR 72203
Fax to:	1-800-259-3562 or (501) 376-2682
Online:	www.ar-newhire.com

Periodic reports

- ☛ Tax withholding: Initially monthly on *Form AR941M,* due within fifteen days of the end of the month; until state informs you in writing that you re exempt; annual reconciliation (*Form AR3 MAR*), due end of February.
- ☛ Unemployment tax: Quarterly wage and contribution reports due end of April, July, October, and January.

When you have no more employees: Complete "date stopped" and "reason closed sections of *Form AR941.*

Employment at will state? Yes

State minimum wage: Same as federal law.

Are you required to carry workers' compensation insurance? No

State anti-discrimination laws: None

Laws concerning references: None

Sex offender registry: Available only through local law enforcement agencies.

CALIFORNIA

Registering as a new employer: Unified registration for both tax withholding and unemployment insurance. Obtain a booklet called *California Employer's Guide*, the *DE-1HW Registration* form, and the tax withholding schedules from:

Employment Development Department
P.O. Box 826880
Sacramento, CA 94280
(916) 654-7041 (registration), (916) 464-3502 (employment taxes)
www.edd.cahwnet.gov (very convenient)
Forms by fax: (916) 654-9211
Local employment tax customer offices:

Bakersfield:	395-2896	Orange:	288-2601
Eureka:	445-6522	Sacramento:	255-1965
Fresno:	445-5132	San Bernadino:	383-4176
Long Beach:	428-0021	San Diego:	284-8615
Los Angeles:	669-7670	San Francisco:	929-5700
Oakland:	577-2396	San Jose:	277-9400

Reporting new hires. For assistance call (916) 657-0529; online at www.edd.cahwnet.gov/txner.htm
☞ Forms: DE-1HW
☞ Filing: Within 15 days

Mail to: Employment Development Dept.
New Hire Reporting
P.O. Box 997016, MIC 23
West Sacramento, CA 95799-7016
Fax to: (916) 653-5214

Periodic reports: Tax withholding and unemployment taxes are reported together quarterly on *Form DE3BHW, Report of Wages & Withholding for Employers of Household Employees*; annual *Payroll Tax Return for Employer of Household Workers (Form DE3HW)*, due by end of January.

When you have no more employees:File annual *DE3HW* payroll tax form, stating that you have no more employees.

Employment at will state? Quasi employment at will; i.e., cannot fire an employee in "bad faith."

State minimum wage: $5.75

Are you required to carry workers' compensation insurance? Yes

State anti-discrimination laws: None

Laws concerning references: Employer immune from suit for giving reference on job performance, reason for termination, and qualifications.

Sex offender registry: www.sexoffender.net (unofficial); or call (916) 227-3288 or 227-3743 or 227-3740

COLORADO

Registering as a new employer:

- ☛ Tax withholding: Not required (optional). If you plan to withhold state income taxes, obtain *Income Tax Withholding Tables for Employers, Employers Withholding Tax Forms*, and *CR100 Business Registration* form from:

> Department of Revenue, Taxpayer Services
> 1375 Sherman Street
> Denver, CO 80261
> (303) 232-2416
> www.state.co.us/gov_dir/revenue_dir/home_rev.html

- ☛ Unemployment insurance: Obtain an *Employer Registration Form* from:

> Department of Labor: Outside Denver: 1-800-480-8299
> Denver: (303) 603-8231 or 603-8235
> Div. of Employment & Training
> P.O. Box 8789
> Denver CO 80201

Reporting new hires. For assistance call (303) 297-2849; online at
www.cdhs.state.co.us/text/oss/CSE/contact.html

- ☛ Forms: Federal W-4
- ☛ Filing: Within 20 days

> Mail to: State Directory of New Hires
> P.O. Box 2920
> Denver, CO 80201
> Fax to: (303) 297-2595

Periodic reports

- ☛ Tax withholding: Quarterly, using withholding coupons sent to you, due end of April, July, October, and January; annual transmittal form for state W-2s (form *DR1093*) due end of February.
- ☛ Unemployment tax: Quarterly wage and contribution reports due end of April, July, October, and January.

When you have no more employees: File form *DR-1095 Account Change or Closure*, available from Labor Department, Division of Employment & Training.

Employment at will state? Yes

State minimum wage: Same as federal.

Are you required to carry workers' compensation insurance? Yes, for full time employees.

State anti-discrimination laws: Unlawful to discriminate based on race, creed, color, sex, age, national origin or ancestry. Discrimination based on disability allowed if reasonably related to ability to perform job.

Laws concerning references: Employer immune from suit for giving reference on job performance.

Sex offender registry: (303) 239-4222

CONNECTICUT

Registering as a new employer
- ☛ Tax withholding: Not required (optional), but you will need to obtain a *CT-W4* form, a *REG-1 Tax Registration Number* form, and *Circular CT, Employer's Tax Guide* from:
     Department of Revenue
     25 Sigourney Street
     Hartford, CT 06106-5032
     Hartford: (860) 297-5962   Outside Hartford: 1-800-382-9463
     www.state.ct.us/drs
     Forms by fax: (860) 297-5698
- ☛ Unemployment insurance: You need form *UC-1A Employer Status Report*. Also helpful is *Employer's Guide to Unemployment Compensation.*
     Department of Labor
     200 Folly Brook Blvd.
     Wethersfield, CT 06109-1114
     Assistance: (860) 263-6550
     Unemployment: (860) 566-4350
     www.ctdol.state.ct.us

Reporting new hires. For assistance call (860) 263-6310
- ☛ Forms: A copy of CT-W4 (included in Tax Guide)
- ☛ Filing: Within 20 days
     Mail to: Department of Labor, New Hire Report
                       200 Folly Brook Blvd.
                       Wethersfield, CT 06109
     Fax to: 1-800-816-1108

Periodic reports
- ☛ Tax withholding: Annual report on form *CT-941* (ignore fact that form says "quarterly"), due April 15; and annual reconciliation (form *CT-W3*), writing in "household employer" in space reserved for tax registration number.
- ☛ Unemployment tax: Quarterly employee earnings report (form *UC-5A*), due end of April, July, October, and January.

When you have no more employees: File form *CT-W4* (tax) and form *UC-5A* (labor)

Employment at will state? Quasi employment at will; i.e., cannot fire an employee in "bad faith."
Restrictions: Cannot fire employee for exercising first amendment rights.

State minimum wage: $5.65 (scheduled to go up to $6.15 on 1/1/2000).

Are you required to carry workers' compensation insurance? Yes

State anti-discrimination laws: Unlawful to discriminate against people who smoke when off duty.

Laws concerning references: None

Sex offender registry: www.state.ct.us/dps/sor.htm; or call (860) 685-8060

DELAWARE

Registering as a new employer:
- ☛ Tax withholding: Not required (optional). If you plan to withhold, you will need to obtain a booklet called *Withholding of Delaware Income Tax* from:
  >Division of Revenue
  >P.O. Box 8995
  >Wilmington, DE 19899
  >(302) 577-8200 (ask for withholding)
  >www.state.de.us/revenue/index.htm
- ☛ Unemployment insurance: Obtain the *Combined Registration Application Packet*, and a *Form UC-1 Initial Liability Report* from:
  >Department of Labor
  >Employer Contributions
  >Div. of Unemployment Insurance
  >P.O. Box 9953
  >Wilmington, DE 19809
  >(302) 761-8482
  >www.state.de.us/labor/aboutdol/ui.shtml

Reporting new hires. For assistance call (302) 577-4815, ext. 249
- ☛ Forms: Federal W4 or state form *SD/W4A*
- ☛ Filing: Within 20 days:
  >Mail to: Division of Child Support Enforcement
  >   P.O. Box 913
  >   New Castle, DE 19720.
  >Fax to: (302) 577-4848

Periodic reports
- ☛ Tax withholding: Quarterly on *Form W-1Q*, due end of April, July, October, and January; annual reconciliation (*Form W-3*), due end of February.
- ☛ Unemployment tax: Quarterly wage and contribution reports due end of April. July, October, and January.

When you have no more employees: Call Labor Department for instructions.

Employment at will state? Quasi employment at will; i.e., cannot fire an employee in "bad faith."

State minimum wage: Same as federal law.

Are you required to carry workers' compensation insurance? Yes

State anti-discrimination laws? None apply to persons with fewer than 4 employees.

Laws concerning references? You are required to provide a reference for a former nanny who is seeking a job in the child-care field.

Sex offender registry: Available through local law enforcement agencies.

DISTRICT OF COLUMBIA

Registering as a new employer: Registration for income tax withholding and unemployment taxes is done on a combined form *FR500 Combined Business Tax Registration Application*. You will also need *FR-230 Income tax Withholding Tables and Instructions*

        Office of Tax and Revenue
        941 N. Capitol Street N.E.
        Washington, DC 20001
        (202) 727-4TAX
        www.dccfo.com/taxpmain.htm

Also helpful is *Unemployment Insurance Compensation Employer's Handbook*, available from:

        Department of Employment Services
        500 C Street, NW
        Washington, DC 20001
        (202) 724-7457, 724-7462, or 724-7472; 639-1383 (tax division)
        http://does.ci.washington.dc/us/

Reporting new hires. For assistance call 1-888-689-6088; or
online at http://does.ci.washington.dc/us/newhiredir.html

- ☛ Forms: Copy of federal W-4 plus cover letter giving employee's date of birth, date of hire, salary, and DC Unemployment Insurance number; or New Hire Registry Reporting Form.
- ☛ Filing: Within 20 days

    Mail to: DC New Hire Registry
                    P.O. Box 97236
                    Washington, DC 20090-7236
    By phone: 1-888-689-6088
    Fax to: 1-888-689-6089

Periodic reports

- ☛ Tax withholding: Annual report on form *FR-900A*.
- ☛ Unemployment tax: Quarterly wage and contribution reports (*UC-30*), due end of April, July, October, and January.

When you have no more employees: File form *UC-30, Report of Change* (included with quarterly forms) and tax forms *FR-900B* and *FR-900W1* final report.

Employment at will state: Yes

State minimum wage: $6.15 (does not apply to maids, cooks, and household help).

Are you required to carry workers' compensation insurance? Yes.

State anti-discrimination laws: None

Laws concerning references: None

Sex offender registry: Inquire at Metropolitan Police Department, 300 Indiana Avenue, N.W., Room 4014; or call (202) 727-4429.

FLORIDA

Registering as a new employer:
- ☞ Tax withholding: Not required; no state income tax
- ☞ Unemployment insurance: Obtain form *UCS-1 Employer Registration Report*. Also recommended is the *Florida Unemployment Compensation Employer Handbook*. Both are available from:
  > Department of Labor
  > Employment Security
  > Division of Unemployment Comp
  > 107 E. Madison Street
  > Tallahassee FL 32399-0233
  > (800) 482-8293, (850) 921-5000, or (850) 921-3108
  > www.state.fl.us/dles/uc/uc_home.htm

Reporting new hires. For assistance call 1-888-854-4791, (850) 656-343; or online at www.fl-newhire.com
- ☞ Forms: New Hire Reporting Form
- ☞ Filing: Within 20 days

Mail to:	Florida New Hire Reporting
	P.O. Box 6500
	Tallahassee, FL 32314
Fax to:	1-888-854-4762 or (850) 656-0528

Periodic reports: Quarterly wage and contribution reports (form *UCT-6*), due end of April, July, October, and January.

When you have no more employees: Report closing of "business" on final quarterly report to Employment Security. Call 1-800-482-8293 for assistance.

Employment at will state: Yes

State minimum wage: None

Are you required to carry workers' compensation insurance? No

State anti-discrimination laws? None

Laws concerning references: Employer immune from suit for giving reference on job performance.

Sex offender registry: www.fdle.state.fl.us/Sexual_Predators/; or call 1-888-357-732 or (850) 410-8572.

GEORGIA

Registering as a new employer
- ☛ Tax withholding: Obtain the *Income Tax Withholding Tables* and *CRF002 Tax Registration Application* from:

> Department of Revenue
> Taxpayer Registration Unit
> P.O. Box 740001
> Atlanta, GA 30374
> (404) 651-8651, 656-4071, or 656-4181
> www.state.ga.us/departments/dor

- ☛ Unemployment insurance: Obtain form *DOL-1A Employer Status Report*. Also helpful is *Information About Unemployment Insurance for Employers*. Both are available from:

> Department of Labor
> Suite 850
> 148 International Blvd. NE
> Atlanta, GA 30303-1751
> New accounts: (404) 656-5590
> General account information: (404) 656-3145
> www.dol.state.ga.us/ui

Reporting new hires. For assistance call 1-888-541-0469; or online at www.ga-newhire.com
- ☛ Forms: New Hire Reporting Form
- ☛ Filing: Within 10 days

> Mail to: New Hire Reporting
> P.O. Box 38480
> Atlanta, GA 30334
>
> Fax to: 1-888-541-0521

Periodic reports
- ☛ Tax withholding: Quarterly withholding tax return (*G-7*), and voucher (*GA-V*).
- ☛ Unemployment tax: Quarterly tax & wage reports (*DOL-4*), due end of April, July, October, and January

When you have no more employees: Check "final" box on quarterly tax form *G-7*. Fill out information in "employer change request" section of quarterly tax & wage report (*DOL-4*).

Employment at will state? Yes

State minimum wage: currently less than federal wage ($3.25) so federal wage applies

Are you required to carry workers' compensation insurance? No

State anti-discrimination laws: Unlawful to discriminate against persons age 40-70.

Laws concerning references: Employer immune from suit for giving reference on job performance, reason for termination, qualifications, and criminal conduct.

Sex offender registry: www.ganet.org/gbi/sorsch.cgi; or call (404) 244-2895; or call your local sheriff's office.

HAWAII

Registering as a new employer:
- ☛ Combined registration for tax withholding and unemployment insurance: Use form *BB-1*, *Basic Business Application*, available from:
  > Business Action Center
  > 1130 N. Nimitz Hwy, Suite A254
  > Honolulu, HI 96817
  > 1-800-468-4644; or (808) 586-2545
  > www.hawaii.gov/dbedt/small.html   or   www.aloha.net/~edpso/
- ☛ Tax withholding: Obtain state *HW-4* forms (you may not use federal W-4), *Booklet A: Employer's Tax Guide,* and a booklet called *Introduction to Withholding State Income Tax By Employers*, from the Business Action Center listed above or from:
  > Taxpayer Services
  > P.O. Box 259
  > Honolulu, HI 96809
  > Oahu: (808) 587-7572   Other islands: 1-800-222-7572
  > www.state.hi.us/tax/tax.html

Reporting new hires. For assistance call (808) 586-8914
- ☛ Forms: *UC-BP-5A*, *Report of New Hire*
- ☛ Filing: Within 5 days (if this is your first employee, within 5 days of receiving form)
  > Mail to: Department of Labor, Employer Services Section
  > 830 Punchbowl Street
  > Honolulu, HI 96813

Periodic reports
- ☛ Tax withholding: Quarterly on *Form HW-14*, due by 15th of April, July, October., and January; annual withholding reconciliation (*Form HW-3*), due end of February.
- ☛ Unemployment tax: Quarterly wage and contribution reports (*UC-B6*), due end of April, July, October, and January.

When you have no more employees: File *GEW-TA-RV-1*, *Notice of Cancellation;* unemployment form *UC-25, Notification of Changes.*

Employment at will state? Yes
Restrictions: cannot fire an employee who refuses to work in unsafe conditions.

State minimum wage: $5.25, but does not apply to most household employees.

Are you required to carry workers' compensation insurance? Yes

State anti-discrimination laws: Unlawful to discriminate based on race, sex, sexual orientation, age, religion, ethnicity, disability, marital status, or previous arrest record.

Laws concerning references: None

Other relevant laws: You must carry "Temporary Disability Insurance" on your household employees.

Sex offender registry: (808) 587-3100

IDAHO

Registering as a new employer.
- ☛ Tax withholding: Not required (optional).
- ☛ Unemployment insurance: You can register for both voluntary income tax withholding and unemployment insurance by filing an *IBR-1, Idaho Business Registration Form*, available from:

    Tax Commission
    P.O. Box 36
    Boise, ID 83722
    1-800-972-7660, or (208) 334-7660
    www.state.id.us/tax/

You also need *A Guide for Idaho Employers*, available from:

    Department of Labor, Job Service
    317 Main Street
    Boise, ID 83735
    1-800-448-2977; (208) 334-6318, 334-6339, or 34-6341
    www.labor.state.id.us

Reporting new hires. For assistance call 1-800-627-3880
- ☛ Forms: Federal W-4 (write in date of hire and your unemployment insurance account number at the bottom of the form)
- ☛ Filing: Within 20 days

    | Mail to: | Department of Labor, New Hire Reporting |
    | | 317 Main Street |
    | | Boise, ID 83735 |
    | Fax to: | (208) 332-7411 |

Periodic reports
- ☛ Tax withholding: Quarterly on *Form 958*, due end of April, July, October, and January; annual reconciliation (*Form 956* and *Form 956-W*), due end of February.
- ☛ Unemployment tax: Quarterly tax report (*TAX020*), due end of April, July, October, and January.

When you have no more employees: No procedure specified.

Employment at will state? Quasi employment at will; i.e., cannot fire an employee in "bad faith."

State minimum wage: Same as federal law

Are you required to carry workers' compensation insurance? No

State anti-discrimination laws: None

Laws concerning references: Employer immune from suit for giving reference on job performance and reason for termination.

Sex offender registry: (208) 884-7305

ILLINOIS

Registering as a new employer
- ☛ Tax withholding: Not required (optional). If you voluntarily withhold, you may obtain *NUC-1-H Household Employer* form and booklet *IL-700-H* withholding guide for household employers from:
  > Department of Revenue
  > P.O. Box 19010
  > Springfield, IL 62794
  > 1-800-732-8866 (info); 1-800-356-6302 (forms)
  > www.revenue.state.il.us
- ☛ Unemployment insurance: Obtain form *UI-1 Report to Determine Liability* from:
  > Employment Security
  > Revenue Division
  > 401 S. State Street
  > Chicago, IL 60605
  > 1-800-247-4984, or (312) 793-4880
  > www.ides.state.il.us

Reporting new hires. For assistance call 1-800-327-HIRE; or online at www.ides.state.il.us/html/idesinfo.htm
- ☛ Forms: IDES New Hire Reporting Form
- ☛ Filing: Within 20 days

Mail to:	New Hire Directory
	P.O. Box 19473
	Springfield, IL 62794
Fax to:	(217) 557-1947

Periodic reports
- ☛ Tax withholding: Annual (state will send you *Booklet IL-700-H* containing form), due April 15.
- ☛ Unemployment tax: Quarterly wage and contribution reports (form *UC-3*), due end of April, July, October, and January.

When you have no more employees: Indicate that you have gone out of "business" on your final quarterly report.

Employment at will state? Yes

State minimum wage: Same as federal law

Are you required to carry worker's compensation insurance? Yes, for full-time employees.

State anti-discrimination laws: Unlawful to discriminate based on physical or mental disability unless reasonably related to ability to perform job.

Laws concerning references: Employer immune from suit for giving reference on job performance.

Sex offender registry: (217) 785-0633

INDIANA

Registering as a new employer
- ☞ Tax withholding: Obtain *Employer's Withholding Guide* and *Business Tax Application* form from:
  > Department of Revenue
  > Taxpayer Services
  > Indiana Govt. Center North, Rm N105
  > Indianapolis, IN 46204-2253
  > (317) 233-4016 (withholding)
  > www.state.in.us/dor/
- ☞ Unemployment insurance: File a *Status Report* form with
  > Department of Workforce Development
  > 10 N. Senate Avenue
  > Indianapolis, IN 46204-2277
  > 1-800-437-9136; or (317) 232-7436 or 232-7698
  > www.dwd.state.in.us

Reporting new hires. For assistance call 1-800-437-9136; or online at www.dwd.state.in.us/ahtml/newhire/sdnh.html
- ☞ Forms: Copy of federal or state W-4
- ☞ Filing: Within 20 days

Mail to:	Department of Workforce Development
	New Hire Directory
	10 N. Senate Avenue
	Indianapolis, IN 46204-2277
Fax to:	1-800-408-1388
Online:	www.dwd.state.in.us

Periodic reports
- ☞ Tax withholding: Quarterly (form *W-1*), due end of April, July, October, and January; annual reconciliation (form *W-3*), due end of February.
- ☞ Unemployment tax: Quarterly wage and tax reports due end of April, July, October, and January.

When you have no more employees: Write "closing business" on final quarterly report to Department of Workforce Development.

Employment at will state? Yes

State minimum wage: Currently less than the federal wage ($2.00), so the federal wage applies

Are you required to carry worker's compensation insurance? No

State anti-discrimination laws: Unlawful to discriminate based on age (40-70).

Laws concerning references: If requested, you are required to supply a letter describing a former employee's job, their dates of employment, and the reason they quit or were fired.

Sex offender registry: www.ai.org/cji/html/sexoffender.html; or call (317) 32301232.

IOWA

Registering as a new employer
- ☞ Tax withholding: Not required (optional). If you plan to withhold state income taxes, obtain a booklet called *Withholding Tax Guide* and the *Business Tax Registration* form from:
  > Department of Revenue
  > Hoover State Office Bldg.
  > Des Moines, IA 50319
  > 1-800-367-3388; or (515) 281-3114
  > www.state.ia.us/tax
  > Forms by fax: 1-800-572-3943
- ☞ Unemployment insurance: Obtain *Report to Determine Liability* form from:
  > Department of Workforce Development
  > Employer Tax Section
  > 1000 E. Grand Avenue
  > Des Moines, IA 50309-9801
  > 1-800-562-4692; or (515) 281-539 or 281-5217
  > www.state.ia.us/iwd

Reporting new hires. For assistance call (515) 281-5331
- ☞ Forms: *Centralized Employee Registry Reporting Form (IA-W)*
- ☞ Filing: Within 15 days
  > Mail to: Employee Registry
  > P.O. Box 10322
  > Des Moines, IA 50306
  > Fax to: 1-800-759-5881

Periodic reports
- ☞ Tax withholding: Quarterly, unless you have several employees (then monthly), on forms the state will send you, due the end of April, July, October, and January; annual verified summary of payments (VSP), due end of February.
- ☞ Unemployment tax: Quarterly contribution and payroll reports, due end of April, July, October, and January.

When you have no more employees: Call local Workforce Development office.

Employment at will state? Yes

State minimum wage: Same as federal law.

Are you required to carry workers' compensation insurance? Yes

State anti-discrimination laws: None

Laws concerning references: If requested, you must provide a former employee with a letter describing their job, their dates of employment, and their wage rate.

Sex offender registry: (515) 281-5138

KANSAS

Registering as a new employer
- ☞ Tax withholding: Obtain *Employer's Withholding Tax Booklet* and a *Business Tax Application (BT/rg-16)*:
  > Department of Revenue
  > Robert B. Docking State Office Bldg.
  > Topeka, KS 66612
  > (785) 296-0222 (general), 296-3059 (withholding), 296-4937 (forms)
  > www.ink.org/public/kdor
  > Forms by fax: (785) 291-3614
- ☞ Unemployment insurance: Obtain form *K-CNS-010 Status Determination Report* (also helpful is *Handbook for Employers*) from:
  > Department of Human Resources
  > Employment Security Division
  > 401 SW Topeka Blvd.
  > Topeka, KS 66603
  > (785) 296-5025; 296-1796; or 296-7082
  > www.hr.state.ks.us/ui/html/EnUI.htm

Reporting new hires. For assistance call (785) 296-5025 (for Topeka); 1-888-219-7801, ext. 100 (for rest of state); or online at: www.hr.state.ks.us/home-html/newhires.htm
- ☞ Forms: *K-CNS104 New Hire Report*, or copy of W-4
- ☞ Filing: Within 20 days

Mail to:	New Hire Directory
	P.O. Box 3510
	Topeka, KS 66601
Fax to:	1-888-219-7798

Periodic reports
- ☞ Tax withholding: Probably annual (state will notify you after you register) form *KW-5*; annual withholding return (*KW-3*), due end of February.
- ☞ Unemployment tax: Employer's quarterly wage reports (*K-CNS100*), due end of April, July, October, and January.

When you have no more employees: File tax form *KW-3* (reconciliation) and *BT/rg-108* (*Notice of Discontinuation of Business*) within 30 days of "close of business." Note "no more employees" on final quarterly wage report to Department of Human Resources.

Employment at will state? Quasi employment at will; i.e., cannot fire an employee in "bad faith."

State minimum wage: Currently less than the federal wage ($2.65), so the federal wage applies.

Are you required to carry workers' compensation insurance? Yes

State anti-discrimination laws: None

Laws concerning references: If requested, you must provide a former employee with a letter describing their job, their dates of employment, and their wage rate.

Sex offender registry: www.ink.org/public/kbi/kbisexpage.html; or call (785) 296-6656 or 296-8277.

KENTUCKY

Registering as a new employer:
- ☞ Tax withholding: Not required (optional). If you plan to withhold state income taxes, obtain *Withholding Kentucky Income Tax* booklet, and *Kentucky Tax Registration Application* form from:
    > Revenue Cabinet, Support Services
    > Station 35
    > Frankfort, KY 40620
    > (502) 564-7287
    > www.state.ky.us/agencies/revenue/revhome.htm
- ☞ Unemployment reporting: Obtain form *UI-1 Application for Unemployment Insurance Reserve Account* from:
    > Workforce Development Cabinet
    > Div. of Unemployment Insurance
    > P.O. Box 948
    > Frankfort, KY 40602
    > 1-800-626-2250; or (502) 564-6606
    > www.des.state.ky.us

Reporting new hires. For assistance call 1-800-817-2262
- ☞ Forms: State form UI-414, or copy of federal W-4
- ☞ Filing: Within 7 days (legislation is pending to change to 20 days)
    > Mail to: Kentucky New Hire Reporting Center
    > P.O. Box 1130
    > Richmond, VA 23219 [Yes! Send it to Virginia]
    > Fax to: 1-800-817-0099

Periodic reports
- ☞ Tax withholding: Either quarterly due end of April, July, October, and January; or yearly, depending upon payroll. Annual *K-3 Return of Income Tax Withheld.*
- ☞ Unemployment tax: Quarterly wage and contribution reports (*UC-3*), due end of April, July, October, and January.

When you have no more employees: File final tax forms *K-2* and *K-3* (fill in bottom section cancelling account); file Workforce Development form *UI-21, Report of Discontinuation of Business.*

Employment at will state? Yes

State minimum wage: Same as federal law.

Are you required to carry workers' compensation insurance? Yes, for full-time employees.

State anti-discrimination laws: If two or more employees, it is unlawful to pay unequally based on gender.

Laws concerning references: None

Other relevant laws: An employee is entitled to "reasonable" personal leave up to six weeks prior to the reception of an adopted child.

Sex offender registry: (502) 227-8700

LOUISIANA

Registering as a new employer
- ☛ Tax withholding: Obtain the booklet *R1306 Withholding Tables and Instructions for Employers*, and *R1609 Application for Louisiana Tax Number* from:
  > Department of Revenue
  > P.O. Box 201
  > Baton Rouge, LA 70821
  > (225) 925-7318 (new registration)
  > (225) 925-4611 (assistance)
  > www.revenue.state.la.us
- ☛ Unemployment insurance: You need a *Status Report* form from:
  > Department of Labor, Employment Security Division
  > P.O. Box 94094
  > Baton Rouge, LA 70804
  > (225) 342-3111, 342-2992, or 342-2944
  > www.ldol.state.la.us

Reporting new hires. For assistance call 1-888-223-1461
- ☛ Forms: copy of W-4
- ☛ Filing: Within 20 days

Mail to:	New Hire Directory
	P.O. Box 2151
	Baton Rouge, LA 70821
Fax to:	1-888-223-1462

Periodic reports
- ☛ Tax withholding: Quarterly on *Form L-1*, due end of April, July, October, and January; annual reconciliation (*Form L-3*), due end of February.
- ☛ Unemployment tax: Quarterly wage and contribution reports (*LDOS-ES4*), due end of April, July, October, and January.

When you have no more employees: Contact Employment Security Division for instructions.

Employment at will state? Yes

State minimum wage: None

Are you required to carry workers' compensation insurance? No

State anti-discrimination laws: Unlawful to discriminate based on race, religion, sex, disability, national origin, because a person has sickle cell trait, or because person smokes when off duty.

Laws concerning references: Employer immune from suit for giving reference on job performance and reason for termination.

Sex offender registry: (225) 925-4867

MAINE

Registering as a new employer
- ☛ Combined registration for tax withholding & unemployment insurance: Obtain *Form A Application for Tax Registration and Unemployment Contributions* from:
  > Department of Labor
  > Central Registration
  > P.O. Box 1057
  > Augusta, ME 04332
  > (207) 287-2338, or 287-3176
  > www.state.me.us/labor/ucd/Default.htm

- ☛ Tax withholding: Obtain *Withholding Tables for Maine Individual Income Tax* from:
  > Revenue Services
  > 24 State House Station
  > Augusta, ME 04333
  > (207) 626-8475 (assistance)
  > (207) 624-7894 (forms)
  > www.janus.state.me.us/revenue

Reporting new hires. For assistance call (207) 287-2886
- ☛ Forms: copy of W-4 or state new hire form
- ☛ Filing: Within 7 days
  > Mail to: New Hire Reporting
  > 11 State House Station
  > Augusta, ME 04330
  > Fax to: (207) 287-6882

Periodic reports: Tax withholding and unemployment taxes reported together quarterly on *Form 941/C1-ME*, due end of April, July, October, and January; annual tax reconciliation (form *W-3ME*), due end of February.

When you have no more employees: Submit final *W-2* and *W-3ME* forms to Revenue Department; complete cancellation notice section on final *Form 941/C1ME*.

Employment at will state? Yes

State minimum wage: Same as federal law.

Are you required to carry worker's compensation insurance? No

State anti-discrimination laws: Unlawful to discriminate based on race, sex, pregnancy, disability, religion, age, ethnicity, membership in the National Guard, or smoking off the job.

Laws concerning references: If requested, you must give a former employee a letter stating the reasons for termination of employment. Employer immune from suit for giving reference on job performance and work record.

Sex offender registry: (207) 624-7009

MARYLAND

Registering as a new employer: Combined tax withholding & unemployment insurance: Obtain form *093*, *Combined Registration Application* by calling (410) 767-1313 (in Baltimore); or 1-800-492-1757 (rest of state).
- ☞ Tax withholding: Obtain an *Employer Withholding Guide and Tables* from:
> Comptroller of Treasury Revenue
> Annapolis, MD 21411-0001
> 1-800-638-2937; or (410) 260-7951
> www.marylandtaxes.com
> Fax number for tax forms: (410) 974-3299
- ☞ Unemployment insurance: Request a copy of *Employer Quick Reference Guide to Unemployment Insurance* from:
> Department of Labor
> 1100 N. Eritaw Street
> Baltimore, MD 21201
> 1-800-492-5524 (employer help line); (410) 767-2414 or 767-2488
> www.comp.state.md.us

Reporting new hires. For assistance call 1-888-MD-HIRES; or (410) 347-9911; or online at www.mdnewhire.com
- ☞ Forms: *MD New Hire Registry Form*
- ☞ Filing: Within 20 days

Mail to:	New Hire Registry
	P.O. Box 1316
	Baltimore, MD 21203
Fax to:	1-888-657-3534 or (410) 347-5993
Online:	www.mdnewhire.com/mdnewhire/method1.html

Periodic reports
- ☞ Tax withholding: Quarterly, due end of April, July, October, and January (if total payroll is very small, you may be permitted to file annually); annual reconciliation due end of February.
- ☞ Unemployment tax: Quarterly wage and contribution reports due end of April, July, October, and January.

When you have no more employees: Call (410) 260-7980, or send "final report form" which is included in the withholding coupon booklet.

Employment at will state? Yes

State minimum wage: Same as federal law.

Are you required to carry workers' compensation insurance? Yes; either through a private carrier or contact state fund at (410) 494-2000.

State anti-discrimination laws: None

Laws concerning references? Employer immune from suit for giving reference on job performance and reason for termination.

Sex offender registry: (410) 764-4006

MASSACHUSETTS

Registering as a new employer:
- ☛ Tax withholding: Not required (optional). If you voluntarily withhold, obtain form *TA-1* and *Circular M - Withholding Tables* (and the helpful *Guide to Withholding Taxes on Wages*) from:
  > Department of Revenue
  > 100 Cambridge Street
  > Boston, MA 02204
  > 1-800-392-6089; or (617) 887-6367
  > www.state.ma.us/dor/
- ☛ Unemployment reporting: Obtain an *Employer Status Report* form and the booklet *Simplifying the Employment and Training Law* from:
  > Bureau of Employment & Training
  > 16 Staniford Street
  > Boston, MA 02114
  > (617) 626-5050, 626-5076, or 626-5078
  > www.detma.org/revenue/

Reporting new hires. For assistance call 1-800-32-273
- ☛ Forms: copy of W-4
- ☛ Filing: Within 14 days

Mail to:	Department of Revenue
	P.O. Box 7032
	Boston, MA 02204
Fax to:	(617) 887-5049

Periodic reports
- ☛ Tax withholding: Quarterly on *Form WR-1*, due by 15th of April, July, October, and January; annual reconciliation *Form M-941A* due end of January.
- ☛ Unemployment tax: Employer's quarterly reports (*Form 0001*), due April, July, October, and January.

When you have no more employees: Call (617) 626-5076 to cancel unemployment insurance; file final wage report.

Employment at will state? Quasi employment at will; i.e., cannot fire an employee in "bad faith."

State minimum wage: $5.25 (maids not included).

Are you required to carry worker's compensation insurance? Yes

State anti-discrimination laws: No

Laws concerning references? No

Other relevant state laws: A female employee may be entitled to eight weeks leave for giving birth or adopting a child. Consult a Massachusetts attorney who specializes in employment law.

Sex offender registry: www.star.net/people/~danvrspd/sexreg.htm; or call (617) 660-4632.

MICHIGAN

Registering as a new employer
- ☛ Combined registration for tax withholding and unemployment insurance. Obtain the *Combined Registration Booklet* from either the Department of Treasury or the Unemployment Agency.
- ☛ Tax withholding: Obtain the *Michigan Tax Withholding Guide* from:
  > Department of Treasury
  > 430 W. Allegan Street
  > Lansing, MI 48922
  > 1-800-487-7000; 1-800-367-6263 (forms); 1-800-373-0888 (withholding)
  > Forms by fax: (517) 241-8730
  > www.treas.state.mi.us
- ☛ Unemployment insurance: Two helpful publications are *Michigan Employment Security Act* and *Employer Guide to Wage Reporting in Paper Format*, available from:
  > Unemployment Agency
  > 7310 Woodward Avenue
  > Detroit, MI 48202
  > 1-800-638-3994; or (313) 876-5131
  > www.cis.state.mi.us/ua/directry.htm

Reporting new hires. For assistance call 1-800-524-9846 or (517) 373-1426; or online at www.new-hires.com/michigan/
- ☛ Forms: state form *MI-W4*
- ☛ Filing: Within 20 days

Mail to:	Department of Treasury New Hire Center
	P.O. Box 85010
	Lansing, MI 48909
Fax to:	(517) 886-9190

Periodic reports
- ☛ Tax withholding: State will send you customized forms with filing deadlines; annual *Return for Sales, Use, or Withheld Taxes* (form *C-3204*)
- ☛ Unemployment tax: Quarterly wage and tax reports (forms *UA-1017* and *UA-1020*) due by 25th of April, July, October, and January.

When you have no more employees: Obtain *Discontinuation of Business* form from Unemployment Agency.

Employment at will state? Yes

State minimum wage: Same as federal law

Are you required to carry workers' compensation insurance? Yes, for full time employees. (517) 322-1195

State anti-discrimination laws: Unlawful to discriminate based on disability, religion, race, ethnicity, age, sex, height, weight, or marital status (hiring maids exempt).

Laws concerning references: Employer immune from suit for giving reference on job performance if documented in personnel file.

Sex offender registry: www.mipsor.state.mi.us; or call (517) 336-6683

MINNESOTA

Registering as a new employer:
- ☛ Tax withholding: Not required (optional). If you plan to withhold state income taxes, you can apply by phone or request a *Form ABR, Application for Business Registration*. You will also need *Income Tax Withholding Instructions and Tax Tables*. These are available from:
  > Department of Revenue, Withholding Tax Division
  > Mail Station 6501
  > St. Paul, MN 55146
  > 1-800-657-3605, 1-800-657-3594, or 1-800-657-3676;
  > for Twin Cities: (651) 282-9999 or 282-5225
  > www.taxes.state.mn.us
- ☛ Unemployment insurance: Obtain a *Report to Determine Liability* form from:
  > Department of Economic Security
  > 390 N. Robert Street
  > St. Paul, MN 55101
  > (651) 296-3736; 296-6141 (information); 296-3643 (forms)
  > www.des.state.mn.us

Reporting new hires. For assistance call 1-800-672-4473 or (651) 227-4661
- ☛ Forms: W-4 with date of birth and date of hire written at bottom, or state *New Hire Reporting* form.
- ☛ Filing: Within 20 days

Mail to:	Minnesota New Hire Reporting Center
	P.O. Box 64212
	St. Paul, MN 55164
Fax to:	1-800-692-4473 or (651) 227-4991

Periodic reports
- ☛ Tax withholding: Either quarterly or annually, depending on a number of factors; the state will send you the appropriate forms after you register.
- ☛ Unemployment tax: Quarterly wage and contribution reports (form *MDES-1*), due end of April, July, October, and January.

When you have no more employees: Contact Department of Economic Security

Employment at will state? Yes

State minimum wage: Complicated law basically tracks federal law

Are you required to carry workers' compensation insurance? Yes

State anti-discrimination laws: Unlawful to discriminate based on race, religion, ethnicity, sex, marital status, welfare status, disability, sexual orientation, age (under 70), AIDS, or smoking/drinking off the job.

Laws concerning references: If requested, you must give a former employee a letter stating the reasons for terminating the job.

Sex offender registry: 1-888-234-1248

MISSISSIPPI

Registering as a new employer
- ☛ Tax withholding: Not required (optional). If you voluntarily withhold, obtain *Registration Application Form* (form *70-001*) and withholding tables from:
  > Tax Commission, Registration Section
  > P.O. Box 1033
  > Jackson, MS 39215
  > (601) 923-7000 or 923-7800
  > www.mstc.state.ms.us
- ☛ Unemployment insurance: Obtain form *UI-1* to determine status, and the booklet *Employer Rights and Responsibilities Under Mississippi Employment Security Law* from:
  > Employment Security Commission
  > P.O. Box 1699
  > Jackson, MS 39215
  > (601) 961-7755
  > www.mesc.state.ms.us/tax

Reporting new hires. For assistance call 1-800-241-1330; or online at www.new-hires.com/mississippi/
- ☛ Forms: Federal W-4 plus employee's date of birth and date of hire; or state new hire form.
- ☛ Filing: Within 15 days

Mail to:	Mississippi Directory of New Hires
	P.O. Box 94673
	Cleveland, OH 44101 [Yes! Send it to Ohio]
Fax to:	1-800-937-8668

Periodic reports
- ☛ Tax withholding: Quarterly report due by 15th of April, July, October, and January; annual reconciliation (form *09-120*) due end of January. State will send you customized forms.
- ☛ Unemployment tax: Quarterly wage and contribution reports (form *UI-2/3*) due end of April, July, October, and January.

When you have no more employees: File *UI-ECR Change of Status* report (employment)

Employment at will state? Yes

State minimum wage: None

Are you required to carry workers' compensation insurance? No

State anti-discrimination laws: Unlawful to discriminate against applicant who smokes off the job.

Laws concerning references: None

Sex offender registry: (601) 987-1592

MISSOURI

Registering as a new employer
- ☞ Tax withholding: Obtain a *Tax Withholding Schedule* and *Form 2643 Tax Registration Application*; and *Employer's Tax Guide* from:
  > Department of Revenue, Tax Administration Bureau
  > P.O. Box 999
  > Jefferson City, MO 65108
  > 1-800-877-6881; or (573) 751-5752
  > http://dor.state.mo.us/
- ☞ Unemployment insurance: Obtain *Form 2699 to Determine Liability Status,* and the booklet *Employer's Rights and Responsibilities* from:
  > Employment Security
  > P.O. Box 59
  > Jefferson City, MO 65104
  > (314) 340-4870, or (573) 751-3328
  > www.dolir.state.mo.us/es/index.htm
- ☞ For general assistance, obtain the publication *Starting a New Business in Missouri* from:
  > Business Assistance Center
  > P.O. BOX 118
  > Jefferson City, MO 65102
  > 1-800-523-1434
  > www.ecodev.state.mo.us/mbac/

Reporting new hires. For assistance call 1-800-859-7999; or online at: www.dss.state.mo.us/ces/newhire.htm
- ☞ Forms: copy of W-4
- ☞ Filing: Within 20 days
  > Mail to: Missouri Department of Revenue, New Hire Report
  > P.O. Box 340
  > Jefferson City, MO 65101
  > Fax to: (573) 526-8079

Periodic reports
- ☞ Tax withholding: Quarterly on *Form MO941,* due end of April, July, October, and January; annual reconciliation due end of January.
- ☞ Unemployment tax: Quarterly wage and contribution reports due in April, July, October, and January.

When you have no more employees: File application to terminate unemployment liability. Contact Business Assistance Center (1-800-523-1434) for instructions.

Employment at will state? Yes

State minimum wage: Same as federal law

Are you required to carry workers' compensation insurance? No

State anti-discrimination laws: None

Laws concerning references: None that apply to household employees.

Sex offender registry: Available at state highway patrol offices.

MONTANA

Registering as a new employer
- ☛ Combined registration for tax withholding and unemployment insurance. Obtain *Employer's Tax Guide* and *Montana Employer Registration* from from:
  > Department of Revenue
  > P.O. Box 5805
  > Helena, MT 59604
  > 1-800-550-1513 or (406) 444-0269
  > www.state.mt.us/revenue/index.htm
- ☛ Unemployment insurance information:
  > Unemployment Insurance Program
  > P.O. Box 6339
  > Helena, MT 59604
  > (406) 444-3834
  > http://uid.dli.state.mt.us/

Reporting new hires. For assistance call 1-888-866-0327 or (406) 444-9290; or online at: www.state.mt.us/revenue/newhire.html
- ☛ Forms: *Montana New Hire Report* form or copy of W-4
- ☛ Filing: Within 20 days
  > Mail to: New Hire Reporting Program
  >   P.O. Box 8013
  >   Helena, MT 59604
  > Fax to: 1-888-272-1990 or (406) 444-0745

Periodic reports
- ☛ Tax withholding: Either quarterly or annually, depending upon several factors. The state will send you the correct forms after you register.
- ☛ Unemployment tax: Quarterly wage and contribution reports due end of April, July, October, and January.

When you have no more employees: Indicate "no employees" on quarterly wage and contribution report.

Employment at will state? No. Employee can be fired only for good cause.

State minimum wage: Nannies and household help not covered

Are you required to carry workers' compensation insurance? No

State anti-discrimination laws: Unlawful to discriminate based on race, religion, ethnicity, age, disability, marital status, gender, or use of tobacco/alcohol off the job; unless reasonably related to ability to perform job.

Laws concerning references: If requested, you are required to provide a fired employee with a statement of reasons.

Sex offender registry: (406) 444-9479, or through local county sheriff's office.

NEBRASKA

Registering as a new employer
- ☛ Tax withholding: Obtain a *Tax Application Form (20)* and *Circular EN* from:
  > Department of Revenue
  > P.O. Box 94818
  > Lincoln, NE 68509
  > Lincoln: (402) 471-5729 or 471-2971; rest of state: 1-800-742-7474
  > www.nol.org/home/NDR/
- ☛ Unemployment insurance: Obtain an *Application for Account (UI-1)* and the booklet *Employer's Guide to Unemployment Insurance* from:
  > Department of Labor
  > P.O. Box 94600
  > Lincoln, NE 68509-4600
  > (402) 471-9839 or 471-9935
  > www.dol.state.ne.us/uihome.htm

Reporting new hires. For assistance call 1-800-256-0293 or (402) 471-9160
- ☛ Forms: W-4
- ☛ Filing: Within 20 days

Mail to:	Directory of New Hires
	P.O. Box 540880
	Omaha, NE 68154
Fax to:	(402)471-9455

Periodic reports
- ☛ Tax withholding: Quarterly on *Form 941N*, due end of April, July, October, and January; annual reconciliation (form *W-3N*), due March 15th.
- ☛ Unemployment tax: Quarterly combined tax reports due end of April, July, October, and January.

When you have no more employees: Fill out *Notice of Change* from included with your quarterly report packet.

Employment at will state? Yes

State minimum wage: Same as federal law.

Are you required to carry workers' compensation insurance? No

State anti-discrimination laws: None

Laws concerning references: None that apply to household employees.

Sex offender registry: (402) 471-4545

NEVADA

Registering as a new employer
- ☛ Tax withholding: Not required; no state income tax.
- ☛ Unemployment insurance: Obtain the *Employer Handbook*, the *Supplemental Registration Form for Domestic Service Employers*, and a *Business Registration Form* from:
    Department of Employment Training
    500 E. Third Street
    Carson City, NV 89713
    (702) 486-7923; or (775) 687-4599, 687-4540, or 687-4545
    www.state.nv.us/detr/

Reporting new hires. For assistance call 1-888-639-7241; or online at: www.state.nv.us/detr/es/newhire.htm
- ☛ Forms: copy of W-4
- ☛ Filing: Within 20 days
    Mail to: New Hire Unit
                    500 E. Third Street
                    Carson City, NV 89713-0033
    Fax to: (775) 684-8681

Periodic reports: Quarterly wage and contribution reports (form *NUC 4072*), due end of April, July, October, and January

When you have no more employees: Write "no more employees" on quarterly wage report.

Employment at will state? Quasi employment at will; i.e., cannot fire an employee in "bad faith."
Restrictions: Cannot fire employee based on witness report without giving him or her a hearing.

State minimum wage: Same as federal law.

Are you required to carry workers' compensation insurance? No

State anti-discrimination laws: None

Laws concerning references: If requested, you must provide a former employee with a letter stating the reasons they left or were fired.

Sex offender registry: (775) 684-2656

NEW HAMPSHIRE

Registering as a new employer:
- ☛ Tax withholding: Not required; no state income tax.
- ☛ Unemployment insurance: Obtain an *Employer Status Report* form from:
  > Employment Security
  > 32 S. Main Street
  > Concord, NH 03301
  > (603) 228-4038 or 224-3311
  > www.nhworks.state.nh.us/agypage.htm

Reporting new hires. For assistance call 1-800-803-4485, or (603) 229-4371
- ☛ Forms: copy of federal W-4 or state New Hire form
- ☛ Filing: Within 20 days

    Mail to: Employer Security, New Hire Registry
                  P.O. Box 2092
                  Concord, NH 03302
    Fax to: 1-800-783-3598 or (603) 229-4324

Periodic reports: Quarterly wage and contribution reports due end of April, July, October, and January

When you have no more employees: Contact Employment Security agency for instructions.

Employment at will state? Yes

State minimum wage: Same as federal law.

Are you required to carry workers' compensation insurance? Yes.

State anti-discrimination laws: None

Laws concerning references: None

Sex offender registry: (603) 271-2663

NEW JERSEY

Registering as a new employer
- ☛ Combined registration for both tax withholding and unemployment insurance. Obtain the *Complete Business Registration Package*. Tax withholding is not required (optional). If you voluntarily withhold, obtain *Gross Income Tax Instructions Booklet* and **Supplement**. These are available from:

    Department of Treasury, Division of Taxation
    P.O. Box 252
    Trenton, NJ 08646
    (609) 292-6400
    www.state.nj.us/treasury/revenue/
- ☛ Unemployment insurance information:

    Department of Labor, Division of Employer Accounts
    CN 947
    Trenton, NJ 08625-0947
    (609) 633-6400
    http://www.state.nj.us/labor/service.htm

Reporting new hires. For assistance call (877) 654-4737
- ☛ Forms: *New Hire Reporting* form, or copy of W-4
- ☛ Filing: Within 20 days

    Mail to: New Hire Operations Center
                    P.O. Box 4654
                    Trenton, NJ 08650
    Fax to: 1-800-304-4901

Periodic reports: Withheld taxes and unemployment payments are made quarterly on form *NJ-927*, due end of April, July, October, and January; annual tax reconciliation (form *NJW-3*) due end of February.

When you have no more employees: File *Change of Registration Information* form, which is included in the *Complete Business Package* or available from Division of Revenue.

Employment at will state? Yes

State minimum wage: Currently less than federal wage ($5.05), so federal wage applies.

Are you required to carry workers' compensation insurance? Yes, for full-time employees.

State anti-discrimination laws: None

Laws concerning references: None

Other relevant laws: All employers must carry Temporary Disability Insurance, which may be purchased either from a private carrier or from the state run plan. Temporary disability includes up to ten weeks maternity leave.

Sex offender registry: (609) 984-2895

NEW MEXICO

Registering as a new employer
- ☛ Tax withholding: Obtain an *Application for Registration* form and *Withholding Tax General Information* packet from:
    > Department of Taxation & Revenue
    > P.O. Box 630
    > Santa Fe, NM 85704
    > (505) 827-0700 (Santa Fe)
    > (505) 841-6200 (Albuquerque)
    > www.state.nm.us/tax
- ☛ Unemployment insurance: Obtain a *Status Report ES-802* form and the booklet *Employer Responsibilities Under the Unemployment Law of New Mexico* from:
    > Department of Employment Security
    > P.O. Box 2281
    > Albuquerque, NM 87103
    > (505) 841-8576 (registration)
    > (505) 841-8568 (wage reporting)

Reporting new hires. For assistance call 1-888-878-1607 or (505) 995-8230; or online at: www.nm-newhire.com
- ☛ Forms: W-4 or state new hire form
- ☛ Filing: Within 20 days
    Mail to: New Mexico New Hires Directory
    > P.O. Box 29480
    > Santa Fe, NM 87592
    Fax to: 1-888-878-1614 or (505) 995-8232

Periodic reports
- ☛ Tax withholding: Quarterly on *Form CRS-1*, due 25th of April, July, October, and January.
- ☛ Unemployment tax: Quarterly wage and contribution report on form *ES-903A*, due end of April, July, October, and January.

When you have no more employees: File *Change Sheet* and final *ES-903A* form with Employment Security; file a *Registration Update* form with Department of Taxation and Revenue.

Employment at will state? Yes

State minimum wage: Currently less than federal wage ($4.25), so federal wage applies

Are you required to carry workers' compensation insurance? No

State anti-discrimination laws: None

Laws concerning references: Employer immune from suit for providing reference.

Sex offender registry: (505) 827-3370

NEW YORK

Registering as a new employer
- ☛ Tax withholding: Not required (optional). If you voluntarily withhold taxes, obtain *Employer's Guide to Unemployment, Wage Reporting and Withholding Tax* from:
  > Department of Taxation, Taxpayer Assistance
  > Harriman Campus
  > Albany, NY 12227
  > 1-800-225-5829 or 1-800-462-8100
  > www.tax.state.ny.us
  > Fax number for tax forms: 1-800-748-3676
- ☛ Unemployment insurance: Obtain *Employer Registration Form for Unemployment Insurance (1A-100)*, and the *Householder's Guide for Unemployment Insurance* from:
  > Business Tax Information Center
  > Department of Labor
  > State Campus Bldg. 12
  > Albany, NY 12240-0372
  > 1-800-972-1233 or (518) 457-4120
  > www.labor.state.ny.us

Reporting new hires. For assistance call 1-800-972-1233
- ☛ Forms: copy of W-4
- ☛ Filing: Within 20 days

Mail to:	New Hire Notification
	P.O. Box 15119
	Albany, NY 12212
Fax to:	(518) 438-3715

Periodic reports: Income and unemployment taxes are reported quarterly on form *NYS-45, Combined Withholding, Wage Reporting and Unemployment Insurance Return*, due end of April, July, October, and January.

When you have no more employees: Send a written request to terminate unemployment insurance liability to: Liability & Determination Section, New York Department of Labor, Albany, NY 12240-032. Also send form *DTF, Change of Business* to Department of Taxation.

Employment at will state? Yes

State minimum wage: Currently less than federal wage ($4.25), so federal wage applies

Are you required to carry workers' compensation insurance? Yes, for full-time employees.

State anti-discrimination laws: None

Laws concerning references: None

Other relevant laws: You must give an employee who leaves the job a Record of Employment (form IA-12.3), available from the Department of Labor Registration Section in Albany, or call (518) 485-8589.

Sex offender registry: (518) 457-6326

NORTH CAROLINA

Registering as a new employer:
- ☛ Tax withholding: Not required (optional). If you voluntarily withhold, obtain *Income Tax Withholding Tables* and *Form AS/RP-1 Application for Withholding Identification Number* from:
  > Department of Revenue
  > P.O. Box 25000
  > Raleigh, NC 27640
  > (919) 733-4626
  > www.dor.state.nc.us/dor/
- ☛ Unemployment insurance: Obtain the booklet *North Carolina Unemployment Tax Information* and *Employer Status Report* (form *NCUI 604*) from:
  > Employment Security Commission
  > Status Unit
  > P.O. Box 26504
  > Raleigh, NC 27611
  > (919) 733-7395 or 733-7156
  > www.esc.state.nc.us

Reporting new hires. For assistance call (919) 571-4114
- ☛ Forms: W-4 or state reporting form
- ☛ Filing: Within 20 days

Mail to:	Department of Human Resources
	New Hire Report
	P.O. Box 900004
	Raleigh, NC 27675-9004
Fax to:	(919) 877-1019

Periodic reports
- ☛ Tax withholding: Quarterly on *Form NC-5 Tax Withholding Report*, due end of April, July, October, and January; annual reconciliation (form *W-3*), due end of February.
- ☛ Unemployment tax: Quarterly tax & wage reports (form *NCUI-101*), due end of April, July, October, and January.

When you have no more employees: File *Out of Business Notification* form with Department of Revenue; file *NCUI-101A* form with Employment Security Commission.

Employment at will state? Yes

State minimum wage: Same as federal law.

Are you required to carry workers' compensation insurance? No

State anti-discrimination laws: If you have 3 or more employees, you may discriminate based on off-the-job use of tobacco or alcohol.

Laws concerning references: You may, but are not required to, provide a reference on a former employee.

Sex offender registry: http://sbi.jus.state.nc.us/sor/

NORTH DAKOTA

Registering as a new employer:
- ☞ Combined tax withholding & unemployment insurance registration: Obtain a *New Business Registration Forms Consolidate Packet*. Tax withholding for household employers is optional; if you voluntarily withhold, you need to obtain *Income Tax Withholding Guidelines* and you will need to file a *Form F-301, Application to Register for Income Tax Withholding*. These are all available from:
    Tax Commission
    600 E. Boulevard Avenue, Dept 127
    Bismarck, ND 58505
    1-800-638-2901 (general)
    (701) 328-3124 or 328-3125 (tax withholding)
    (701) 328-2868 (unemployment insurance)
    www.state.nd.us/taxdpt
- ☞ Unemployment insurance: Obtain *Report to Determine Liability* (included in the packet mentioned above).
    Job Service
    P.O. Box 5507
    Bismarck, ND 58506
    1-800-472-2952; or (701) 328-2868 or 328-2814
    www.state.nd.us/jsnd/uins.htm

Reporting new hires. For assistance call 1-800-755-8530 or (701) 328-3582
- ☞ Forms: copy of W-4
- ☞ Filing: Within 20 days
    Mail to: Child Support Enforcement Agency
                    P.O. Box 7369
                    Bismarck, ND 58507
    Fax to: (701) 328-5497

Periodic reports
- ☞ Tax withholding: Quarterly on *Form F-306*, due end of April, July, October, and January; annual transmittal (Form *F-307*), due end of February.
- ☞ Unemployment tax: Quarterly wage and contribution reports due end of April, July, October, and January.

When you have no more employees: Call or write both Tax Commission and Job Service

Employment at will state? Yes

State minimum wage: Same as federal law.

Are you required to carry workers' compensation insurance? No

State anti-discrimination laws: None

Laws concerning references: None

Sex offender registry: (701) 328-5500

OHIO

Registering as a new employer
- ☛ Tax withholding: Not required (optional). If you plan to withhold state income taxes, obtain an *Application for Registration as Ohio Withholding Agent* (form *IT-1*), and *Employer's Income Tax Withholding Tables* from:
  > Department of Taxation
  > P.O. Box 2476
  > Columbus, OH 43216
  > (614) 466-3960
  > www.state.oh.us/tax
- ☛ Unemployment insurance: Obtain form *UCO-1, Report to Determine Liability* from:
  > Employment Services
  > P.O. Box 923
  > Columbus, OH 43216
  > (614) 466-2319
  > www.state.oh.us/obes

Reporting new hires. For assistance call 1-800-208-8887, or online at: www.new-hires.com
- ☛ Forms: copy of W-4
- ☛ Filing: Within 20 days
  Mail to: Ohio New Hire Reporting Program
  > P.O. Box 44972
  > Cleveland, OH 44101
  Fax to: (440) 808-8021

Periodic reports
- ☛ Tax withholding: Quarterly on payment voucher for withheld taxes (*Form IT-50*), due end of April, July, October, and January; annual transmittal and reconciliation forms (*Form IT-3* and *Form IT-941*), due end of February.
- ☛ Unemployment tax: Quarterly wage and contribution reports due end of April, July, October, and January.

When you have no more employees: File *UCD-384, Disposition of Business* form with Bureau of Employment Services.

Employment at will state? Yes

State minimum wage: Varies depending on a number of conditions, but all at or less than federal level, so federal law applies.

State anti-discrimination laws: None

Are you required to carry workers' compensation insurance? Yes.

Laws concerning references: Employer immune from suit for giving reference on job performance.

Sex offender registry: (614) 466-8204, ext. 224

OKLAHOMA

Registering as a new employer:
- ☛ Tax withholding: Not required (optional). If you voluntarily withhold, obtain a *Business Registration* packet and *Oklahoma Income Tax Withholding Tables* from:
  > Tax Commission
  > 2501 N. Lincoln Blvd.
  > Oklahoma City, OK 73194
  > 1-800-522-8165 or (405) 521-3279
  > www.oktax.state.ok.us/oktax
- ☛ Unemployment insurance: Obtain an *Employer Status Report for Domestic Employment* form, and the booklet *Employer's Information About Unemployment Insurance* from:
  > Employment Security Commission
  > P.O. Box 52003
  > Oklahoma City, OK 73152
  > 1-800-317-3785; or (405) 557-7138 or 557-7135
  > www.oesc.state.ok.us

Reporting new hires. For assistance call 1-800-317-3785, or (405) 522-2550; or online at: www.oesc.state.ok,us/newhire
- ☛ Forms: W-4 or state new hire form
- ☛ Filing: Within 20 days

Mail to:	New Hire Reporting Center
	P.O. 52004
	Oklahoma City, OK 73152
Fax to:	1-800-317-3786 or (405) 557-5350

Periodic reports
- ☛ Tax withholding: Quarterly withheld tax return due by 15th day of April, July, October, and January.
- ☛ Unemployment tax: Quarterly wage and contribution reports (form *OES3-A*), due end of April, July, October, and January.

When you have no more employees: Check the appropriate box on back of quarterly withholding tax return.

Employment at will state? Yes

State minimum wage: Same as federal law.

State anti-discrimination laws: None

Are you required to carry workers' compensation insurance? Yes.

Laws concerning references? You are authorized but not required to provide a reference letter. Employer immune from suit for giving reference on job performance.

Sex offender registry: (405) 425-2872

OREGON

Registering as a new employer:
- ☞ Combined tax withholding & unemployment insurance registration: Obtain a *Combined Employer's Registration* form, and the *Oregon Withholding Tax Tables* from:
  > Department of Revenue
  > P.O. Box 14800
  > Salem, OR 97309
  > (503) 378-4988 or 945-8091
  > www.dor.state.or.us/
- ☞ Employment information: Obtain the helpful booklet, *Oregon Business Guide*, from:
  > Business Information Center, Public Services Bldg.
  > 255 Capitol St NE
  > Salem, OR 97310-2222
  > (503) 986-2222
- ☞ If you have questions about unemployment insurance:
  > Department of Employment
  > 875 Union Street NE
  > Salem, OR 97311
  > (503) 947-1488
  > e-mail: taxinfo@emp.state.or.us
  > www.emp.state.or.us/tax

Reporting new hires. For assistance call (503) 986-6053
- ☞ Forms: Federal W4
- ☞ Filing: Within 20 days
  >   Mail to: Department of Justice, Support Enforcement Division
  >   1495 Edgewater NW
  >   Salem, OR 97304-9902.

Periodic reports
- ☞ Tax withholding: Quarterly *Form* OQ (combined tax report and payment coupon), due end of April, July, October, and January.
- ☞ Unemployment tax: Quarterly wage detail report (form *132*), due in April, July, October, and January.

When you have no more employees: Send request in writing that your account be closed to: Employment Department, 875 Union Street NE, Rm 107, Salem OR 97311

Employment at will state? Yes

State minimum wage: $6.50, but does not apply to nannies and household employees.

Are you required to carry workers' compensation insurance? No

State anti-discrimination laws: Unlawful to discriminate based on race, religion, ethnicity, sex, marital status, pregnancy, childbirth, sexual orientation, AIDS, age, disability, or use of tobacco off the job.

Laws concerning references: Employer immune from suit for giving reference on job performance.

Sex offender registry: (503) 378-3720, ext. 4418

PENNSYLVANIA

Registering as a new employer:
- ☛ Tax withholding: Not required (optional). If you intend to withhold taxes, obtain the *Instructions for Employer Withholding of Pennsylvania Personal Income* tax booklet, and a *Form PA-100, Pennsylvania Enterprise Registration Form and Instructions* from:
  > Department of Revenue
  > Bureau of Business Trust Fund Taxes, Dept. 280901
  > Harrisburg, PA 17128-0901
  > (717) 783-1488
  > www.revenue.state.pa.us
- ☛ Unemployment insurance: Obtain Form *UC-2, Employer's Report for Unemployment Compensation* and the helpful booklet *Unemployment Compensation Information for Contributing Employers* from:
  > Department of Labor & Industry
  > P.O. Box 60849
  > Harrisburg, PA 17106
  > (717) 787-7613, 787-5279, or 787-2097
  > www.li.state.pa.us

Reporting new hires. For assistance call 1-888-724-4737 or (717) 787-6466; or online at: www.panewhires.com
- ☛ Forms: *New Hire Reporting* form
- ☛ Filing: Within 20 days
  > Mail to: Pennsylvania New Hire Reporting Program
  >   P.O. Box 69400
  >   Harrisburg, PA 17106
  > Fax to: (717) 657-4473

Periodic reports
- ☛ Tax withholding: Quarterly *Deposit Statement and Return of Income Tax Withheld* (form *PA501R*), due end of April, July, October, and January; annual final report (form *PA-W3R*), due end of January.
- ☛ Unemployment tax: Quarterly wage and contribution reports (form *U2-C*), due end of April, July, October, and January.

When you have no more employees: File *Change/Correction Form REV-1705* with Department of Revenue.

Employment at will state? Yes

State minimum wage: Same as federal law.

Are you required to carry workers' compensation insurance? No

State anti-discrimination laws: None

Laws concerning references: None

Sex offender registry: (717) 783-4363

RHODE ISLAND

Registering as a new employer: Obtain a *Business Application and Registration* form, which is used to register employers for tax withholding, unemployment, and disability taxes from:

Department of Administration - Division of Taxation
Employer Tax Section
1 Capitol Hill, Suite 36
Providence, RI 02908
(401) 222-6323 (general)
(401) 222-2909 (forms & tax withholding)
(401) 222-2905 (taxpayer assistance)
(401) 222-3696 (employer registration)
www.tax.state.ri.us/

Reporting new hires. For assistance call 1-888-870-6461 or (401) 277-2303; or online at: www.RInewhire.com
- ☛ Forms: State New Hire form, or copy of W-4 with "no health insurance" written on the bottom.
- ☛ Filing: Within 14 days

Mail to:	Rhode Island New Hire Reports
	P.O. Box 540229
	Omaha, NE 68154 (Yes! Send it to Nebraska)
Fax to:	1-888-430-6907
Telephone:	1-888-870-6461

Periodic reports
- ☛ Tax withholding: Quarterly on *Form 941-Q-RI*, due end of April, July, October, and January; annual reconciliation (*Form W-3-RI*), due end of February.
- ☛ Unemployment tax: Quarterly wage and tax reports due end of April, July, October, and January.

When you have no more employees: Call (401) 222-6323 or 222-2909

Employment at will state? Yes

State minimum wage: Same as federal law.

Are you required to carry worker's compensation insurance? No, but you are required to carry Temporary Disability Insurance, administered through the Employment Security Commission. Information is contained with the *Business Application & Registration* form.

State anti-discrimination laws: None

Laws concerning references: None

Sex offender registry: (401) 274-4400, ext. 2352

SOUTH CAROLINA

Registering as a new employer:
- ☛ Tax withholding: Not required (optional). If you plan to withhold, obtain an *Income Tax Withholding Package* from:
  > Department of Revenue
  > Withholding Tax
  > P.O. Box 125
  > Columbia, SC 29214
  > (803) 898-5752
  > www.dor.state.sc.us/
- ☛ Unemployment insurance: Obtain booklet *South Carolina Business Registration Forms*, which contains *Form UCE-151, Employer Status Report*; and *Form SCTS-111, Business Tax Registration*; available from:
  > Employment Security Commission
  > P.O. Box 995
  > Columbia, SC 29202
  > (803) 737-3070, 737-3075, or 737-3080
  > www.sces.org/ui/employer

Reporting new hires. For assistance call 1-800-768-5858
- ☛ Forms: W-4
- ☛ Filing: Within 20 days

Mail to:	South Carolina Department of Social Services
	Child Support Division, New Hire Reporting Program
	P.O. Box 1469
	Columbia, SC 29202-1469
Fax to:	(803) 898-9100

Periodic reports
- ☛ Tax withholding: Quarterly report on *Form WH-1605* and payment with coupon *WH-1601*, due end of April, July, October, and January; annual reconciliation (*Form WH-1606*), due end of February.
- ☛ Unemployment tax: Quarterly wage and contribution reports (form *UCE-101*), due end of April, July, October, and January.

When you have no more employees: File a *WH-398, Business Closure Form*, available from the Department of Revenue.

Employment at will state? Yes
Restrictions: Cannot fire someone for their political opinions or activities

State minimum wage: None

Are you required to carry workers' compensation insurance? No

State anti-discrimination laws: None

Laws concerning references: None

Sex offender registry: www.scattorneygeneral.com/public/registry.html; or call (803) 896-7051

SOUTH DAKOTA

Registering as a new employer:
- ☞ Tax withholding: Not required; no state income tax.
- ☞ Unemployment insurance: Obtain an *Employer's Report to Determine Liability* form, and the helpful *Handbook for Employers* from:
    Department of Labor,
    Unemployment Insurance Division
    P.O. Box 4730
    Aberdeen, SD 57402
    (605) 626-2312 or 626-2310
    www.state.sd.us/dol/ui/ui-home.htm

Reporting new hires. For assistance call 1-888-827-6078
- ☞ Forms: copy of W-4
- ☞ Filing: Within 20 days
    Mail to: South Dakota New Hire Reporting Center
                    P.O. Box 4700
                    Aberdeen, SD 57402
    Fax to: 1-888-835-8659

Periodic reports: Quarterly wage and contribution reports (form *DOL-UID-21*), due end of April, July, October, and January.

When you have no more employees: Contact Department of Labor, Unemployment Insurance Division.

Employment at will state? Yes

State minimum wage: Same as federal law.

Are you required to carry workers' compensation insurance? Yes.

State anti-discrimination laws: Unlawful to discriminate based on race, religion, sex, ethnicity, disability, refusal to participate in an abortion, or off-duty use of tobacco.

Laws concerning references: Employer immune from suit for giving reference on job performance.

Sex offender registry: (605) 773-4614 or 773-3331

TENNESSEE

Registering as a new employer:
- ☛ Tax withholding: Not required; no state income tax.
- ☛ Unemployment insurance: Obtain a *Report to Determine Status & Application for Employer Number* form from:

> Employer Services
> Department of Employment Security
> 500 James Robertson Pkwy.
> Nashville, TN 37245
> (615) 741-2486 or 741-2346
> www.state.tn.us/empsec/

Reporting new hires. For assistance call 1-888-715-2280
- ☛ Forms: State form DES-230-11C
- ☛ Filing: Within 20 days

> Mail to: New Hire Operations Center
> P.O. Box 140700
> Nashville, TN 37214
> Fax to: (615) 884-2827

Periodic reports: Quarterly unemployment tax reports due end of April, July, October, and January.

When you have no more employees: Contact Department of Employment Security.

Employment at will state? Yes

State minimum wage: None

Are you required to carry workers' compensation insurance? No

State anti-discrimination laws: None

Laws concerning references: Employer immune from suit for giving reference on job performance.

Sex offender registry: www.yicic.state.tn.us/sexoffender.htm; or contact local law enforcement agency.

TEXAS

Registering as a new employer:
- ☞ Tax withholding: Not required; no state income tax
- ☞ Unemployment insurance: Obtain *Form C-1, Employer's Status Report*; and the helpful booklet called *Especially for Texas Employers* from:
  > Workforce Commission
  > 101 E. 15th Street, Rm 624
  > Austin, TX 78778-0001
  > 1-800-832-9394, or (512) 463-2731
  > www.twc.state.tx.us

Reporting new hires. For assistance call 1-888-839-4473
- ☞ Forms: *New Hire Reporting* form
- ☞ Filing: Within 20 days

Mail to:	New Hire Reporting Center
	P.O. Box 149224
	Austin, TX 78714
Fax to:	1-800-732-5015

Periodic reports: Quarterly unemployment tax reports (form C-3), due end of April, July, October, and January.

When you have no more employees: File *Form C-13, Notice That Employment or Business has Been Discontinued*, available from Workforce Commission.

Employment at will state? Yes

State minimum wage: Currently less than federal wage ($3.35), so federal wage applies

Are you required to carry workers' compensation insurance? No

State anti-discrimination laws: None

Laws concerning references: Employer immune from suit for giving reference on job performance and reason for termination.

Sex offender registry: (512) 424-2200

UTAH

Registering as a new employer:

☛ Tax withholding: Obtain a *TC69 - Utah State Business and Tax Registration* form, and the state *Withholding Tax Guide* from:

>Tax Commission
>210 North 1950 West
>Salt Lake City, UT 84134
>(801) 297-2200
>www.tax.ex.state.ut.us

☛ Unemployment insurance: Obtain a *Status Report* form, and the helpful *Employer Handbook* from:

>Workforce Services
>P.O. Box 45288
>Salt Lake City, UT 84145
>(801) 526-9400 or 536-7755
>www.dws.state.ut.us

Reporting new hires: Obtain the *New Hire Reporting* booklet, which contains the necessary form, by calling Department of Workplace Services at (801) 526-4361; fax: (801) 526-4391; or online at: www.dwsa.state.ut.us

☛ Forms: Utah New Hire Registry Reporting Form
☛ Filing: Within 20 days

>Mail to: New Hire Registry
>P.O. Box 45247
>Salt Lake City, UT 84145
>Fax to: (801) 526-4391

Periodic reports

☛ Tax withholding: Quarterly on *Form TC-96Q*, due end of April, July, October, and January; annual reconciliation (coupon *TC-96R*), due end of February.

☛ Unemployment tax: Quarterly wage and contribution reports (form 3), due end of April, July, October, and January.

When you have no more employees: Inform Tax Commission in writing.

Employment at will state? Quasi employment at will; i.e., cannot fire an employee in "bad faith."

State minimum wage: Same as federal law.

Are you required to carry workers' compensation insurance? Yes, for full-time employees.

State anti-discrimination laws: None

Laws concerning references: Employer immune from suit for giving reference on job performance, reason for termination, and qualifications.

Sex offender registry: (801) 265-5626

VERMONT

Registering as a new employer:
- ☛ Tax withholding: Obtain *Income Tax Withholding Tables and Instructions* booklet, and a *Form S1 - Registration and Vermont Business Account Number Application* from:

  > Taxpayer Services
  > 109 State Street
  > Montpelier, VT 05609-1401
  > (802) 828-2551, or 828-2505
  > www.state.vt.us/tax/

- ☛ Unemployment insurance: Obtain *Form C-1, Status Report,* and the helpful *Unemployment Compensation Employer Information Manual* from:

  > Department of Employment Training
  > P.O. Box 488
  > Montpelier, VT 05601
  > (802) 828-4252 or 828-4242
  > www.det.state.vt.us

Reporting new hires:
- ☛ Forms: *New Hire Reporting Form*, available online at www.det.state.vt.us/empsvc.htm; or by mail from the Department of Employment & Training.
- ☛ Filing: Within 20 days

Mail to:	Vermont Dept. of Employment & Training
	P.O. Box 488
	Montpelier, VT 05601-0488
Fax to:	(802) 828-4286
Online:	www.det.state.vt.us/empsvc/vtnhlogin.cfm

Periodic reports
- ☛ Tax withholding: Quarterly reports due end of April, July, October, and January; annual reconciliation (form *WH-434*), due end of February.
- ☛ Unemployment tax: Quarterly wage and tax reports (form *C-101*), due end of April, July, October, and January.

When you have no more employees: File *Notice of Change* (form *C-36*) with Employer Service Unit, Department of Employment, (802) 828-4251.

Employment at will state? Yes

State minimum wage: $5.25 (does not apply to maids)

Are you required to carry worker's compensation insurance? No

State anti-discrimination laws: Unlawful to discriminate based on race, religion, ethnicity, sex, sexual orientation, age, disability, or positive AIDS test, except where a bona fide occupational qualification.

Laws concerning references: None

Sex offender registry: (802) 244-8727

VIRGINIA

Registering as a new employer: Obtain the *Business Registration Guide*, which contains all instructions and forms for both tax and employment registration. This booklet is available from either agency listed below:
- ☞ Tax withholding: File a *Combined Registration Application Form* (form *R-1*). You will also need *Employer Income Tax Withholding Instructions*. These are available from:

     Department of Taxation
     P.O. Box 1115
     Richmond, VA 23218
     (804) 367-8037
     www.state.vs.us/tax
- ☞ New employer: File a *Report to Determine Liability for State Unemployment Tax*, available from:

     Employment Commission
     P.O. Box 1358
     Richmond, VA 23218
     (804) 786-7159
     www.vec.state.va.us/

Reporting new hires. For assistance call 1-800-979-9014, or (804) 771-9733
- ☞ Forms: copy of W-4 or *Virginia New Hire Reporting* form
- ☞ Filing: Within 20 days

     Mail to: Virginia New Hire Reporting Center
                        P.O. Box 25309
                        Richmond, VA 23260
     Fax to: 1-800-688-2680, or (804) 771-9709

Periodic reports
- ☞ Tax withholding: Quarterly *Form VA-5, Return of Virginia Income Tax Withheld*, due end of April, July, October, and January; annual reconciliation (*Form VA-6*), due end of February.
- ☞ Unemployment tax: Quarterly reports due in April, July, October, and January.

When you have no more employees: Contact the Employment Commission; file *Form R-3, Registration Change Request* and final *Form VA-6* with Department of Taxation.

Employment at will state? Yes

State minimum wage: Same as federal law.

Are you required to carry workers' compensation insurance? No

State anti-discrimination laws: Unlawful to discriminate based on race, religion, national origin, sex, age, marital status or disability.

Laws concerning references: You may, but are not required to, supply a letter of reference.

Sex offender registry: http://sex-offender.vsp.state.va.us/cool-ICE; or call (804) 674-2147.

WASHINGTON

Registering as a new employer:
- ☞ Tax withholding: Not required; no state income tax.
- ☞ Unemployment insurance: Obtain *Unemployment Insurance Tax Information*, and *Master Application* form for registering a new business from:

> Employment Security
> P.O. Box 9046
> Olympia, WA 98507
> (360) 902-9360 or 902-9554
> www.wa.gov/esd

- ☞ Master Application form also available from:

> Department of Licensing
> P.O. Box 9034
> Olympia, WA 98507
> (360) 664-1400

Reporting new hires. For assistance call 1-800-562-0479; or online at: www.wa.gov/dshs/newhire/index.html
- ☞ Forms: Federal W-4 and write in employee's date of birth.
- ☞ Filing: Within 20 days

Mail to:	Washington New Hire Directory
	P.O. Box 9023
	Olympia, WA 98507
Fax to:	1-800-782-0624 (statewide); 586-7804 (Olympia)

Periodic reports: *Employer's Quarterly Report* (form *EMS 5208*), due in April, July, October, and January.

When you have no more employees: File *Business Change Form* (form *5208C*) with Employment Security department.

Employment at will state? Yes

State minimum wage: $5.70 (scheduled to go up to $6.50 on 1/1/2000).

Are you required to carry workers' compensation insurance? Yes, for full-time employees.

State anti-discrimination laws: None

Laws concerning references: If requested, you must give a former employee a letter stating the reasons for, and date of, discharge.

Other relevant laws: You may be required to provide twelve weeks of family to allow an employee to care for a newborn, newly adopted, or terminally ill child. Consult a Washington attorney who specializes in employment law.

Sex offender registry: (360) 705-5100

WEST VIRGINIA

Registering as a new employer:
- ☛ Tax withholding: Obtain the *Employer's Withholding Instructions and Tax Tables*, and *Taxpayer Registration Application* from:
  - Department of Tax & Revenue
  - Taxpayer Services
  - P.O. Box 3784
  - Charleston, WV 25337
  - 1-800-982-8297; or (304) 558-3333
  - www.state.wv.us/taxdiv
- ☛ Unemployment insurance: Obtain the *Employer's Initial Statement* form, and the helpful *Handbook for Employers* from:
  - Bureau of Employment Programs
  - 112 California Avenue
  - Charleston, WV 25305
  - (304) 558-2677 or 558-2675
  - www.state.wv.us/bep

Reporting new hires. For assistance call 1-800-835-4683
- ☛ Forms: Federal W-4 with employee's date of hire written on it
- ☛ Filing: Within 14 days mail to:　State Directory of New Hires
  - Bureau of Child Support Enforcement
  - Bldg. 6, Rm. 817
  - 1900 Kanawha Blvd. East
  - Charleston, WV 25305

Periodic reports
- ☛ Tax withholding: Quarterly on *Form WV/IT-101, Return of Income Tax Withheld*, due end of April, July, October, and January; annual reconciliation (*Form WV/IT-103*), due end of February.
- ☛ Unemployment tax: Quarterly wage and contribution reports (*Form WVUC-A-154*), due end of April, July, October, and January.

When you have no more employees: Fill out "Employer Account Update" section of *Form WVUC-A-154*.

Employment at will state? Yes

State minimum wage: Same as federal law.

Are you required to carry workers' compensation insurance? No

State anti-discrimination laws? None

Laws concerning references? None

Sex offender registry: (304) 746-213

WISCONSIN

Registering as a new employer:
- ☛ Tax withholding: Not required (optional). If you wish to withhold state income tax, obtain *Wisconsin Employer's Withholding Tax Guide* and *Application for Permit/Certificate* from:
  > Department of Revenue Income Tax Division
  > P.O. Box 8902
  > Madison, WI 53708
  > (608) 266-2776
  > www.dor.state.wi.us
- ☛ Unemployment insurance: Obtain a *Domestic Employer's Report* form from:
  > Department of Workforce Development
  > P.O. Box 7942
  > Madison, WI 53707
  > (608) 261-6700
  > www.dwd.state.wi.us.ui

Reporting new hires. For assistance call 1-888-300-4473
- ☛ Forms: State *WT-4, Employee's Wisconsin Withholding Exemption Certificate/New Hire Reporting*, available from the Department of Revenue
- ☛ Filing: Within 20 days
  > Mail to: Department of Workforce Development
  > New Hire Reporting
  > P.O. Box 14431
  > Madison, WI 53714
  > Fax to: 1-800-277-8075

Periodic reports
- ☛ Tax withholding: Quarterly on *Form WT-6*, due end of April, July, October, and January; annual reconciliation (*Form WT-7*), due end of February.
- ☛ Unemployment tax: Quarterly wage and contribution reports due in April, July, October, and January.

When you have no more employees: File *Information Correction Form*, which is included in booklet of quarterly tax withholding coupons; call Division of Unemployment Insurance.

Employment at will state? Yes

State minimum wage: Same as federal law.

Are you required to carry workers' compensation insurance? No

State anti-discrimination laws: Unlawful to discriminate based on age, race, creed, color, disability, marital status, sex, pregnancy, sexual orientation, national origin, ancestry, criminal record, membership in the national guard, or use of tobacco or alcohol off the job.

Laws concerning references: You may but are not required to give a former employee a letter of reference.

Sex offender registry: badger.state.wi.us/agencies/doc/html/sexofender.html; or call 1-800-398-2408 or (608) 266-3831.

WYOMING

Registering as a new employer:
- ☛ Tax withholding: Not required; no state income tax.
- ☛ Unemployment insurance: Obtain the *Employer Handbook*, and *Wyoming Business Registration Form* from:

> Department of Employment
> P.O. Box 2760
> Casper, WY 82602
> (307) 235-3200 or 235-32-1 (to request forms); 235-3203 (new accounts).
> wydoe.state.wy.us

Reporting new hires. For assistance call (307) 970-9258
- ☛ Forms: Federal W-4
- ☛ Filing: Within 20 days, mail to: New Hire Reporting Center
> P.O. Box 1408
> Cheyenne, WY 82003-1408

Periodic reports: Quarterly wage and unemployment contribution reports (form *WYO-47*), due end of April, July, October, and January.

When you have no more employees: Notify Department of Employment, Employer Resources Division, at (307) 473-3893

Employment at will state? Quasi employment at will; i.e., cannot fire an employee in "bad faith."

State minimum wage: Currently less than federal wage ($1.60), so federal wage applies.

Are you required to carry workers' compensation insurance? No

State anti-discrimination laws: If you have two or more employees, it is unlawful to discriminate based on age, sex, race, creed, ethnicity, military service, smoking off the job, or refusal to participate in an abortion.

Laws concerning references: None

Sex offender registry: (307) 777-7881

Appendix B
Forms

The following is a list of the blank forms found in this appendix. Each form is designated by a number in the upper outside corner. The page number where the form begins is also listed below.

Table of Forms

Employment Application

1. Date: _____

2. Name: _____
            (last)   (first)   (middle)

3. Have you ever had a different name? ___Yes   ___No

   If yes, what was that name? _____

4. Address: _____
               _____

5. How long have you lived there? _____

   If less than 3 years, what was your previous address?
   _____
   _____

6. Date of Birth: _____

7. Place of Birth: _____

8. Social security number: _____

9. Education:
   ___ Did not finish high school
   ___ High school graduate
   ___ Some college or technical school   Name of college: _____
   ___ College/technical school graduate   In what city? _____
   ___ Other education. Explain: _____
                               _____

10. Have you participated in any other apprenticeships or training programs?

    ___Yes ___No

    If yes, explain: _____
    _____

-employment application page 1-

11. Please describe your previous work experience for the past 5 years.

    a. Current or most recent job:
      Name of employer: _____
      Address, if known: _____
      City: _____ State: _____ Zip: _____
      Date started: _____ Date stopped: _____
      Reason for leaving:

      Describe your job and its duties:

    b. Previous job:
      Name of employer: _____
      Address, if known: _____
      City: _____ State: _____ Zip: _____
      Date started: _____ Date stopped: _____
      Reason for leaving:

      Describe your job and its duties:

    c. Previous job:
      Name of employer: _____
      Address, if known: _____
      City: _____ State: _____ Zip: _____
      Date started: _____ Date stopped: _____
      Reason for leaving:

      Describe your job and its duties:

12. Have you ever been convicted of a crime? ___Yes   ___No

If yes, please explain;

13. If your job may include driving, do you have a driver's license? ___Yes   ___No

Driver's license number: _____ State:_____
What kind of license? ___Operator   ___Commercial   ___Chauffeur

Have you ever been involved in any accidents in the last 3 years? ___Yes   ___No
If yes, please explain:

Have you ever received any traffic tickets in the last 3 years?   ___Yes   ___No
If yes, please explain:

14. Please list 3 references who are not members of your family:

a. Name: _____ Tel. number: _____
   Address: _____
   _____

b. Name: _____ Tel. number: _____
   Address: _____
   _____

c. Name: _____ Tel. number: _____
   Address: _____
   _____

-employment application page 3-

15. When can you start work? _____

16. Are you available to work occasional weekends as needed?   ___Yes   ___No
    If no, please explain limitations:

17. Are you available to work occasional weekday evenings or nights as needed?
    ___Yes   ___No
    If no, please explain limitations:

_____

All information you have provided will be kept strictly confidential.
_____

Please read over your application to check for accuracy and sign it.

I certify that the statements I have made are true and correct to the best of my knowledge.

Signed: _____   Date:_____

DISCLOSURE OF INTENT TO REQUEST CONSUMER REPORTS

YOU HAVE SUBMITTED AN EMPLOYMENT APPLICATION TO:

Name of employer:

Address:

FOR A POSITION AS A DOMESTIC EMPLOYEE. THE EMPLOYMENT PROCESS FOR THIS POSITION INCLUDES A REVIEW OF YOUR CREDIT HISTORY AND OTHER BACKGROUND INFORMATION. FOR THIS PURPOSE, I WILL REQUIRE YOUR WRITTEN CONSENT TO AUTHORIZE ME TO OBTAIN A COPY OF YOUR CREDIT REPORT FROM A CREDIT REPORTING AGENCY.

THE INFORMATION OBTAINED WILL BE USED FOR THE SOLE PURPOSE OF EVALUATING YOUR EMPLOYMENT APPLICATION, AND WILL REMAIN CONFIDENTIAL.

I have read and understood the above disclosure regarding _____

_____'s intent to obtain my consumer report for the
                         (name of employer)

purpose of my employment.

Date: _____

_____
Applicant's Signature

_____
Print Name

CONSENT TO DISCLOSURE OF CONSUMER CREDIT REPORT

I have submitted an employment application to _____
_____.

(name and address of employer)

I have received written disclosure that the above named employer intends to request a copy of my consumer credit report prior to my employment. I hereby give your agency my consent to provide my potential employer with a copy of my consumer report.

Date: _____

Applicant's signature: _____

Printed name: _____

Address: _____

              _____

Date of birth: _____

Social Security Number: _____-_____-_____

CONSENT TO RELEASE OF INFORMATION FROM REFERENCES

I have submitted an employment application to _____

_____ for a job as a domestic service employee.

                             (name of employer)

I hereby authorize any person or company to disclose in good faith any information they may have regarding my character, past job performance, qualifications, and fitness for employment. I will former employers and other persons giving references free of liability for the exchange of any information reasonably related to the employment process.

Signed: _____

Printed Name: _____

Date: _____

CERTIFICATION TO CREDIT REPORTING AGENCY

I, _____, under penalties of perjury, hereby certify:
(name of employer)

1.   I am seeking a consumer report on _____,
Social Security Number _____, an applicant for employment with me.

2.   I have provided the applicant with a written, clear, and conspicuous disclosure of my intentions.

3.   I have received the written consent of the applicant to procure a copy of his/her consumer credit report.

4.   I will not use the information I receive against the applicant until I have provide him/her with a copy of the report and a written description of his/her consumer rights afforded him/her under Federal law.

5.   I will not use the information I receive in any way which violates Federal or State equal employment opportunity laws or regulations.

I affirm under the penalties of perjury that the foregoing representations are true to the best of my knowledge and belief.

Date: _____

Signature: _____

Printed Name: _____

Address: _____

_____

Greetings:

This letter shall serve as my request for a consumer report on the following individual:

Name: _____   Date of birth: _____

Address: _____   Social Security #: _____-_____-_____
_____

I have enclosed the required certification, a copy of the disclosure, and the applicant's written consent for your records.

Please send a copy of the consumer report to:

Name: _____

Address: _____
_____

Telephone: _____

Sincerely,

EMPLOYMENT REFERENCE RELEASE

I request that _____ {name of employer}
respond to reference requests from any prospective employer that may be considering me
for a job. I authorize him/her/them to disclose any employment-related information that
they determine is appropriate to disclose, including their personal opinion and evaluation of
my job performance. I understand that such evaluation may contain some criticisms or
negative comments.

In consideration for _____ {name of employer}
providing such references, I agree to release and discharge him/her/them for any claim or
potential claim for damages caused in whole or in part by their reference, including, but not
limited to, claims of defamation, negligence, or interference with contract.

I have read and understand the provisions of this release. I was given an opportunity to
consult with an attorney before signing this release, and I am signing it voluntarily and
without coercion.

Date: _____

Signed: _____
(name of employee)

EMPLOYMENT AGREEMENT

This Agreement is made effective on _____ *{date}*, between

_____

(referred to in this Agreement as "Employer,") and _____

(referred to in this Agreement as "Employee."

RECITALS

1.   Employer and Employee are individuals, residents of _____ *{state}*, and are over the age of eighteen.

2.   Employee is willing to be employed by Employer, and Employer is willing to employ Employee, on the terms and conditions set forth in this Agreement.

A. EMPLOYMENT

1.   Employer is hiring Employee to perform the usual and customary duties of _____, including but not limited to:

2.   Employee shall work at the convenience of Employer, arriving and leaving at times to be specified by Employer, up to _____ hours per week. Employee shall not be required to work more than _____ hours per week, but may consent to do so.

B. COMPENSATION

1.   Employer agrees to pay Employee gross compensation at the rate of $_____ per _____.

2.   Employer shall withhold appropriate amounts from Employee's gross pay as required by tax and social security laws.

3.   Employer shall pay Employee once weekly on the Friday of each week while this Agreement is in force.

4. Employee shall receive a wage 1.5 times the usual hourly rate for every hour worked over 40 hours per week.

5. In the event Employee works more than 8 hours in any one day, Employer may compensate Employee by either paying overtime or by giving Employee compensatory time off during the same week, at the option of Employer.

6. Employer and Employee may agree to increases or decreases in Employee's compensation as may be mutually agreed upon. Such modifications must be in writing and signed by both parties.

C. TERMS AND CONDITIONS

1. Employee may not smoke, drink an alcoholic beverage, or use illegal drugs in Employer's house or car.

2. Employer shall provide Employee with funds for expenses which Employer deems are necessary in connection with Employee's job duties. Should it become necessary for Employee to expend such funds, Employer shall reimburse Employee so long as Employee provides Employer with a receipt or explanation why no receipt is available. Reimbursements of such expenses will be made at least once per week.

3. The parties agree to the following terms and conditions: ❑ None

D. TERMINATION OF AGREEMENT

1. Employer may terminate this Agreement without notice and for any cause whatsoever. in the event Employer terminates this Agreement, all compensation and other benefits shall accrue and be paid to Employee on the date of termination. Employee shall not be entitled to any compensation after such termination. It is understood that the duration of employment is unspecified, and is solely in the discretion of Employer.

2. Employee may terminate this Agreement upon giving Employer 30 days' notice, either orally or in writing. Employee's right to vacation and sick leave is terminated by the giving of such notice. Once Employee has given such notice, Employer may not fire Employee prior to the end of the 30-day period, except for absence from work, neglect of duty, or failure to perform duties in a reasonable manner.

3. This Agreement terminates upon the death of Employee, and no rights will accrue to Employee's estate, heirs, or successors, except that Employer shall pay to the estate any salary earned for actual services rendered prior to death.

E. BENEFITS

1. Employee is entitled to _____ days of paid vacation per year, at times to be scheduled in advance and agreed to by Employer. Vacation pay is based upon normal pay for a 40 hour work week, without consideration to bonuses or other supplemental compensation.

2. Employee is entitled to _____ days per year as sick leave with pay. Sick leave may not be accumulted from year to year. Sick leave benefits are not convertible into, and cannot be taken in, cash compensation. All of Employee's rights to sick leave benefits end and will be forfeited on termination of employment.

F. MODIFICATION AND INTERPRETATION

1. It is mutually understood that the precise duties assigned to Employee may change at the election of Employer, and that the assignment of specific duties beyond those contained in this Agreement does not have to be in writing.

2. The terms of this Agreement may be modified in writing signed by both parties.

3. This Agreement is to be interpreted at all times to reflect the broadest range of custom, usage, and customary practice concerning the scope of the duties and responsibilities of Employee.

Date: _____

_____   _____
Signature of Employer   Signature of Employee

_____
Signature of Employer

EMPLOYMENT AGREEMENT

This Agreement is made effective on _____ *{date}*, between

_____

(referred to in this Agreement as "Employer,") and _____ (referred to in this Agreement as "Nanny."

RECITALS

1.   Employer and Nanny are individuals, residents of _____ *{state}*, and are over the age of eighteen.

2.   Nanny is willing to be employed by Employer, and Employer is willing to employ Nanny, on the terms and conditions set forth in this Agreement.

A. EMPLOYMENT

1.   Employer is hiring Nanny to perform the usual and customary duties of a nanny, including but not limited to: supervising, feeding, clothing, bathing, playing with, reading to, and educating Employer's child(ren); taking the child(ren) to museums, parks, movies, plays, and other entertaining events; participating in toilet training of the child(ren); keeping the child(ren)'s rooms and play areas neat, clean, and orderly; transporting the child(ren) to and from activities; and arranging for a transporting the child(ren) to and from medical care appointments.

2.   Nanny shall work at the convenience of Employer, arriving and leaving at times to be specified by Employer, up to _____ hours per week. Nanny shall not be required to work more than _____ hours per week, but may consent to do so.

3.   Nanny may not slap, strike, shake, spank, or hit the child(ren) for discipline or any other any reason. The parties agree that she is to use a "time out" method of discipline, in which a misbehaving child is isolated for a maximum of ten minutes per incident in a room designated by Employer for that purpose.

4.   Nanny may not permit the child(ren) to watch television for more than _____ hours per day.

5.   Nanny must take the child(ren) outside for play or recreation at least _____ hour(s) per day, except when weather or the illness of a child would make it unreasonable.

6.   To the best of her ability, Nanny agrees to follow a schedule of meals and naps as determined by Employer.

7.   Nanny accepts and agrees to perform these duties subject to the general supervision and direction of Employer.

8.   Nanny shall render other services and duties as may be assigned to her from time to time by Employer as long as they pose no threat to the health and safety of Nanny.

9.   Nanny agrees that she will, at all time, faithfully and to the best of her ability, experience, and talents perform all the duties that may be required of her pursuant to the terms of this Agreement and to the reasonable satisfaction of Employer.

B. COMPENSATION

1.   Employer agrees to pay Nanny gross compensation at the rate of $_____ per _____.

2.   Employer shall withhold appropriate amounts from Nanny's gross pay as required by tax and social security laws.

3.   Employer shall pay Nanny once weekly on the Friday of each week while this Agreement is in force.

4.   Employee shall receive a wage 1.5 times the usual hourly rate for every hour she works over 40 hours per week.

5.   In the event Nanny works more than 8 hours in any one day, Employer may compensate Nanny by either paying her overtime or by giving her compensatory time off during the same week, at the option of Employer.

6.   Employer and Nanny may agree to increases or decreases in Nanny's compensation as may be mutually agreed upon. Such modifications must be in writing and signed by both parties.

C. SMOKING, ALCOHOL, AND DRUGS

1.   While on duty, under no circumstances may Nanny smoke, drink an alcoholic beverage, or use illegal drugs within sight of the child(ren).

2.   Nanny may not smoke, drink an alcoholic beverage, or use illegal drugs in Employer's house or car, regardless of whether the children are present.

3.   If the children are not present and it will not interfere with her ability to supervise them, Nanny may smoke during working hours as long as she does so outdoors. The use of alcohol or illegal drugs during working hours is strictly forbidden.

D. TERMS AND CONDITIONS

1.   Employer shall provide Nanny with funds for the purpose of travel and entertainment in connection with the care of the child(ren). Employer shall provide for Nanny' expenses relating to said travel and entertainment. Should it become necessary for Nanny to expend additional funds for travel and entertainment, Employer shall reimburse Nanny for those expenses so long as Nanny provides Employer with a receipt or explanation why no receipt is available. Reimbursements of expenses will be made at the convenience of Employer, but will be made at least once per week.

2.   Nanny shall furnish he own automobile to perform the duties required by this Agreement and shall keep it maintained, repaired, and in good driving condition, Nanny shall maintain full-coverage insurance on the automobile as defined by Employer's insurance carrier. A certificate of Nanny's insurance showing coverage must be given to Employer. All the requirements of this section shall be complied with at Nanny's cost.

3.   Nanny shall not allow her friends or members of her own family to come into Employer's home without the express consent of Employer.

4.   Nanny shall not watch or babysit other children while supervising Employer's child(ren).

5.   The parties agree to the following additional terms and conditions: ❏ None

E. TERMINATION OF AGREEMENT

1.   Employer may terminate this Agreement without notice and for any cause whatsoever. in the event Employer terminates this Agreement, all compensation and other benefits shall accrue and be paid to Nanny on the date of termination. Nanny shall not be entitled to any compensation after such termination. It is understood that the duration of employment is unspecified, and is solely in the discretion of Employer.

2.   Nanny may terminate this Agreement upon giving Employer 30 days' notice, either orally or in writing. Nanny's right to vacation and sick leave is terminated by the giving of such notice. Once Nanny has given such notice, Employer may not fire Nanny prior to the end of the 30-day period, except for absence from work, neglect of duty, or failure to perform duties in a reasonable manner.

3.   This Agreement terminates upon the death of Nanny, and no rights will accrue to Nanny's estate, heirs, or successors, except that Employer shall pay to the estate any salary earned for actual services rendered prior to death.

F. DRUG TESTING AND PHYSICALS

1.   It is understood that Nanny's job involves an issue of safety to the child(ren). For that reason, Nanny agrees to submit to a drug test at Employer's request and expense, by a physician of Employer's choice, if Employer has reasonable grounds to suspect drug use by Nanny. Nanny understands that if she fails to pass the test, she will not be retained in Employer's service. Employer may terminate this Ageement if Nanny refuses to submit to a drug test.

2.   Nanny agrees that, if at any time Nanny shall make a claim against Employer for personal injuries, whether or not covered by Workers' Compensation, Nanny shall submit herself to examination by a physician or physicians of Employer's selection as often as a reasonably necessary.

G. BENEFITS

1.   Nanny is entitled to _____ days of paid vacation per year, at times to be scheduled in advance and agreed to by Employer. Vacation pay is based upon normal pay for a 40 hour work week, without consideration for bonuses or other supplemental compensation.

2.   Nanny is entitled to _____ days of unpaid vacation per year, which may be taken all at once or separately. These days are to be scheduled in advance to the mutual convenience of the Nanny and Employer.

3.   Nanny is entitled to the following holidays off with pay: July 4, Thanksgiving, Christmas, New Year's Day, and up to _____ days per year for religious observation.

4.   After completion of _____ months of employment, Nanny shall be entitled to _____ days per year as sick leave with pay. Nanny may take up to _____ additional days of sick leave without pay. Sick leave may not be accumulted from year to year. Sick leave benefits are not convertible into, and cannot be taken in, cash compensation. All of Nanny's rights to sick leave benefits end and will be forfeited on termination of employment.

5. Nanny is entitled to up to _____ days' consecutive leave per year with pay for pesonal and family emergencies, including; death or serious illness of a close family member; significant damage to Nanny's home be fire, storm, or other cause; arrest of the filing of criminal charges against a close family member; the Nanny or Nanny's spouse's maternity, pregnancy, or adoption. Nanny may take additional time in connection with personal and family emergencies without pay.

H. MODIFICATION AND INTERPRETATION

1. It is mutually understood that the precise duties assigned to Nanny may change at the election of Employer, and that the assignment of specific duties beyond those contained in this Agreement does not have to be in writing.

2. The terms of this Agreement may be modified in writing signed by both parties.

3. This Agreement is to be interpreted at all times to reflect the broadest range of custom, usage, and customary practice concerning the scope of the duties and responsibilities of a Nanny.

Date: _____

_____
Signature of Employer

_____
Signature of Nanny

_____
Signature of Employer

Form SS-8 (Rev. June 1997) Department of the Treasury Internal Revenue Service	**Determination of Employee Work Status for Purposes of Federal Employment Taxes and Income Tax Withholding**	OMB No. 1545-0004

Paperwork Reduction Act Notice

We ask for the information on this form to carry out the Internal Revenue laws of the United States. You are required to give us the information. We need it to ensure that you are complying with these laws and to allow us to figure and collect the right amount of tax.

You are not required to provide the information requested on a form that is subject to the Paperwork Reduction Act unless the form displays a valid OMB control number. Books or records relating to a form or its instructions must be retained as long as their contents may become material in the administration of any Internal Revenue law. Generally, tax returns and return information are confidential, as required by Code section 6103.

The time needed to complete and file this form will vary depending on individual circumstances. The estimated average time is: **Recordkeeping,** 34 hr., 55 min.; **Learning about the law or the form,** 12 min.; and **Preparing and sending the form to the IRS,** 46 min. If you have comments concerning the accuracy of these time estimates or suggestions for making this form simpler, we would be happy to hear from you. You can write to the Tax Forms Committee, Western Area Distribution Center, Rancho Cordova, CA 95743-0001. **DO NOT** send the tax form to this address. Instead, see **General Information** for where to file.

Purpose

Employers and workers file Form SS-8 to get a determination as to whether a worker is an employee for purposes of Federal employment taxes and income tax withholding.

General Information

Complete this form carefully. If the firm is completing the form, complete it for **ONE** individual who is representative of the class of workers whose status is in question. If you want a written determination for more than one class of workers, complete a separate Form SS-8 for one worker

from each class whose status is typical of that class. A written determination for any worker will apply to other workers of the same class if the facts are not materially different from those of the worker whose status was ruled upon.

Caution: Form SS-8 is not a claim for refund of social security and Medicare taxes or Federal income tax withholding. Also, a determination that an individual is an employee does not necessarily reduce any current or prior tax liability. A worker must file his or her income tax return even if a determination has not been made by the due date of the return.

Where to file.—In the list below, find the state where your legal residence, principal place of business, office, or agency is located. Send Form SS-8 to the address listed for your location.

Location:	Send to:
Alaska, Arizona, Arkansas, California, Colorado, Hawaii, Idaho, Illinois, Iowa, Kansas, Minnesota, Missouri, Montana, Nebraska, Nevada, New Mexico, North Dakota, Oklahoma, Oregon, South Dakota, Texas, Utah, Washington, Wisconsin, Wyoming	Internal Revenue Service SS-8 Determinations P.O. Box 1231, Stop 4106 AUSC Austin, TX 78767
Alabama, Connecticut, Delaware, District of Columbia, Florida, Georgia, Indiana, Kentucky, Louisiana, Maine, Maryland, Massachusetts, Michigan, Mississippi, New Hampshire, New Jersey, New York, North Carolina, Ohio, Pennsylvania, Rhode Island, South Carolina, Tennessee, Vermont, Virginia, West Virginia, All other locations not listed	Internal Revenue Service SS-8 Determinations Two Lakemont Road Newport, VT 05855-1555
American Samoa, Guam, Puerto Rico, U.S. Virgin Islands	Internal Revenue Service Mercantile Plaza 2 Avenue Ponce de Leon San Juan, Puerto Rico 00918

Name of firm (or person) for whom the worker performed services	Name of worker	
Address of firm (include street address, apt. or suite no., city, state, and ZIP code)	Address of worker (include street address, apt. or suite no., city, state, and ZIP code)	
Trade name	Telephone number (include area code) ( )	Worker's social security number
Telephone number (include area code) ( )	Firm's employer identification number	

Check type of firm for which the work relationship is in question:

☐ Individual ☐ Partnership ☐ Corporation ☐ Other (specify) ▶ ....

Important Information Needed To Process Your Request

This form is being completed by: ☐ Firm ☐ Worker

If this form is being completed by the worker, the IRS **must** have your permission to disclose your name to the firm.

Do you object to disclosing your name and the information on this form to the firm? . . . . ☐ Yes ☐ No

If you answer "Yes," the IRS cannot act on your request. **Do not complete the rest of this form unless the IRS asks for it.**

Under section 6110 of the Internal Revenue Code, the information on this form and related file documents will be open to the public if any ruling or determination is made. However, names, addresses, and taxpayer identification numbers will be removed before the information is made public.

Is there any other information you want removed? . . . . ☐ Yes ☐ No

If you check "Yes," we cannot process your request unless you submit a copy of this form and copies of all supporting documents showing, in brackets, the information you want removed. Attach a separate statement showing which specific exemption of section 6110(c) applies to each bracketed part.

This form is designed to cover many work activities, so some of the questions may not apply to you. You must answer ALL items or mark them "Unknown" or "Does not apply." If you need more space, attach another sheet.

Total number of workers in this class. (Attach names and addresses. If more than 10 workers, list only 10.) ▶ _____

This information is about services performed by the worker from _____ to _____
                                                                (month, day, year)   (month, day, year)

Is the worker still performing services for the firm? . . . . ☐ **Yes** ☐ **No**

● If "No," what was the date of termination? ▶ _____
                                                (month, day, year)

1a Describe the firm's business ....

b Describe the work done by the worker ....

....

2a If the work is done under a written agreement between the firm and the worker, attach a copy.

b If the agreement is not in writing, describe the terms and conditions of the work arrangement ....

....

c If the actual working arrangement differs in any way from the agreement, explain the differences and why they occur ......

....

....

3a Is the worker given training by the firm? . . . . ☐ **Yes** ☐ **No**
  ● If "Yes," what kind? ....
  ● How often? ....

b Is the worker given instructions in the way the work is to be done (exclusive of actual training in 3a)? . ☐ **Yes** ☐ **No**
  ● If "Yes," give specific examples ....

c Attach samples of any written instructions or procedures.

d Does the firm have the right to change the methods used by the worker or direct that person on how to do the work? . . . . ☐ **Yes** ☐ **No**
  ● Explain your answer ....

....

e Does the operation of the firm's business require that the worker be supervised or controlled in the performance of the service? . . . . ☐ **Yes** ☐ **No**
  ● Explain your answer ....

....

4a The firm engages the worker:
  ☐ To perform and complete a particular job only
  ☐ To work at a job for an indefinite period of time
  ☐ Other (explain) ....

b Is the worker required to follow a routine or a schedule established by the firm? . . . . ☐ **Yes** ☐ **No**
  ● If "Yes," what is the routine or schedule? ....

....

....

c Does the worker report to the firm or its representative?. . . . . ☐ **Yes** ☐ **No**
  ● If "Yes," how often? ....
  ● For what purpose? ....
  ● In what manner (in person, in writing, by telephone, etc.)? ....
  ● Attach copies of any report forms used in reporting to the firm.

d Does the worker furnish a time record to the firm? . . . . ☐ **Yes** ☐ **No**
  ● If "Yes," attach copies of time records.

5a State the kind and value of tools, equipment, supplies, and materials furnished by:
  ● The firm ....

....

  ● The worker ....

....

b What expenses are incurred by the worker in the performance of services for the firm? ....

....

c Does the firm reimburse the worker for any expenses? . . . . ☐ **Yes** ☐ **No**
  ● If "Yes," specify the reimbursed expenses ....

Form SS-8 (Rev. 6-97)

6a Will the worker perform the services personally? . . . . ☐ Yes ☐ No
  b Does the worker have helpers? . . . . ☐ Yes ☐ No
   • If "Yes," who hires the helpers? ☐ Firm ☐ Worker
   • If the helpers are hired by the worker, is the firm's approval necessary? . . . . ☐ Yes ☐ No
   • Who pays the helpers? ☐ Firm ☐ Worker
   • If the worker pays the helpers, does the firm repay the worker? . . . . ☐ Yes ☐ No
   • Are social security and Medicare taxes and Federal income tax withheld from the helpers' pay? . . ☐ Yes ☐ No
   • If "Yes," who reports and pays these taxes? ☐ Firm ☐ Worker
   • Who reports the helpers' earnings to the Internal Revenue Service? ☐ Firm ☐ Worker
   • What services do the helpers perform? ....
7 At what location are the services performed? ☐ Firm's ☐ Worker's ☐ Other (specify) ....
8a Type of pay worker receives:
   ☐ Salary ☐ Commission ☐ Hourly wage ☐ Piecework ☐ Lump sum ☐ Other (specify) ....
  b Does the firm guarantee a minimum amount of pay to the worker? . . . . ☐ Yes ☐ No
  c Does the firm allow the worker a drawing account or advances against pay? . . . . ☐ Yes ☐ No
   • If "Yes," is the worker paid such advances on a regular basis? . . . . ☐ Yes ☐ No
  d How does the worker repay such advances? ....
9a Is the worker eligible for a pension, bonus, paid vacations, sick pay, etc.? . . . . ☐ Yes ☐ No
   • If "Yes," specify ....
  b Does the firm carry worker's compensation insurance on the worker? . . . . ☐ Yes ☐ No
  c Does the firm withhold social security and Medicare taxes from amounts paid the worker? . . . . . ☐ Yes ☐ No
  d Does the firm withhold Federal income tax from amounts paid the worker? . . . . ☐ Yes ☐ No
  e How does the firm report the worker's earnings to the Internal Revenue Service?
   ☐ Form W-2 ☐ Form 1099-MISC ☐ Does not report ☐ Other (specify) ....
   • Attach a copy.
  f Does the firm bond the worker? . . . . ☐ Yes ☐ No
10a Approximately how many hours a day does the worker perform services for the firm? ....
  b Does the firm set hours of work for the worker? . . . . ☐ Yes ☐ No
   • If "Yes," what are the worker's set hours? _____ a.m./p.m. to _____ a.m./p.m. (Circle whether a.m. or p.m.)
  c Does the worker perform similar services for others? . . . . ☐ Yes ☐ No ☐ Unknown
   • If "Yes," are these services performed on a daily basis for other firms? . . . . . ☐ Yes ☐ No ☐ Unknown
   • Percentage of time spent in performing these services for:
    This firm .... % Other firms .... % ☐ Unknown
   • Does the firm have priority on the worker's time? . . . . ☐ Yes ☐ No
   • If "No," explain ....
  d Is the worker prohibited from competing with the firm either while performing services or during any later
    period? . . . . ☐ Yes ☐ No
11a Can the firm discharge the worker at any time without incurring a liability? . . . . ☐ Yes ☐ No
   • If "No," explain ....
  b Can the worker terminate the services at any time without incurring a liability? . . . . ☐ Yes ☐ No
   • If "No," explain ....
12a Does the worker perform services for the firm under:
   ☐ The firm's business name ☐ The worker's own business name ☐ Other (specify) ....
  b Does the worker advertise or maintain a business listing in the telephone directory, a trade
    journal, etc.? . . . . ☐ Yes ☐ No ☐ Unknown
   • If "Yes," specify ....
  c Does the worker represent himself or herself to the public as being in business to perform
    the same or similar services? . . . . ☐ Yes ☐ No ☐ Unknown
   • If "Yes," how? ....
  d Does the worker have his or her own shop or office? . . . . ☐ Yes ☐ No ☐ Unknown
   • If "Yes," where? ....
  e Does the firm represent the worker as an employee of the firm to its customers? . . . . ☐ Yes ☐ No
   • If "No," how is the worker represented? ....
  f How did the firm learn of the worker's services? ....
13 Is a license necessary for the work? . . . . ☐ Yes ☐ No ☐ Unknown
   • If "Yes," what kind of license is required? ....
   • Who issues the license? ....
   • Who pays the license fee?

14 Does the worker have a financial investment in a business related to the services performed? . . . . □ **Yes** □ **No** □ **Unknown**
  - If "Yes," specify and give amount of the investment _____

15 Can the worker incur a loss in the performance of the service for the firm? . . . . □ **Yes** □ **No**
  - If "Yes," how? _____

16a Has any other government agency ruled on the status of the firm's workers? . . . . □ **Yes** □ **No**
  - If "Yes," attach a copy of the ruling.

  b Is the same issue being considered by any IRS office in connection with the audit of the worker's tax return or the firm's tax return, or has it been considered recently? . . . . □ **Yes** □ **No**
  - If "Yes," for which year(s)? _____

17 Does the worker assemble or process a product at home or away from the firm's place of business? □ **Yes** □ **No**
  - If "Yes," who furnishes materials or goods used by the worker? □ **Firm**   □ **Worker**   □ **Other**
  - Is the worker furnished a pattern or given instructions to follow in making the product? . . . . . □ **Yes** □ **No**
  - Is the worker required to return the finished product to the firm or to someone designated by the firm? □ **Yes** □ **No**

18 Attach a detailed explanation of any other reason why you believe the worker is an employee or an independent contractor.

Answer items 19a through o only if the worker is a salesperson or provides a service directly to customers.

19a Are leads to prospective customers furnished by the firm? . . . . □ **Yes** □ **No**   □ **Does not apply**
  b Is the worker required to pursue or report on leads? . . . . □ **Yes** □ **No**   □ **Does not apply**
  c Is the worker required to adhere to prices, terms, and conditions of sale established by the firm? . . □ **Yes** □ **No**
  d Are orders submitted to and subject to approval by the firm? . . . . □ **Yes** □ **No**
  e Is the worker expected to attend sales meetings? . . . . □ **Yes** □ **No**
  - If "Yes," is the worker subject to any kind of penalty for failing to attend? . . . . □ **Yes** □ **No**
  f Does the firm assign a specific territory to the worker? . . . . □ **Yes** □ **No**
  g Whom does the customer pay?   □ **Firm**   □ **Worker**
  - If worker, does the worker remit the total amount to the firm? . . . . □ **Yes** □ **No**
  h Does the worker sell a consumer product in a home or establishment other than a permanent retail establishment? . . . . □ **Yes** □ **No**
  i List the products and/or services distributed by the worker, such as meat, vegetables, fruit, bakery products, beverages (other than milk), or laundry or dry cleaning services. If more than one type of product and/or service is distributed, specify the principal one _____
  j Did the firm or another person assign the route or territory and a list of customers to the worker? . . □ **Yes** □ **No**
  - If "Yes," enter the name and job title of the person who made the assignment _____
  k Did the worker pay the firm or person for the privilege of serving customers on the route or in the territory? □ **Yes** □ **No**
  - If "Yes," how much did the worker pay (not including any amount paid for a truck or racks, etc.)? $ _____
  - What factors were considered in determining the value of the route or territory? _____
  l How are new customers obtained by the worker? Explain fully, showing whether the new customers called the firm for service, were solicited by the worker, or both _____
  m Does the worker sell life insurance? . . . . □ **Yes** □ **No**
  - If "Yes," is the selling of life insurance or annuity contracts for the firm the worker's entire business activity? . . . . □ **Yes** □ **No**
  - If "No," list the other business activities and the amount of time spent on them _____
  n Does the worker sell other types of insurance for the firm? . . . . □ **Yes** □ **No**
  - If "Yes," state the percentage of the worker's total working time spent in selling other types of insurance _____ %
  - At the time the contract was entered into between the firm and the worker, was it their intention that the worker sell life insurance for the firm: □ on a full-time basis   □ on a part-time basis
  - State the manner in which the intention was expressed _____
  o Is the worker a traveling or city salesperson? . . . . □ **Yes** □ **No**
  - If "Yes," from whom does the worker principally solicit orders for the firm? _____
  - If the worker solicits orders from wholesalers, retailers, contractors, or operators of hotels, restaurants, or other similar establishments, specify the percentage of the worker's time spent in the solicitation _____ %
  - Is the merchandise purchased by the customers for resale or for use in their business operations? If used by the customers in their business operations, describe the merchandise and state whether it is equipment installed on their premises or a consumable supply _____

Under penalties of perjury, I declare that I have examined this request, including accompanying documents, and to the best of my knowledge and belief, the facts presented are true, correct, and complete.

Signature ▶ _____   Title ▶ _____   Date ▶ _____

If the firm is completing this form, an officer or member of the firm must sign it. If the worker is completing this form, the worker must sign it. If the worker wants a written determination about services performed for two or more firms, a separate form must be completed and signed for each firm. Additional copies of this form may be obtained by calling 1-800-TAX-FORM (1-800-829-3676).

U.S. Department of Justice
Immigration and Naturalization Service

OMB No. 1115-0136
Employment Eligibility Verification

Please read instructions carefully before completing this form. The instructions must be available during completion of this form. **ANTI-DISCRIMINATION NOTICE.** It is illegal to discriminate against work eligible individuals. Employers CANNOT specify which document(s) they will accept from an employee. The refusal to hire an individual because of a future expiration date may also constitute illegal discrimination.

Section 1. Employee Information and Verification. To be completed and signed by employee at the time employment begins

Print Name: Last	First	Middle Initial	Maiden Name

Address (Street Name and Number)   Apt. #   Date of Birth (month/day/year)

City   State   Zip Code   Social Security #

I am aware that federal law provides for imprisonment and/or fines for false statements or use of false documents in connection with the completion of this form.

I attest, under penalty of perjury, that I am (check one of the following):
☐ A citizen or national of the United States
☐ A Lawful Permanent Resident (Alien # A_____)
☐ An alien authorized to work until____/____/____
(Alien # or Admission #_____)

Employee's Signature   Date (month/day/year)

Preparer and/or Translator Certification. (To be completed and signed if Section 1 is prepared by a person other than the employee.) I attest, under penalty of perjury, that I have assisted in the completion of this form and that to the best of my knowledge the information is true and correct.

Preparer's/Translator's Signature   Print Name

Address (Street Name and Number, City, State, Zip Code)   Date (month/day/year)

Section 2. Employer Review and Verification. To be completed and signed by employer. Examine one document from List A OR examine one document from List B **and** one from List C as listed on the reverse of this form and record the title, number and expiration date, if any, of the document(s)

List A	OR	List B	AND	List C
Document title: _____		_____		_____
Issuing authority: _____		_____		_____
Document #: _____		_____		_____
Expiration Date (if any): __/__/__		__/__/__		__/__/__
Document #: _____				
Expiration Date (if any): __/__/__				

CERTIFICATION - I attest, under penalty of perjury, that I have examined the document(s) presented by the above-named employee, that the above-listed document(s) appear to be genuine and to relate to the employee named, that the employee began employment on (month/day/year) ____/____/____ and that to the best of my knowledge the employee is eligible to work in the United States. (State employment agencies may omit the date the employee began employment).

Signature of Employer or Authorized Representative   Print Name   Title

Business or Organization Name   Address (Street Name and Number, City, State, Zip Code)   Date (month/day/year)

Section 3. Updating and Reverification. To be completed and signed by employer

A. New Name (if applicable)   B. Date of rehire (month/day/year) (if applicable)

C. If employee's previous grant of work authorization has expired, provide the information below for the document that establishes current employment eligibility.

Document Title:_____ Document #:_____ Expiration Date (if any):__/__/__

I attest, under penalty of perjury, that to the best of my knowledge, this employee is eligible to work in the United States, and if the employee presented document(s), the document(s) I have examined appear to be genuine and to relate to the individual.

Signature of Employer or Authorized Representative   Date (month/day/year)

Form I-9 (Rev. 11-21-91) N

SS-4

Application for Employer Identification Number

February 1998

Department of the Treasury
Internal Revenue Service

(For use by employers, corporations, partnerships, trusts, estates, churches, government agencies, certain individuals, and others. See instructions.)

▶ Keep a copy for your records.

EIN

OMB No. 1545-0003

1 Name of applicant (legal name) (see instructions)

2 Trade name of business (if different from name on line 1)

3 Executor, trustee, "care of" name

4a Mailing address (street address) (room, apt., or suite no.)

5a Business address (if different from address on lines 4a and 4b)

4b City, state, and ZIP code

5b City, state, and ZIP code

6 County and state where principal business is located

7 Name of principal officer, general partner, grantor, owner, or trustor—SSN or ITIN may be required (see instructions) ▶

Type of entity (Check only one box.) (see instructions)

Caution: *If applicant is a limited liability company, see the instructions for line 8a.*

☐ Sole proprietor (SSN) _____
☐ Partnership ☐ Personal service corp.
☐ REMIC ☐ National Guard
☐ State/local government ☐ Farmers' cooperative
☐ Church or church-controlled organization
☐ Other nonprofit organization (specify) ▶ _____
☐ Other (specify) ▶

☐ Estate (SSN of decedent) _____
☐ Plan administrator (SSN) _____
☐ Other corporation (specify) ▶ _____
☐ Trust
☐ Federal government/military
_____ (enter GEN if applicable) _____

If a corporation, name the state or foreign country (if applicable) where incorporated

State

Foreign country

Reason for applying (Check only one box.) (see instructions)
☐ Started new business (specify type) ▶ _____
_____
☐ Hired employees (Check the box and see line 12.)
☐ Created a pension plan (specify type) ▶

☐ Banking purpose (specify purpose) ▶ _____
☐ Changed type of organization (specify new type) ▶ _____
☐ Purchased going business
☐ Created a trust (specify type) ▶ _____
☐ Other (specify) ▶

Date business started or acquired (month, day, year) (see instructions)

11 Closing month of accounting year (see instructions)

First date wages or annuities were paid or will be paid (month, day, year). **Note:** *If applicant is a withholding agent, enter date income will first be paid to nonresident alien. (month, day, year)* . . . . ▶

Highest number of employees expected in the next 12 months. **Note:** *If the applicant does not expect to have any employees during the period, enter -0-. (see instructions)* . . . . ▶

Nonagricultural	Agricultural	Household

Principal activity (see instructions) ▶

Is the principal business activity manufacturing? . . . . ☐ Yes ☐ No
If "Yes," principal product and raw material used ▶

To whom are most of the products or services sold? Please check one box.
☐ Public (retail) ☐ Other (specify) ▶ ☐ Business (wholesale) ☐ N/A

Has the applicant ever applied for an employer identification number for this or any other business? . . . . ☐ Yes ☐ No
Note: *If "Yes," please complete lines 17b and 17c.*

If you checked "Yes" on line 17a, give applicant's legal name and trade name shown on prior application, if different from line 1 or 2 above.
Legal name ▶ Trade name ▶

Approximate date when and city and state where the application was filed. Enter previous employer identification number if known.

Approximate date when filed (mo., day, year)	City and state where filed	Previous EIN

Under penalties of perjury, I declare that I have examined this application, and to the best of my knowledge and belief, it is true, correct, and complete.

Business telephone number (include area code)

Fax telephone number (include area code)

Name and title (Please type or print clearly.) ▶

Signature ▶

Date ▶

Note: *Do not write below this line. For official use only.*

Please leave blank ▶

Geo.	Ind.	Class	Size	Reason for applying

Paperwork Reduction Act Notice, see page 4.

Cat. No. 16055N

Form **SS-4** (Rev. 2-98)

Form **8822** (Rev. Oct. 1997) Department of the Treasury Internal Revenue Service	**Change of Address** ▶ **Please type or print.** ▶ **See instructions on back.** ▶ **Do not attach this form to your return.**	OMB No. 1545-1163

Complete This Part To Change Your Home Mailing Address

Check **ALL** boxes this change affects:

1 ☐ Individual income tax returns (Forms 1040, 1040A, 1040EZ, 1040NR, etc.)

　　▶ If your last return was a joint return and you are now establishing a residence separate
　　from the spouse with whom you filed that return, check here . . . . ▶ ☐

2 ☐ Gift, estate, or generation-skipping transfer tax returns (Forms 706, 709, etc.)

　　▶ For Forms 706 and 706-NA, enter the decedent's name and social security number below.

　　▶ Decedent's name　　　　　　　　　　▶ Social security number

3a Your name (first name, initial, and last name)	**3b** Your social security number
4a Spouse's name (first name, initial, and last name)	**4b** Spouse's social security number

5　Prior name(s). See instructions.

6a Old address (no., street, city or town, state, and ZIP code). If a P.O. box or foreign address, see instructions.	Apt. no.
6b Spouse's old address, if different from line 6a (no., street, city or town, state, and ZIP code). If a P.O. box or foreign address, see instructions.	Apt. no.
7 New address (no., street, city or town, state, and ZIP code). If a P.O. box or foreign address, see instructions.	Apt. no.

Complete This Part To Change Your Business Mailing Address or Business Location

Check **ALL** boxes this change affects:

8 ☐ Employment, excise, and other business returns (Forms 720, 940, 940-EZ, 941, 990, 1041, 1065, 1120, etc.)
9 ☐ Employee plan returns (Forms 5500, 5500-C/R, and 5500-EZ). See instructions.
10 ☐ Business location

11a Business name	**11b** Employer identification number
12 Old mailing address (no., street, city or town, state, and ZIP code). If a P.O. box or foreign address, see instructions.	Room or suite no.
13 New mailing address (no., street, city or town, state, and ZIP code). If a P.O. box or foreign address, see instructions.	Room or suite no.
14 New business location (no., street, city or town, state, and ZIP code). If a foreign address, see instructions.	Room or suite no.

Signature

Daytime telephone number of person to contact (optional) ▶ ( )

Please Sign Here	▶ Your signature　　　　　　　Date	▶ If Part II completed, signature of owner, officer, or representative　Date
	▶ If joint return, spouse's signature　　Date	▶ Title

For Privacy Act and Paperwork Reduction Act Notice, see back of form.　　　Cat. No. 12081V　　　Form **8822** (Rev. 10-97)

Form W-4 (1998)

Purpose. Complete Form W-4 so your employer can withhold the correct Federal income tax from your pay. Because your tax situation may change, you may want to refigure your withholding each year.

Exemption from withholding. *If you are exempt, complete only lines 1, 2, 3, 4, and 7, and sign the form to validate it. Your exemption for 1998 expires February 16, 1999.*

Note: *You cannot claim exemption from withholding if (1) your income exceeds $700 and includes unearned income (e.g., interest and dividends) and (2) another person can claim you as a dependent on their tax return.*

Basic instructions. If you are not exempt, complete the Personal Allowances Worksheet. The worksheets on page 2 adjust your withholding allowances based on itemized deductions, adjustments to income, or two-earner/two-job situations. Complete all worksheets that apply. They will help you figure the number of withholding allowances you are entitled to claim. However, you may claim fewer allowances.

New—Child tax and higher education credits. For details on adjusting withholding for these and other credits, see **Pub. 919,** Is My Withholding Correct for 1998?

Head of household. Generally, you may claim head of household filing status on your tax return only if you are unmarried and pay more than 50% of the costs of keeping up a home for yourself and your dependent(s) or other qualifying individuals.

Nonwage income. If you have a large amount of nonwage income, such as interest or dividends, you should consider making estimated tax payments using Form 1040-ES. Otherwise, you may owe additional tax.

Two earners/two jobs. If you have a working spouse or more than one job, figure the total number of allowances you are entitled to claim on all jobs using worksheets from only one W-4. Your withholding will usually be most accurate when all allowances are claimed on the W-4 filed for the highest paying job and zero allowances are claimed for the others.

Check your withholding. After your W-4 takes effect, use Pub. 919 to see how the dollar amount you are having withheld compares to your estimated total annual tax. Get Pub. 919 especially if you used the Two-Earner/Two-Job Worksheet and your earnings exceed $150,000 (Single) or $200,000 (Married). To order Pub. 919, call 1-800-829-3676. Check your telephone directory for the IRS assistance number for further help.

Sign this form. Form W-4 is not valid unless you sign it.

Personal Allowances Worksheet

A Enter "1" for **yourself** if no one else can claim you as a dependent . . . . **A** _____

B Enter "1" if: {
- You are single and have only one job; or
- You are married, have only one job, and your spouse does not work; or
- Your wages from a second job or your spouse's wages (or the total of both) are $1,000 or less.
} . . **B** _____

C Enter "1" for your **spouse.** But, you may choose to enter -0- if you are married and have either a working spouse or more than one job. (This may help you avoid having too little tax withheld.) . . . . **C** _____

D Enter number of **dependents** (other than your spouse or yourself) you will claim on your tax return . . . . **D** _____

E Enter "1" if you will file as **head of household** on your tax return (see conditions under **Head of household** above) **E** _____

F Enter "1" if you have at least $1,500 of **child or dependent care expenses** for which you plan to claim a credit . . **F** _____

G **New—Child Tax Credit:** • If your total income will be between $16,500 and $47,000 ($21,000 and $60,000 if married), enter "1" for each eligible child. • If your total income will be between $47,000 and $80,000 ($60,000 and $115,000 if married), enter "1" if you have two or three eligible children, or enter "2" if you have four or more . . . . **G** _____

H Add lines A through G and enter total here. **Note:** This amount may be different from the number of exemptions you claim on your return. ▶ **H** _____

For accuracy, complete all worksheets that apply.
- If you plan to **itemize or claim adjustments to income** and want to reduce your withholding, see the Deductions and Adjustments Worksheet on page 2.
- If you are **single,** have **more than one job,** and your combined earnings from all jobs exceed $32,000 OR if you are **married** and have a **working spouse or more than one job,** and the combined earnings from all jobs exceed $55,000, see the Two-Earner/Two-Job Worksheet on page 2 to avoid having too little tax withheld.
- If **neither** of the above situations applies, **stop here** and enter the number from line H on line 5 of Form W-4 below.

---------- **Cut here and give the certificate to your employer. Keep the top part for your records.** ----------

| Form **W-4** Department of the Treasury Internal Revenue Service | **Employee's Withholding Allowance Certificate** ▶ **For Privacy Act and Paperwork Reduction Act Notice, see page 2.** | OMB No. 1545-0010 **1998** |

1 Type or print your first name and middle initial | Last name | **2** Your social security number

Home address (number and street or rural route)

3 ☐ Single ☐ Married ☐ Married, but withhold at higher Single rate.
Note: *If married, but legally separated, or spouse is a nonresident alien, check the Single box.*

City or town, state, and ZIP code

4 If your last name differs from that on your social security card, check here and call 1-800-772-1213 for a new card . . . . . . ▶ ☐

5 Total number of allowances you are claiming (from line H above or from the worksheets on page 2 if they apply) . | **5** _____

6 Additional amount, if any, you want withheld from each paycheck . . . . | **6** $ _____

7 I claim exemption from withholding for 1998, and I certify that I meet **BOTH** of the following conditions for exemption:
- Last year I had a right to a refund of **ALL** Federal income tax withheld because I had **NO** tax liability **AND**
- This year I expect a refund of **ALL** Federal income tax withheld because I expect to have **NO** tax liability.
If you meet both conditions, enter "EXEMPT" here . . . . ▶ | **7** _____

Under penalties of perjury, I certify that I am entitled to the number of withholding allowances claimed on this certificate or entitled to claim exempt status.

Employee's signature ▶ | Date ▶ _____, 19__

8 Employer's name and address (Employer: Complete 8 and 10 only if sending to the IRS) | **9** Office code (optional) | **10** Employer identification number

Cat. No. 10220Q

Deductions and Adjustments Worksheet

Note: *Use this worksheet only if you plan to itemize deductions or claim adjustments to income on your 1998 tax return.*

1   Enter an estimate of your 1998 itemized deductions. These include qualifying home mortgage interest, charitable contributions, state and local taxes (but not sales taxes), medical expenses in excess of 7.5% of your income, and miscellaneous deductions. (For 1998, you may have to reduce your itemized deductions if your income is over $124,500 ($62,250 if married filing separately). Get Pub. 919 for details.)   **1** $ _____

2   Enter: { $7,100 if married filing jointly or qualifying widow(er)
$6,250 if head of household
$4,250 if single
$3,550 if married filing separately }   . . . .   **2** $ _____

3   **Subtract** line 2 from line 1. If line 2 is greater than line 1, enter -0-   . . . . . .   **3** $ _____

4   Enter an estimate of your 1998 adjustments to income, including alimony, deductible IRA contributions, and education loan interest   **4** $ _____

5   **Add** lines 3 and 4 and enter the total   . . . .   **5** $ _____

6   Enter an estimate of your 1998 nonwage income (such as dividends or interest)   . . . .   **6** $ _____

7   **Subtract** line 6 from line 5. Enter the result, but not less than -0-   . . . .   **7** $ _____

8   **Divide** the amount on line 7 by $2,500 and enter the result here. Drop any fraction   . . .   **8**   _____

9   Enter the number from Personal Allowances Worksheet, line H, on page 1   . . . . . .   **9**   _____

10   **Add** lines 8 and 9 and enter the total here. If you plan to use the Two-Earner/Two-Job Worksheet, also enter this total on line 1 below. Otherwise, **stop here** and enter this total on Form W-4, line 5, on page 1 . . . . .   **10**   _____

Two-Earner/Two-Job Worksheet

Note: *Use this worksheet only if the instructions for line H on page 1 direct you here.*

1   Enter the number from line H on page 1 (or from line 10 above if you used the Deductions and Adjustments Worksheet)   **1**   _____

2   Find the number in **Table 1** below that applies to the **LOWEST** paying job and enter it here   . . . .   **2**   _____

3   If line 1 is **GREATER THAN OR EQUAL TO** line 2, subtract line 2 from line 1. Enter the result here (if zero, enter -0-) and on Form W-4, line 5, on page 1. **DO NOT** use the rest of this worksheet   . . .   **3**   _____

Note: *If line 1 is LESS THAN line 2, enter -0- on Form W-4, line 5, on page 1. Complete lines 4–9 to calculate the additional withholding amount necessary to avoid a year end tax bill.*

4   Enter the number from line 2 of this worksheet   . . . .   **4**   _____

5   Enter the number from line 1 of this worksheet   . . . .   **5**   _____

6   **Subtract** line 5 from line 4   . . . .   **6**   _____

7   Find the amount in **Table 2** below that applies to the **HIGHEST** paying job and enter it here   . . . .   **7** $ _____

8   **Multiply** line 7 by line 6 and enter the result here. This is the additional annual withholding amount needed   **8** $ _____

9   Divide line 8 by the number of pay periods remaining in 1998. (For example, divide by 26 if you are paid every other week and you complete this form in December 1997.) Enter the result here and on Form W-4, line 6, page 1. This is the additional amount to be withheld from each paycheck   . . . .   **9** $ _____

Table 1: Two-Earner/Two-Job Worksheet

Married Filing Jointly				All Others			
If wages from **LOWEST** paying job are—	Enter on line 2 above	If wages from **LOWEST** paying job are—	Enter on line 2 above	If wages from **LOWEST** paying job are—	Enter on line 2 above	If wages from **LOWEST** paying job are—	Enter on line 2 above
0 - $4,000	0	38,001 - 43,000	8	0 - $5,000	0	70,001 - 85,000	8
4,001 - 7,000	1	43,001 - 54,000	9	5,001 - 11,000	1	85,001 - 100,000	9
7,001 - 12,000	2	54,001 - 62,000	10	11,001 - 16,000	2	100,001 and over	10
12,001 - 18,000	3	62,001 - 70,000	11	16,001 - 21,000	3		
18,001 - 24,000	4	70,001 - 85,000	12	21,001 - 25,000	4		
24,001 - 28,000	5	85,001 - 100,000	13	25,001 - 42,000	5		
28,001 - 33,000	6	100,001 - 110,000	14	42,001 - 55,000	6		
33,001 - 38,000	7	110,001 and over	15	55,001 - 70,000	7		

Table 2: Two-Earner/Two-Job Worksheet

Married Filing Jointly		All Others	
If wages from **HIGHEST** paying job are—	Enter on line 7 above	If wages from **HIGHEST** paying job are—	Enter on line 7 above
0 - $50,000	$400	0 - $30,000	$400
50,001 - 100,000	760	30,001 - 60,000	760
100,001 - 130,000	840	60,001 - 120,000	840
130,001 - 240,000	970	120,001 - 250,000	970
240,001 and over	1,070	250,001 and over	1,070

INDEX

Your #1 Source for Real World Legal Information...

SPHINX® PUBLISHING
A Division of Sourcebooks, Inc.®

- Written by lawyers
- Simple English explanation of the law
- Forms and instructions included

HOW TO FORM YOUR OWN CORPORATION, 2ND ED.

Protect yourself from personal liability by incorporating your business. Contains a summary of the laws and forms with instruction for forming a corporation in all 50 states and the District of Columbia. Saves entrepeneurs precious capital!

208 pages; $19.95;
ISBN 1-57071-227-1

LEGAL RESEARCH MADE EASY, 2ND ED.

Simplify the process of doing your own legal research in law libraries and on computers. This book explains how to research statutes, case law, databases, law reports and more Learn how to access your state's statutes on the Internet. Save yourself enormous amounts of time and money.

128 pages; $14.95;
ISBN 1-57071-400-2

THE MOST VALUABLE BUSINESS LEGAL FORMS YOU'LL EVER NEED, 2ND ED.

Using the right legal forms can add to your profits and help you avoid legal problems. This book provides businesses with the many and varied legal forms they will need. They are so simple and standard, you will wonder why anyone would pay a lawyer to fill them out!

140 pages; $19.95;
ISBN 1-57071-345-6

See the following order form for books written specifically for California, Florida, Georgia, Illinois, Massachusetts, Michigan, Minnesota, New York, North Carolina, Pennsylvania, and Texas! *Coming soon—Ohio and New Jersey!*

What our customers say about our books:

"It couldn't be more clear for the lay person." —R.D.

"I want you to know I really appreciate your book. It has saved me a lot of time and money." —L.T.

"Your real estate contracts book has saved me nearly $12,000.00 in closing costs over the past year." —A.B.

"...many of the legal questions that I have had over the years were answered clearly and concisely through your plain English interpretation of the law." —C.E.H.

"If there weren't people out there like you I'd be lost. You have the best books of this type out there." —S.B.

"...your forms and directions are easy to follow." —C.V.M.

SPHINX® PUBLISHING'S NATIONAL TITLES
Valid in All 50 States

LEGAL SURVIVAL IN BUSINESS

How to Form a Limited Liability Company	$19.95
How to Form Your Own Corporation (2E)	$19.95
How to Form Your Own Partnership	$19.95
How to Register Your Own Copyright (2E)	$19.95
How to Register Your Own Trademark (3E)	$19.95
Most Valuable Business Legal Forms You'll Ever Need (2E)	$19.95
Most Valuable Corporate Forms You'll Ever Need (2E)	$24.95
Software Law (with diskette)	$29.95

LEGAL SURVIVAL IN COURT

Crime Victim's Guide to Justice	$19.95
Debtors' Rights (3E)	$12.95
Defend Yourself against Criminal Charges	$19.95
Grandparents' Rights (2E)	$19.95
Help Your Lawyer Win Your Case (2E)	$12.95
Jurors' Rights (2E)	$9.95
Legal Malpractice and Other Claims against Your Lawyer	$18.95
Legal Research Made Easy (2E)	$14.95
Simple Ways to Protect Yourself from Lawsuits	$24.95
Victims' Rights	$12.95
Winning Your Personal Injury Claim	$19.95

LEGAL SURVIVAL IN REAL ESTATE

How to Buy a Condominium or Townhome	$16.95
How to Negotiate Real Estate Contracts (3E)	$16.95
How to Negotiate Real Estate Leases (3E)	$16.95
Successful Real Estate Brokerage Management	$19.95

LEGAL SURVIVAL IN PERSONAL AFFAIRS

Your Right to Child Custody, Visitation and Support	$19.95
The Nanny and Domestic Help Legal Kit	$19.95
How to File Your Own Bankruptcy (4E)	$19.95
How to File Your Own Divorce (3E)	$19.95
How to Make Your Own Will	$12.95
How to Write Your Own Living Will	$9.95
How to Write Your Own Premarital Agreement (2E)	$19.95
How to Win Your Unemployment Compensation Claim	$19.95
Living Trusts and Simple Ways to Avoid Probate (2E)	$19.95
Neighbor v. Neighbor (2E)	$12.95
The Power of Attorney Handbook (3E)	$19.95
Simple Ways to Protect Yourself from Lawsuits	$24.95
Social Security Benefits Handbook (2E)	$14.95
Unmarried Parents' Rights	$19.95
U.S.A. Immigration Guide (3E)	$19.95
Guia de Inmigracion a Estados Unidos (2E)	$19.95

Legal Survival Guides are directly available from Sourcebooks, Inc., or from your local bookstores.

*For credit card orders call 1–800–43–BRIGHT, write P.O. Box 372, Naperville, IL 60566,
or fax 630-961-2168*

SPHINX® PUBLISHING ORDER FORM

BILL TO:		SHIP TO:	
Phone #	Terms	F.O.B. Chicago, IL	Ship Date

Charge my: ☐ VISA ☐ MasterCard ☐ American Express

☐ **Money Order or Personal Check**

Credit Card Number

Expiration Date

Qty	ISBN	Title	Retail	Ext.
		SPHINX PUBLISHING NATIONAL TITLES		
	1-57071-166-6	Crime Victim's Guide to Justice	$19.95	
	1-57071-342-1	Debtors' Rights (3E)	$12.95	
	1-57071-162-3	Defend Yourself against Criminal Charges	$19.95	
	1-57248-082-3	Grandparents' Rights (2E)	$19.95	
	1-57248-087-4	Guia de Inmigracion a Estados Unidos (2E)	$19.95	
	1-57248-103-X	Help Your Lawyer Win Your Case (2E)	$12.95	
	1-57071-164-X	How to Buy a Condominium or Townhome	$16.95	
	1-57071-223-9	How to File Your Own Bankruptcy (4E)	$19.95	
	1-57071-224-7	How to File Your Own Divorce (3E)	$19.95	
	1-57248-083-1	How to Form a Limited Liability Company	$19.95	
	1-57248-099-8	How to Form a Nonprofit Corporation	$24.95	
	1-57071-227-1	How to Form Your Own Corporation (2E)	$19.95	
	1-57071-343-X	How to Form Your Own Partnership	$19.95	
	1-57071-228-X	How to Make Your Own Will	$12.95	
	1-57071-331-6	How to Negotiate Real Estate Contracts (3E)	$16.95	
	1-57071-332-4	How to Negotiate Real Estate Leases (3E)	$16.95	
	1-57071-225-5	How to Register Your Own Copyright (2E)	$19.95	
	1-57248-104-8	How to Register Your Own Trademark (3E)	$19.95	
	1-57071-349-9	How to Win Your Unemployment Compensation Claim	$19.95	
	1-57071-167-4	How to Write Your Own Living Will	$9.95	
	1-57071-344-8	How to Write Your Own Premarital Agreement (2E)	$19.95	
	1-57071-333-2	Jurors' Rights (2E)	$9.95	
	1-57248-032-7	Legal Malpractice and Other Claims against...	$18.95	
	1-57071-400-2	Legal Research Made Easy (2E)	$14.95	
	1-57071-336-7	Living Trusts and Simple Ways to Avoid Probate (2E)	$19.95	
	1-57071-345-6	Most Valuable Bus. Legal Forms You'll Ever Need (2E)	$19.95	
	1-57071-346-4	Most Valuable Corporate Forms You'll Ever Need (2E)	$24.95	
	1-57248-089-0	Neighbor v. Neighbor (2E)	$12.95	
	1-57071-348-0	The Power of Attorney Handbook (3E)	$19.95	
	1-57248-020-3	Simple Ways to Protect Yourself from Lawsuits	$24.95	
	1-57071-337-5	Social Security Benefits Handbook (2E)	$14.95	
	1-57071-163-1	Software Law (w/diskette)	$29.95	
	0-913825-86-7	Successful Real Estate Brokerage Mgmt.	$19.95	
	1-57248-098-X	The Nanny and Domestic Help Legal Kit	$19.95	
	1-57071-399-5	Unmarried Parents' Rights	$19.95	
	1-57071-354-5	U.S.A. Immigration Guide (3E)	$19.95	
	0-913825-82-4	Victims' Rights	$12.95	
	1-57071-165-8	Winning Your Personal Injury Claim	$19.95	
	1-57248-097-1	Your Right to Child Custody, Visitation and Support	$19.95	
		CALIFORNIA TITLES		
	1-57071-360-X	CA Power of Attorney Handbook	$12.95	
	1-57071-355-3	How to File for Divorce in CA	$19.95	
	1-57071-356-1	How to Make a CA Will	$12.95	
	1-57071-408-8	How to Probate an Estate in CA	$19.95	
	1-57071-357-X	How to Start a Business in CA	$16.95	
	1-57071-358-8	How to Win in Small Claims Court in CA	$14.95	
	1-57071-359-6	Landlords' Rights and Duties in CA	$19.95	
		NEW YORK TITLES		
	1-57071-184-4	How to File for Divorce in NY	$19.95	
		FLORIDA TITLES		
	1-57071-363-4	Florida Power of Attorney Handbook (2E)	$12.95	
	1-57248-093-9	How to File for Divorce in FL (6E)	$21.95	
	1-57248-086-6	How to Form a Limited Liability Co. in FL	$19.95	
	1-57071-401-0	How to Form a Partnership in FL	$19.95	
	1-57071-380-4	How to Form a Corporation in FL (4E)	$19.95	
	1-57071-361-8	How to Make a FL Will (5E)	$12.95	
	1-57248-088-2	How to Modify Your FL Divorce Judgment (4E)	$22.95	

Form Continued on Following Page   **SUBTOTAL** _____

To order, call Sourcebooks at 1-800-43-BRIGHT or FAX (630)961-2168 (Bookstores, libraries, wholesalers—please call for discount)

SPHINX® PUBLISHING ORDER FORM

Qty	ISBN	Title	Retail	Ext.
		FLORIDA TITLES (CONT'D)		
_____	1-57071-364-2	How to Probate an Estate in FL (3E)	$24.95	_____
_____	1-57248-081-5	How to Start a Business in FL (5E)	$16.95	_____
_____	1-57071-362-6	How to Win in Small Claims Court in FL (6E)	$14.95	_____
_____	1-57071-335-9	Landlords' Rights and Duties in FL (7E)	$19.95	_____
_____	1-57071-334-0	Land Trusts in FL (5E)	$24.95	_____
_____	0-913825-73-5	Women's Legal Rights in FL	$19.95	_____
		GEORGIA TITLES		
_____	1-57071-376-6	How to File for Divorce in GA (3E)	$19.95	_____
_____	1-57248-075-0	How to Make a GA Will (3E)	$12.95	_____
_____	1-57248-076-9	How to Start a Business in Georgia (3E)	$16.95	_____
		ILLINOIS TITLES		
_____	1-57071-405-3	How to File for Divorce in IL (2E)	$19.95	_____
_____	1-57071-415-0	How to Make an IL Will (2E)	$12.95	_____
_____	1-57071-416-9	How to Start a Business in IL (2E)	$16.95	_____
_____	1-57248-078-5	Landlords' Rights & Duties in IL	$19.95	_____
		MASSACHUSETTS TITLES		
_____	1-57071-329-4	How to File for Divorce in MA (2E)	$19.95	_____
_____	1-57248-108-0	How to Make a MA Will (2E)	$12.95	_____
_____	1-57248-109-9	How to Probate an Estate in MA (2E)	$19.95	_____
_____	1-57248-106-4	How to Start a Business in MA (2E)	$16.95	_____
_____	1-57248-107-2	Landlords' Rights and Duties in MA (2E)	$19.95	_____
		MICHIGAN TITLES		
_____	1-57071-409-6	How to File for Divorce in MI (2E)	$19.95	_____
_____	1-57248-077-7	How to Make a MI Will (2E)	$12.95	_____
_____	1-57071-407-X	How to Start a Business in MI (2E)	$16.95	_____
		MINNESOTA TITLES		
_____	1-57248-039-4	How to File for Divorce in MN	$19.95	_____
_____	1-57248-040-8	How to Form a Simple Corporation in MN	$19.95	_____
_____	1-57248-037-8	How to Make a MN Will	$9.95	_____
_____	1-57248-038-6	How to Start a Business in MN	$16.95	_____
		NEVADA TITLES		
_____	1-57248-101-3	How to Form a Corporation in NV	$19.95	_____
		NEW YORK TITLES		
_____	1-57071-184-4	How to File for Divorce in NY	$19.95	_____

Qty	ISBN	Title	Retail	Ext.
_____	1-57248-105-6	How to Form a Corporation in NY	$19.95	_____
_____	1-57248-095-5	How to Make a NY Will (2E)	$12.95	_____
_____	1-57071-185-2	How to Start a Business in NY	$16.95	_____
_____	1-57071-187-9	How to Win in Small Claims Court in NY	$14.95	_____
_____	1-57071-186-0	Landlords' Rights and Duties in NY	$19.95	_____
_____	1-57071-188-7	New York Power of Attorney Handbook	$19.95	_____
		NORTH CAROLINA TITLES		
_____	1-57248-326-X	How to File for Divorce in NC (2E)	$19.95	_____
_____	1-57071-327-8	How to Make a NC Will (2E)	$12.95	_____
_____	1-57248-096-3	How to Start a Business in NC (2E)	$16.95	_____
_____	1-57248-091-2	Landlords' Rights & Duties in NC	$19.95	_____
		OHIO TITLES		
_____	1-57248-102-1	How to File for Divorce in OH	$19.95	_____
		PENNSYLVANIA TITLES		
_____	1-57071-177-1	How to File for Divorce in PA	$19.95	_____
_____	1-57248-094-7	How to Make a PA Will (2E)	$12.95	_____
_____	1-57248-112-9	How to Start a Business in PA (2E)	$16.95	_____
_____	1-57071-179-8	Landlords' Rights and Duties in PA	$19.95	_____
		TEXAS TITLES		
_____	1-57071-330-8	How to File for Divorce in TX (2E)	$19.95	_____
_____	1-57248-009-2	How to Form a Simple Corporation in TX	$19.95	_____
_____	1-57071-417-7	How to Make a TX Will (2E)	$12.95	_____
_____	1-57071-418-5	How to Probate an Estate in TX (2E)	$19.95	_____
_____	1-57071-365-0	How to Start a Business in TX (2E)	$16.95	_____
_____	1-57248-111-0	How to Win in Small Claims Court in TX (2E)	$14.95	_____
_____	1-57248-110-2	Landlords' Rights and Duties in TX (2E)	$19.95	_____

SUBTOTAL THIS PAGE _____

SUBTOTAL PREVIOUS PAGE _____

Illinois residents add 6.75% sales tax _____

Florida residents add 6% state sales tax plus applicable discretionary surtax _____

Shipping— $4.00 for 1st book, $1.00 each additional _____

TOTAL _____